# THE AGE OF INIGO JONES

1 The Banqueting House, Whitehall, 1619-22.

*By Inigo Jones. Details of a Water Colour by Thomas Malton, junr. (1781)*

# THE AGE OF
# INIGO JONES

*James Lees-Milne*

LONDON
**B. T. BATSFORD LTD**

For

ALVILDE

*First Published* 1953

MADE AND PRINTED IN GREAT BRITAIN BY
WILLIAM CLOWES AND SONS, LIMITED, LONDON AND BECCLES
FOR THE PUBLISHERS
B. T. BATSFORD LTD
4 FITZHARDINGE STREET, PORTMAN SQUARE
LONDON, W.I

# PREFACE

" . . . on the sudden
A Roman thought hath struck him."
*Antony and Cleopatra, Act 1, Sc. 2*

INDEED, it came like a thunderbolt, the conviction that buildings in England must, in order to be beautiful, conform absolutely to the ideals set by ancient Rome. Accordingly Inigo Jones brought about the most momentous revolution that English architecture has experienced. Yet the biographies of the father of our classical architecture are remarkably few. There is the section in Horace Walpole's *Anecdotes of Painting*. There are Allan Cunningham's (1831) and Peter Cunningham's (1848) *Lives*; W. J. Loftie's *Inigo Jones and Christopher Wren* (1895) and H. I. Triggs and H. Tanner's *Some Architectural Works of Inigo Jones* (1901). There are Stanley Ramsey's monograph, *Inigo Jones* (1924), and J. A. Gotch's *Inigo Jones* (1928). Of them all the last is by far the most valuable because Mr. Gotch had done an immense amount of original research. It is still the standard biography of Inigo Jones, to which all students of the architect are bound to refer. Concerning his life few fresh facts have been unearthed during the past quarter of a century, and so in the following pages I have condensed my biographical material. This has given me room to cover not only Jones's work but that of his contemporaries, who tried with varying successes to build in his manner. Nevertheless, I have not attempted to include all those buildings at one time or another ascribed to Inigo's design. I have purposely extended the age of Inigo Jones beyond his death up to the Restoration of Charles II. If I occasionally stray over the year 1660, it is in pursuit of his contemporaries who had the temerity to survive him, or of a younger generation of architects and craftsmen who continued to work under his influence. I do not include men like Hugh May and William Winde who never practised before the Restoration and, after it, were to build under the influence of Wren.

*The Age of Inigo Jones* may not be read as literature. It is frankly a reference book, without being a work of scholarship. There is little to be found in it that has not been recorded elsewhere, "for I am"—to purloin the words of Sir Henry Wotton —"but a gatherer and disposer of other men's stuff". My book is rather an attempt to collate what has appeared in numerous learned articles published both before and since Mr. Gotch's book. Since these are scattered in many different periodicals they are not always easily procurable. Lack of space has not allowed me to refer to more than a fraction of them in my text. For the same reason I have not been able to acknowledge all the books from which I have gleaned information. Yet I must express particular indebtedness to P. Simpson and C. F. Bell's *Designs of Inigo Jones for Masques and Plays* (Vol. XII of the Walpole Society, 1924) and to Allardyce Nicoll's *Stuart Masques* (1937). As regards the buildings themselves which I have mentioned, my strongest suit is perhaps that I have at least seen and studied at different times all of those that survive. If my readers shall complain that I have described too many buildings which have already disappeared, well—I can only deplore the circumstances that have brought about their destruction. It is an accepted paradox of the present age that the more we learn about old buildings, the faster do we pull them down.

I am greatly beholden to many friends for help in various ways—to the Duchess of Devonshire for letting me handle all the Inigo Jones drawings and papers at Chatsworth; Lord Herbert, certain documents relating to Wilton; and Sir Gyles Isham, the Webb correspondence at Lamport: to Mr. Ralph Arnold for supplying me with particulars of Cobham Hall; Mr. Rupert Gunnis and Mr. Howard Colvin, with data about to be published by them in their respective dictionaries; and Mr. Wyndham Ketton-Cremer, with information about the Paston collections: to Mr. Noel Blakiston for clearing a path for me in the Public Record Office, Mr. Derek Hill for searching (in vain, as it turned out) for references to Inigo Jones in the archives of the Biblioteca Nazionale at Florence, and Miss Dorothy Margaret Stuart for reading and correcting my text. I also thank Lord Stanhope for his kindness in taking measurements for me of the "Webb" rooms at Chevening; Dr. H. Langberg for giving me particulars of the buildings in Denmark erroneously associated with Inigo Jones; Monsignore A. Mercati for consulting records in the Vatican Library and Dr. Ugo Tucci for enabling me to look through relevant papers in the Archivio di Stato in Venice.

In my quotations I have throughout modernised the spelling of words (except in cases where the meaning of certain archaic words is ambiguous), but retained the original spelling of names of persons and places.

J. L-M.

# CONTENTS

Page

PREFACE     7

LIST OF ILLUSTRATIONS     11

ACKNOWLEDGMENT     17

*Chapter*

I    INIGO JONES—ARTIST AND MASQUE PRODUCER     19

II    INIGO JONES—CHARACTER AND STATUS     45

III    INIGO JONES—DOCUMENTED BUILDINGS
*House for Lord Arundel at Greenwich and Arundel House in the Strand, 1615–17; Newmarket, Cambridgeshire: royal lodging, brewhouse, stable and kennels, 1616–23; Oatlands, Surrey, 1616–17; The Queen's House, Greenwich, 1616–35; Holyroodhouse, Edinburgh, 1617; Whitehall, work for Lord Buckingham, 1618; Queen Anne's Hearse, 1619; The Banqueting House, Whitehall, 1619–22; Chiswick House, gateway, 1621; New Hall, Essex: alterations, 1622; Theobalds Palace, Hertfordshire: a stable, 1623, and a banqueting house, 1624; Marlborough House Chapel, 1623–6; King James I's Hearse, 1625; Covent Garden Piazza and St. Paul's Church, 1631–8; Somerset House and Chapel, 1632–8; Chapman's Monument, St. Giles-in-the-Fields, 1634; Winchester Cathedral Screen, 1634–8; St. Paul's Cathedral, 1634–43; The Barber Surgeons' Hall, 1636; Wilton House, Wiltshire, 1649–53*     63

IV    INIGO JONES—SOME ATTRIBUTED BUILDINGS
*Houghton Conquest House, Bedfordshire, 1615–21; Lincoln's Inn Chapel, London, 1618–23; Raynham Hall, Norfolk, 1619–22–37; Boston Manor, Brentford, 1622–3, c. 1670?; Castle Ashby, Northamptonshire, 1624–30; Forty Hall, Enfield, 1629–36; Chevening, Kent: before 1630; Charlton House, Greenwich: garden house, c. 1630; Becket Park, Berkshire: fishing lodge, c. 1630–40; Stoke Bruerne Park, Northamptonshire, 1630–6; Chesterton Windmill, Warwickshire, 1632; Ham House, Surrey: alterations, 1637–9; Kirby Hall, Northamptonshire, 1638–40; Ashburnham House, Westminster, c. 1640; Lindsey House, Lincoln's Inn Fields, c. 1640; Cranborne Manor, Dorset, 1647; Forde Abbey, Dorset, 1658*     105

V   NICHOLAS STONE AND THE FLEMISH TRADITION
*York House Watergate, 1624–6; The Physic Garden, Oxford, 1631–2;
Cornbury Park, Oxfordshire, 1632–3; The Goldsmith's Hall, Foster Lane,
1634–40; St. Mary's Portico, Oxford, 1637; St. Catherine Cree, Leadenhall
Street, 1630; St. Helen's, Bishopsgate: door, 1633; St. John's College,
Oxford, 1631–6; Lambeth Palace, 1633–63; Brasenose College Chapel,
Oxford, 1656–9; Burford Priory Chapel, 1661–2; Holy Trinity Church,
Berwick-on-Tweed, 1652; Clare College, Cambridge, 1638–42; Christ's
College, Cambridge: Fellows Building, 1640–2*   135

VI   JOHN WEBB AND THE PALLADIAN TRADITION
*Lamport Hall, Northamptonshire, 1654–7; Drayton House, Northampton-
shire, 1653–5; Belvoir Castle, Rutland, 1654; The Vyne, Hampshire, 1654;
Northumberland House, Charing Cross, 1657–8; Gunnersbury House, Middle-
sex, 1658; Amesbury Abbey, Wiltshire, 1661; Greenwich Palace, 1663–8;
Lees Court, Kent, 1652; Cobham Hall, Kent, 1662; Farnham Castle,
Surrey, 1662–72*   159

VII   GERBIER, MILLS, PRATT AND THE RUBENS SCHOOL
*Swakeleys House, near Uxbridge, Middlesex, 1629–38; Kew Palace, 1631;
Broome Park, Kent, 1635–8; Hampstead Marshall, Berkshire, 1662; Crom-
well House, Highgate, 1637–8; Balls Park, Hertford, c. 1640; Tyttenhanger
Park, Hertfordshire, c. 1640–54; Great Queen Street houses, Lincoln's Inn
Fields, c. 1640; Thorpe Hall, Northamptonshire, 1654–6; Wisbech Castle,
Cambridgeshire, 1658; Thorney Abbey House, Cambridgeshire, 1660; South
Luffenham Hall, Rutland; Lyndon Hall, Rutland, 1668; Walcot Hall,
Northamptonshire, 1674; Coleshill House, Berkshire, 1650–62; Kingston
Lacy, Dorset, 1663–5; Horseheath, Cambridgeshire, 1663–5; Clarendon
House, Piccadilly, London, 1664–6; Ryston Hall, Norfolk, 1669*   191

VIII   CAROLEAN CONCLUSION   222

INDEX   235

# LIST OF ILLUSTRATIONS

*Figure*                                                                                          *Page*

1   The Banqueting House, Whitehall. From a water-colour by Thomas
    Malton, jun.   .   .   .   .   .   .   .   .   *frontispiece*

2   Heriot's Hospital, Edinburgh. One of numerous buildings erroneously
    ascribed to Inigo Jones   .   .   .   .   .   .   .   .   23

3   Drawing by Inigo Jones of "A Page, like a Fiery Spirit" for Thomas
    Campion's *The Lord's Masque*   .   .   .   .   .   .   24

4   Sketch by Inigo Jones for Scene II, "The City of Sleep", of Sir William
    Davenant's masque, *Luminalia*   .   .   .   .   .   .   37

5   Sketch by Inigo Jones for Scene I, "Night", of Sir William Davenant's
    masque, *Luminalia* .   .   .   .   .   .   .   .   37

6   Drawing by Inigo Jones in his Sketch Book   .   .   .   .   .   38

7   Inigo Jones in his old age. A study by William Dobson for the finished
    portrait in Chiswick House   .   .   .   .   .   .   .   47

8   Santa Susanna, Rome .   .   .   .   .   .   .   .   .   48

9   Scene probably connected with Ben Jonson's Masque *Oberon*   .   .   57

10  "The House of Fame". Drawing by Inigo Jones for Ben Jonson's *Masque
    of Queens*   .   .   .   .   .   .   .   .   .   .   57

11  Drawing by Inigo Jones of his Catafalque for King James I   .   .   58

12  Inigo Jones: a self-portrait .   .   .   .   .   .   .   .   62

13  Plan of the Queen's House, Greenwich   .   .   .   .   .   66

14  The Queen's House, Greenwich: the South Front   .   .   .   .   67

| Figure | | Page |
|---|---|---|

15    The Queen's House, Greenwich: the Galleried Hall.    .    .    .    68

16    Covent Garden: Doorway of Inigo Jones's still surviving within North Arcade    .   .   .   .   .   .   .   .   .   77

17    Chiswick House: Gateway by Inigo Jones    .   .   .   77

18    "The Queen's Chapel" at Marlborough House, London, built by Inigo Jones .   .   .   .   .   .   .   .   .   78

19    Covent Garden: the North Side, showing the Church and part of the East Side    .   .   .   .   .   .   .   87

20    St. Paul's, Covent Garden .   .   .   .   .   .   87

21    Somerset House, London, showing classical block by Inigo Jones    .   88

22    Old St. Paul's Cathedral, showing Inigo Jones's refacing of West End and Portico    .   .   .   .   .   .   .   .   88

23    Wilton Park, Wiltshire: the Grotto    .   .   .   .   97

24    Winchester Cathedral: Choir Screen, designed by Inigo Jones    .   .   97

25    Wilton House, Wiltshire: the centre of the South Front    .   .   98

26    Wilton House, Wiltshire: the Stables    .   .   .   .   100

27    Wilton House, Wiltshire: the Double Cube Room by Inigo Jones and John Webb    .   .   .   .   .   .   .   107

28    Houghton Conquest, Bedfordshire: Centrepiece of North Front .   .   108

29    Houghton Conquest: remains of Centrepiece of West Front    .   .   108

30    Castle Ashby, Northamptonshire: part of connecting screen    .   .   117

31    Raynham Hall, Norfolk: East Centrepiece    .   .   .   117

32    Becket Park, Berkshire: the Fishing Lodge, once a brewhouse    .   .   118

33    Charlton House, Greenwich: Garden House .   .   .   118

| Figure | | Page |
|---|---|---|
| 34 | Chesterton Windmill, Warwickshire . . . . . | 118 |
| 35 | Plan of Stoke Bruerne, Northamptonshire . . . . | 121 |
| 36 | Stoke Bruerne Park, Northamptonshire: one of the Pavilion wings . | 123 |
| 37 | Lindsey House, Lincoln's Inn Fields, probably by Inigo Jones . . | 123 |
| 38 | Kirby Hall, Northamptonshire: Garden Portal . . . | 124 |
| 39 | Kirby Hall: Entrance to Great Hall . . . . | 124 |
| 40 | Kirby Hall: Forecourt Gateway . . . . . . | 124 |
| 41 | Forde Abbey, Dorset: the Saloon . . . . . | 133 |
| 42 | Forde Abbey: a Ceiling Panel . . . . . . | 133 |
| 43 | Ashburnham House, Westminster: the Staircase, attributed to John Webb | 134 |
| 44 | Monument of the Hon. Francis Holles, Westminster Abbey . . | 139 |
| 45 | Standing Effigy of Dr. John Donne, St. Paul's Cathedral . . | 139 |
| 46 | Charles I's Equestrian statue at Charing Cross, by Hubert le Sueur . | 140 |
| 47 | Physic Garden, Oxford: Great Gateway built by Nicholas Stone . | 149 |
| 48 | York House Watergate, Buckingham Street, Strand . . | 149 |
| 49 | St. Mary's, Oxford: Portico added by Nicholas Stone . . | 150 |
| 50 | Speaker Lenthall's Chapel, Burford Priory, Oxfordshire . . | 155 |
| 51 | St. Catherine Cree, Leadenhall Street, London: interior . . | 155 |
| 52 | St. Helen's, Bishopsgate: South Door . . . . | 156 |
| 53 | Brasenose College Chapel, Oxford . . . . . | 156 |
| 54 | Clare College, Cambridge: East Range . . . . . | 156 |

| Figure | | Page |
|---|---|---|
| 55 | Holy Trinity, Berwick-on-Tweed . . . . . . | 165 |
| 56 | St. John's College, Oxford: Frontispiece of Quadrangle . . . | 165 |
| 57 | Amesbury Abbey, Wiltshire: original façade by John Webb . . | 166 |
| 58 | Belvoir Castle, Rutland: façade designed by John Webb . . . | 166 |
| 59 | Oatlands Palace, Surrey: Garden Portal by Inigo Jones . . . | 166 |
| 60 | Whitehall Palace: a picture by Thomas Sandby showing how Jones's and Webb's scheme for the Royal Palace might have appeared . . | 171 |
| 61 | Lees Court, Kent: corner of the Hall . . . . . . | 171 |
| 62 | Lamport Hall, Northamptonshire: Hall Fireplace designed by John Webb | 171 |
| 63 | The Vyne, Hampshire: Portico built by Edward Marshall . . . | 172 |
| 64 | The Vyne: Garden House possibly designed by John Webb . . | 172 |
| 65 | Gunnersbury House, Middlesex . . . . . . . | 181 |
| 66 | Chevening, Kent, probably designed by Inigo Jones . . . . | 181 |
| 67 | Lamport Hall, Northamptonshire . . . . . . . | 182 |
| 68 | King Charles II's Block, Greenwich Palace . . . . . | 182 |
| 69 | Lees Court, Kent . . . . . . . . . | 187 |
| 70 | Swakeleys House, Middlesex: Gable . . . . . . | 188 |
| 71 | Hampstead Marshall, Berkshire: pair of Gatepiers designed by Sir Balthazar Gerbier . . . . . . . . | 188 |
| 72 | Swakeleys House, Middlesex: Hall Screen . . . . . | 188 |
| 73 | Rubens's House, Antwerp: part of Stone Screen and Garden Pavilion designed by the artist . . . . . . . | 197 |

| *Figure* | | *Page* |
|---|---|---|
| 74 | Cromwell House, Highgate, possibly built by Sir Balthazar Gerbier under the influence of Rubens . . . . . . . . | 198 |
| 75 | Cromwell House: the Staircase . . . . . . . | 198 |
| 76 | Old Grammar School, Rye, Sussex . . . . . . | 203 |
| 77 | Balls Park, Hertford . . . . . . . . . | 203 |
| 78 | Thorpe Hall, Northamptonshire, the outcome of the Rubens influence . | 204 |
| 79 | Thorney Abbey House, Cambridgeshire . . . . . | 204 |
| 80 | Kew Palace, Surrey; the Dutch type of house . . . . | 204 |
| 81 | Plan of Coleshill . . . . . . . . . | 212 |
| 82 | Broome Park, Kent: the most elaborate of the Dutch Skylines . . | 213 |
| 83 | Coleshill House, Berkshire: the perfection of English seventeenth-century classicism . . . . . . . . . | 213 |
| 84 | Coleshill House: Staircase Hall . . . . . . . | 214 |
| 85 | Wisbech Castle, Cambridgeshire, from a contemporary painting in Wisbech Museum . . . . . . . . . | 219 |
| 86 | Kingston Lacy, Dorset, from an original drawing in the house . . | 219 |
| 87 | Lodge Park, Sherborne, Gloucestershire . . . . . | 220 |
| 88 | Aldermaston Court, Berkshire: early regional classical work . . | 220 |
| 89 | Brympton D'Evercy, Somerset: provincial classical façade . . | 229 |
| 90 | West Woodhay House, Berkshire: provincial classical doorway . . | 230 |
| 91 | Design by Inigo Jones for a Cabinet . . . . . | 230 |
| 92 | Stanway House, Gloucestershire: the Gatehouse, an example of Cotswold compromise between Gothic and classical . . . . | 230 |

# ACKNOWLEDGMENT

THE Author and Publishers wish to thank the following for permission to reproduce the illustrations appearing in this book: The Trustees of the British Museum, for fig. 60; The Trustees of the Chatsworth Settlement, for figs. 3–6 and 12; *Country Life,* for figs. 14, 15, 31, 50, 77, 78, and 82–6; The Courtauld Institute, for figs. 6 and 87; the Director, The Ashmolean Museum, Oxford, for fig. 91; Gevaert Photo-Producten N.V., Antwerp, for fig. 73; W. Gibson, for fig. 44; A. F. Kersting, F.R.P.S., for figs. 16, 25, 27, 30, 32, 33, 37, 38, 40–2, 45, 48, 49, 51, 52, 63, 64, 69, 71, 76, 79, 89 and 92; McLeish and Macaulay, for fig. 2; the Ministry of Works, for fig. 39; the National Buildings Record, for figs. 55, 62 and 67; E. Richter, Rome, for fig. 8; the Royal Commission on Historical Monuments, for figs. 68, 70, 72, 74 and 75; P. S. Spokes, for fig. 90; Stearn of Cambridge, for fig. 54; Topical Press Agency Ltd., for fig. 46; The Trustees of the Victoria & Albert Museum, for figs. 1 and 28; the Warburg Institute, for figs. 17 and 43; Reece Winstone, A.R.P.S., for fig. 56.

Fig. 19 is reproduced by permission of The Lord Herbert; fig. 7 by permission of Spink & Son, Ltd.; fig. 21 by permission of Lady Stanley; fig. 85 by permission of the Curator of Wisbech Museum; fig. 11 by permission of the Provost and Fellows of Worcester College, Oxford.

Figs. 29 and 34 are from photographs by the Author.

Figs. 68, 70, 72, 74 and 75 are Crown Copyright, and are reproduced by permission of the Controller of Her Majesty's Stationery Office.

17

# CHAPTER ONE

# INIGO JONES—ARTIST AND MASQUE PRODUCER

"ENEYO JONES the son of Eneyo Jones was christened the XIX day of July", we read in the church register of St. Bartholomew-the-Less, Smithfield, in the City of London. This entry comes under the year 1573. In St. Bartholomew's parish the great cloth fair of England had been held since time immemorial. The elder Eneyo, or Inigo, was by trade a clothworker, perhaps originally from Wales as his surname suggests, and up till his death resident in the neighbouring parish of St. Benet, Paul's Wharf. That he was not rich is apparent from the record of a legal action brought against him in 1589 by one Richard Baker, to whom he owed the sum of £55. The Court of Requests, which was the poor man's court, generously allowed him to clear off the debt at the rate of ten shillings a month. At this rate of payment the debt cannot have been discharged before the elder Inigo died in 1597. It is not therefore surprising that in his will, which was proved on the 5th April, little enough was left to be divided equally between his only son and three daughters, Joan, Judith and Mary, and that the unfortunate children were directed "to pay my debts so far forth as they may be received".

Nothing for certain is known of the future architect's upbringing and education; nothing much of the first thirty years of his life. We can only surmise that Inigo's education was scanty, for he never showed any traces of strict academic training. Throughout his life his spelling, even in an age of considerable orthographical licence, when Shakespeare used six variants of his own surname, was unashamedly phonetic. Ben Jonson was in years to come to make mock of his bad Latin and his malapropisms. Jones may therefore have been almost wholly self-taught. Yet he was blessed with a compulsive instinct to probe the minds of men and the mysteries of the world he lived in; and with an immense capacity for concentration and work. His achievements, remarkable as they were, are those of the amateur rather than the professional, the aesthete rather than the intellectual, and should not accordingly be judged by the definitive standards of the modern art and architectural historian. George Vertue, the antiquary, was told by Wren, on the authority of a Doctor Harwood, that in early youth Inigo was apprenticed to a joiner in St. Paul's churchyard. This perfectly credible tradition is to some extent corroborated by Ben Jonson, who in his malicious *Tale of a Tub* makes Medlay, the character impersonating Jones, say:

> And he named me In-and-Inn Medlay; which serves
> A joiner's craft, because that we do lay
> Things in and in, in our work. But I am truly
> Architectonicus Professor rather.

John Webb, the architect's faithful disciple, wrote [1] "there is no certain account how he passed his younger years", but added, "he was early distinguished by his inclination to drawing and design and was particularly taken notice of for his skill in the practice of landskip-painting". Jones tells us himself [2] that "being naturally inclined in my younger years to study the arts of design I passed into foreign parts to converse with the great masters thereof in Italy, where I applied myself to search out the ruins of those ancient buildings which, in despite of time itself and the violence of barbarians, are yet remaining. Having satisfied myself in these, and returning to my native country, I applied my mind more particularly to the study of architecture."

At this unspecified juncture of his career we are plunged into uncertainties and speculations. Unfortunately neither Webb nor Jones thought it worth while to furnish us with dates. The expression "in my younger years" might in Elizabethan times, when the normal span of life was short, be taken to apply to a man at the age of fifteen to twenty. To Inigo Jones, who lived to be nearly eighty, the expression, if recorded in his old age, probably signified from twenty-five to thirty years of age. We know that he was in England in 1597, when he proved his father's will. It is quite likely that until that event the joiner's apprentice would not have dared, under the parental eye, to abandon good business prospects for the gamble of an artist's career. Maybe soon after his father was out of the way he decided to take the risk. But even so, in Tudor times the only way in which a poor man's son could travel abroad was to attach himself to the retinue of some aristocratic patron. Now Lloyd,[3] Vertue and Webb all implied that Inigo's early patron was William Herbert, 3rd Earl of Pembroke. Lloyd even said he was "brought up by" Pembroke, surely a slight exaggeration, since the ward was certainly seven years older than the putative patron—unless Lloyd meant the father, Henry, 2nd Earl and husband of the immortal "subject of all verse", Mary, Sir Philip Sidney's sister. Webb went so far as to say that William Herbert actually paid for Jones's travels to Italy and Europe. Herbert, who was not independent of his family nor settled in London before 1598, did not succeed to the earldom until 1601, when he was twenty-one years of age. "Exceedingly beloved of all men" he liked to consort with artists and men of letters, such as his cousin George Herbert, the parson poet of Bemerton, John Donne and

---

[1] *A Vindication of Stone Heng restored*, 1665.
[2] *The Most Notable Antiquity . . . vulgarly called Stoneheng . . . restored*, 1655.
[3] David Lloyd, Bishop of St. Asaph, *Memoirs of the lives, actions . . . of Excellent Personages*, 1667.

Ben Jonson, to whom each New Year's day he regularly sent a present of £20 with which to buy books. His lasting epitaph will always be the dedicatory words in the first folio of Shakespeare's work, recording that he and his brother Philip, "the incomparable pair of brethren", had "prosequuted both them [Shakespeare's poems] and their author living with so much favour".

This handsome and fascinating nobleman, who was painted by Rubens and Mytens and sculptured by Le Sueur, was, we are told by a rueful contemporary, "immoderately given up to women", and before his succession became involved in an affair with the Queen's Maid of Honour, the quondam dark lady of the sonnets, Mary Fitton. In March 1601 she gave birth to a son, and Herbert found himself in deep disgrace with Elizabeth. In consequence throughout the summer he repeatedly begged permission to go abroad—"the change of climate may purge me of melancholy", he pleaded—but whether permission was granted we cannot be sure. It very probably was, since nothing is heard of him until Christmas of the following year, when he stayed at Exton with the Harington family. Now there is a fairly convincing record that in 1601, if not before, Inigo Jones was abroad; for in his cherished copy of Palladio's *Quattro Libri Dell'Architettura,* in the margin of which he was to make copious notes over a period of thirty-nine years, he inscribed under his name the following: "1601. In loccato Ven-." If then Jones was not in the company of William Herbert when he bought his Palladio (incidentally for two ducats) in Venice, or at least Veneto, he must have been in the retinue of some other nobleman.[1] Exactly how long he remained in Italy is also unknown, but in referring to John Webb once more we read: "Christianus IV [of Denmark] first engrossed him to himself sending for him out of Italy, where especially at Venice he had many years resided." If Webb knew what he was writing about—and there is no reason to suspect from his unblemished record of veracity and loyalty to his master that he was romancing—a residence in Italy of "many years" presupposes more than two or three. For reasons which shall be dealt with immediately, the limits of the many years cannot have extended beyond 1603 nor, in view of the father's death, before 1597. The period can only have fallen between these two dates, which amounted to six years at most. Moreover, if William Herbert paid for the whole of Inigo's sojourn abroad it is natural to suppose that he would have met his protégé somewhere on the Continent during his temporary exile.

Among the household accounts at Belvoir Castle of Roger, 5th Earl of Rutland,[2] occurs the following entry under the year 1603: "Item, 28 Junii, to Henygo Jones, a picture maker X$^{li}$". It implies that Inigo was in England at this date, or to be

[1] Francis Manners, later to become 6th Earl of Rutland, was in Venice from 1599 to the summer of 1600. Until James I's reign few English nobles visited Venice. The archives of the Consiglio de' Dieci ordered official welcomes to be accorded only to two parties of English visitors between 1597 and 1603, whereas an average of twelve a year were given to French, Spanish, German and other foreign visitors of distinction.

[2] 5th Earl of Rutland, 1576–1612: went to Paris 1597; was in Germany that March; back in Plymouth that July; went to Holland 1600; was implicated in the Essex rebellion; in the Tower 1601; at Belvoir 1602–3.

more precise, had been the previous day, when the Earl with a large retinue of gentlemen, trumpeters and cooks, dined at Gravesend before sailing on board the *Lion* for Denmark, there to present on behalf of his sovereign the Order of the Garter, and on his own behalf several rich jewels, to King Christianus IV. Either the payment to Jones was retrospective for services rendered recently, possibly a landscape or two, or in advance, for expenses over the forthcoming visit. The solitary Belvoir account does not of course prove that Inigo Jones was included in Lord Rutland's embassy. But the eventuality is fairly plausible. The Danish King, who fancied himself an architectural draftsman and genuinely loved to surround himself with foreign artists, may well have been struck with Inigo's talent and made it worth his while to stay behind when the Rutland mission was over. After all, he kept the English lutanist and song-writer, John Dowland, for eight years in Copenhagen at the huge salary of 500 dalers per annum, which was comparable to that of a Danish Minister of State.

Now Webb's version of the Danish visit was that the King, having heard through his representatives of Inigo's presence in Venice, engaged him to come straight from there to Denmark. It would not have been extraordinary for Inigo to travel to Denmark via England, where he would attach himself temporarily to the suite of an illustrious person like Rutland and thus work the long and expensive passage across the North Sea. Inigo may have stayed a year in Denmark, and returned with Dowland [1] the following autumn in the suite of the King's younger brother, then on a visit to their sister Anne, the Queen Consort of England. Christianus himself followed in August 1606 (incidentally bringing Paul van Somer to this country), and Webb tells us that Inigo Jones waited upon him in London. We know too that the young artist's first employer was Anne of Denmark, a fact which Ben Jonson grudgingly acknowledged in an ungracious couplet:

> He's warm on his feet now he says and can
> Swim without cork: why thank the good Queen Anne.

The tradition, born since Webb's day, that Jones designed the Frederiksborg and Rosenborg Castles and the Børsen in Copenhagen, because they bear certain resemblances in style to Heriot's Hospital in Edinburgh (2), cannot very seriously be maintained. It is true that no names of Danish architects are associated with these three buildings. On the other hand, the names of several native craftsmen who worked upon them are preserved among the archives of Copenhagen. The dates when the buildings were begun do not coincide with Jones's supposed visit to Denmark. Frederiksborg was begun before, Rosenborg and Børsen after it.[2] It is not impossible that the King personally dictated the designs of each. He was fully qualified to do so, since there exist architectural sketches in his own hand, worked

---

[1] It is significant that on his return to England Dowland was immediately appointed court lutanist to Queen Anne through the influence of the Danish king, her brother, and van Somer became her court painter.

[2] Frederiksborg, 1602–14; Rosenborg, 1606–34; Børsen, 1619–31.

2  Heriot's Hospital, Edinburgh, 1628–58. One of numerous buildings erroneously ascribed to Inigo Jones

*Master masons: William Wallace and William Aytoun*

3   Drawing by Inigo Jones of "A Page, like a Fiery Spirit" for Thomas Campion's
*The Lord's Masque*, 1613. The original is coloured

over by a more professional one. If it is true that he was Inigo's patron he may conceivably have obtained from him rough plans for Rosenborg and Børsen. But more than that it is rash to conjecture. As for Heriot's Hospital, there is no reason whatever to trust the old legend that Inigo Jones was its architect. This enormous establishment was built between 1628 and 1658 in accordance with the will of King James I's rich jeweller, George Heriot. Here the names of the master masons and builders have been preserved. They appear all to have been Scots. The first to be appointed master mason was William Wallace, who on his premature death was praised by the governors of the hospital for the "extraordinary pains and great care he had in that work, both by his advice and in the building of the same". William Aytoun succeeded him, and in his contract bound himself "to devise, plot, and set down what he shall think meetest for the decoration of the said work, and pattern thereof already begun . . . and to make with his own hands the hall moulds as well of timber as of stone". Built like a Scandinavian fortress round a central courtyard, Heriot's Hospital, with its great corner towers, its octagonal cupolas and pepper-pot turrets, its immature gateways and alcoves, has little in common with the undeviating classicism of Jones's documented buildings.

*     *     *

Anne of Denmark, that much underestimated consort, shared with her cultivated, if boorish brother Christianus a sincere and passionate love of all artistic enterprise. It was she who reinstituted what had first been held in England under Henry VIII—the court masques. And she set about the business with such gusto and liberality that the artists whom she commissioned to produce the masques endured none of the usual drawbacks of patronage, namely interference and parsimony. She commanded the foremost poets to write the scripts, artists to design the stage effects and dresses, musicians to compose the interludes and airs. In her efforts she received nothing but compliance and encouragement from King James. Throughout the masques of his reign only the name of the greatest poet of all ages is conspicuously absent; and even he did not escape the royal patronage. Shakespeare's plays were performed in London contemporaneously with the masques between 1604 and 1611. That Jones may on occasion have designed dresses for them is suggested by some rough sketches for figures, entitled "Romeo", a "good pilgrim" in a cape—possibly Juliet's friar—and an elderly man with a great belly, mustachios and a bald head, against which are scribbled the words "like a Sr. Jon fall staff". Yet the masquers, unlike His Majesty's Players who performed in public, were socially exclusive. They consisted of members of the royal family and leading courtiers, who performed strictly within the palace walls. On Twelfth Night of the year 1605 [1] one of these court entertainments was performed at Whitehall with the title *The Queen's Masque of Blackness*.

[1] Throughout this book I intend to interpret the dates of the year by the modern method and not to write either 6th January 1604 Old Style, or 6th January 1604/5 but 6th January 1605.

The *Masque of Blackness* was the first of a long series of masques to be produced by Ben Jonson and Inigo Jones in partnership on a scale far more lavish than ever before in England. It is to this country's credit that at last the chief participants in a vast artistic enterprise were not foreigners, and to Queen Anne's that the two Englishmen chosen were men of exceptional abilities. Jonson brought to the masques the fruits of his deep reading of the classics, Jones the fruits of several years' study of ancient and renaissance art; and both of them the vigour and originality of creative genius. Now we can see to what purpose the "good" and certainly discriminating Queen Anne had put her new protégé.

The *Masque of Blackness* indicates the beginning of a new phase in Ben Jonson's literary life. The poet and playwright had become masque-composer as well. Although most of the occasions for masques were frivolous ones—to celebrate a society wedding and enliven a festival on the long, dull evenings of mid-winter—Jonson took care that a bored court had diversions that would tax the knowledge of the most learned among them. He fairly crammed his masques full of Platonic meanings, mythological references and humanistic doctrines, so that his plots and characters were only properly understandable by the erudite. It is highly questionable whether performers or spectators ever fully appreciated their abstruse mysteries or more than vaguely gleaned what the author was propounding. For his material Jonson drew largely on the Italian manuals of the sixteenth century which described for an artist's benefit the relevant personalities of the innumerable deities of Greece and Rome. Perhaps the most widely consulted of these manuals was Caesare Ripa's *Iconologia,* or *Descrittione di Diverse Imagini,* published in Rome in 1603.

Many detailed descriptions were given by Jonson and Jones, as well as by favourable and critical spectators, of the masques produced during the reigns of James I and Charles I. Jones contributed his share to twenty-three, excluding pastorals and plays. Fortunately an enormous number of his drawings for their settings and costumes (3-5, 9,10) are preserved at Chatsworth in the Duke of Devonshire's library. They will always remain the most vivid and beautiful witnesses of his share in these productions.[1] Later we shall discuss the influence his masque drawings had upon his architecture. The early masques, beginning with *Blackness,* were accounted so spectacular and so novel that when eye-witnesses have recorded their impressions it seems a pity to overlook them altogether. For a start, let us consider the effect the *Masque of Blackness* had upon the beholders. "The masquers", records Ben Jonson after a description of the scenery, "were placed in a great concave shell, like mother of pearl, curiously made to move on the waters, and rise with the billow", a feat of engineering for those days that must have amazed the audience. The top of the shell was struck by a chevron of light. By the sides of it swam six sea monsters, carrying on their backs twelve torch-bearers. The masquers, their faces and hands blackened, were dressed in azure and silver, with classical headdresses of feathers and jewels

[1] Messrs. Percy Simpson and C. F. Bell in Vol. XII of the Walpole Society, published 1924, give as complete a descriptive catalogue with illustrations of the drawings as could be desired.

interlaced with ropes of pearl: the bearers wore their hair loose and flowing, garlanded with seaweed and branches of coral. The carefully staged perspective of the ocean scenery caught the eye "with a wondering beauty, to which was added an obscure and cloudy night-piece that made the whole set-off. So much", concludes the dramatist, "for the bodily part which was of Master Inigo Jones's design and art." The performance indicated long preparation, and was replete with ingenuity and artistry.

The following August Inigo Jones prepared for Oxford University's reception of the King and Queen in Christ Church Hall three plays which unfortunately were not accounted a success. An eye-witness wrote: "They also hired one Mr. Jones, a great traveller, who undertook to further them much, and furnish them with rare devices, but performed very little to that which was expected. He had for his pains, as I heard constantly reported, 50<sup>lib</sup>.". In spite of an elaborate machinery set at the upper end of the hall whereby the wings were actually made to revolve, and so in one tragedy display three different scenes of false walls, "fair painted and adorned with stately pillars", the whole novelty was "utterly disliked" by the conservative dons, the King was bored stiff and fell asleep, and worse still, the Queen was deeply shocked by the unexpected entry of some naked and unnecessarily hairy men. It is gratifying to learn that not only the production but the acting was considered at fault.

The reference by the member of the Oxford audience to Inigo as a great traveller to some extent supports Mr. Gotch's theory that he had only just returned from another and brief visit to Italy.[1] Mr. Gotch's theory was derived from a note made by Inigo during his stay in Rome nine years later, on the back of a drawing of the Castle of St. Angelo: "Roma 29 Maggio 1614 this night I saw again the Girandola and focci articcale, the Procession Corpus Domini at Coronation di P. Paulo V", thereby implying that he was present at the firework display at the enthronement of Camillo Borghese, which took place in May 1605. It is of course conceivable that Jones had managed to attach himself to a royal mission of congratulation to the new Pope on that historic occasion.

After the temporary set-back at Oxford Inigo soon got to work to retrieve his reputation by preparing with Ben Jonson the epithalamium masque *Hymenaei,* which was performed two nights running early in January 1606. It was ostensibly "the auspicious celebrating" of what turned out to be one of the most disastrous marriages of the seventeenth century, namely that between the luckless young Earl of Essex and the completely amoral Lady Frances Howard. The couple were destined to a very scandalous divorce a few years later, when the wife, after conniving at the poisoning of Sir Thomas Overbury, married her fellow-murderer, Lord Somerset, with whom she had all along been cohabiting. But on Twelfth Night of this year nothing but triumph and glory encompassed the blissful pair. Into the masque, which took the form of a Roman marriage ceremony, the author wove a double

---

[1] J. Alfred Gotch, *Inigo Jones,* 1928.

significance in the Union of England and Scotland, by way of compliment to the Stuart King. On every score the masque seems to have been a success. "Both Inigo, Ben, and the actors, men and women, did their parts with great commendation . . ." wrote Mr. John Pory, himself a wide traveller to the courts of Europe and that of Turkey. And Jonson recorded of this ephemeral performance: "There was not wanting either in riches, or strangeness of the habits, delicacy of dances, magnificence of the scene, or divine rapture of music [which was played by a leading composer, Alfonso Ferrobosco, the second of that name]. Only the envy was, that it lasted not still, or, now it is passed, cannot by imagination, much less description, be recovered to a part of that spirit, with which it glided by." The spectacle must indeed have been magnificent, with an enormous globe of the earth as if suspended in the air, in which the masquers sat and were slowy revolved by Jonson, ensconced behind the sacrificial altar. It is pleasant too to recall the generous words which the author wrote about his colleague, the originator of these gorgeous fantasies: "the design and art together with the devices and their habits, belong properly to the merit and reputation of Mr. Inigo Jones, to whom I take modest occasion, in this fit place, to remember lest his own worth might excuse me of an ignorant neglect, from my silence". It was not long before Jonson was inspired by very different sentiments.

For the rest of this year and the whole of the following we hear nothing of Inigo's movements. Was he once again in Italy? The only basis for such a conjecture lies in a Latin dedication in a New Year book for 1607 given him by his friend, the Roman Catholic scholar and historian Edmund Bolton.[1] Bolton's inscription, as translated, is to Inigo Jones "through whom there is hope that sculpture, modelling, architecture, painting, acting and all that is praiseworthy in the elegant arts of the ancients, may one day find their way across the Alps into our England". The inference is implicit in the last words, and in the fact that the book, relating to Pope Sixtus V, was published, and so presumably presented to Bolton's friend, in Rome. Certainly Inigo was not concerned with the masque given at Whitehall that January. Nor does he appear at court again until Shrove Tuesday of the following year, when his and Jonson's joint production, the *Hue and Cry after Cupid* was performed in honour of Lord Haddington's marriage. The cost of this masque amounted to the enormous sum for those days of £20,000 of which £1,000 alone was spent on the music by William Lawes. Once again Jonson was to pay tribute to "that admirable artist, Mr. Inego Jones, Master Surveyor of the King's work . . . for his rare decorements . . . who to every act, nay almost to every scene, by his excellent inventions, gave such extraordinary lustre; upon every occasion changing the stage to the admiration of all the spectators". Among the masquers were Inigo's supposed patron, William Earl of Pembroke, his brother Philip, recently created, on account of his exceptional good looks, Earl of Montgomery, and a future patron, Thomas Earl of Arundel.

[1] Bolton's life ambition, never realized, was to establish in England a Royal Academy of Letters and Science.

Inigo's next appearance was on 1st January 1609, when he asked the Lord High Treasurer for £150 with which "he hopeth to discharge the residue of that work which appertaineth to the show—for provision of barriers",[1] or lists for the tilting yard. His production of Jonson's *Masque of Queens* took place before the court on 2nd February. The scenery was quite the most splendid up to date. In fact the French Ambassador, who was present, found it rather ornate than artistic. Some of the settings were deliberately modelled upon the intermezzi staged by Giulio Paragi between the acts of M. A. Buonarotti's opera, *Il Giudizio di Paridi,* which had been performed in Florence the previous October in honour of Cosimo II's marriage to Maria Maddalena of Austria. Consequently the question arises whether Inigo had not again been in Italy and a spectator of the opera. It is otherwise difficult to understand how within so short an interval he could have had access to Paragi's designs or even to reproductions of them.

Anne of Denmark took the closest personal interest in the performance of the *Masque of Queens,* and to some extent dictated the patterns of the dresses and chose the colours. There is a deferential little note from Inigo to the Queen desiring to receive Her Majesty's commands, admitting that the colours of her dress are entirely her choice, but respectfully suggesting that in his opinion grass green mixed with gold and silver will be appropriate.

In the summer of 1609 Inigo Jones was sent as King's Messenger to France, carrying James I's letters to the court of Henri IV. There is a note of Inigo's which begins "being in Paris the year 1609 . . .", but all that it tells is that he witnessed an unsuccessful experiment on perpetual motion. It seems to have been the only special visit he ever made to France, which he must have crossed and recrossed repeatedly on his journeys to Italy. Not a word is vouchsafed on what he noticed of painting or architecture in Paris. In fact the buildings of Inigo Jones point to few French manifestations of style; and among the forty books from his library preserved at Worcester College, Oxford, Philibert de l'Orme's *Le Premier tome de l'architecture* is the only French one. By December Jones was back in England, for on the 11th of that month he was authorized to spend money on the "Princes' exercises at the barriers".

In 1610 the young Prince Henry was created Prince of Wales and in the middle of the summer a masque, *Tethys Festival,* was held in his honour. This time the author was Samuel Daniel, with Inigo Jones as producer. Among Jones's sketches is one for Prince Charles, then aged nine and a half, who made his first appearance on the stage dressed as Zephyrus, in a robe of green satin embroidered with golden flowers. Daniel tactfully gave credit for the success of the performance to Jones. "The art and invention of the architect", he wrote, and this is an early reference to Inigo in such a capacity, "gives the greatest grace and is of most importance, ours the least part"; though whether this observation, which precisely coincided with Ben Jonson's complaints of a few years later, was made with bitterness, we are left to

1 Letter from Sir Thomas Chaloner to the Earl of Salisbury—Hodgkin MSS.

wonder. On 13th January of the next year Inigo Jones was appointed Surveyor to the Prince of Wales.

*      *      *

With the year 1611 begins a short but significant interlude in Inigo's life. By now he was thirty-eight years old, already highly esteemed within a small but influential circle on account of his travels, his knowledge of classical art, his competence as a painter, his ingenuity in devising stage scenery and his capacity to organize superb masques. He could hardly be esteemed as an architect, for so far he had built nothing permanent (and it is unlikely that more than a handful of cognoscenti recognized in his stage sets the revolutionary turn to English architecture which this classical purist was destined to bring about).

The Prince, whom Inigo was henceforth to regard as his master and who now held a separate court of his own, was a prodigiously precocious youth of seventeen. "He had," wrote Francis Bacon after the boy's premature death, "by the excellence of his disposition, excited high expectations among great numbers of all ranks, nor had, through the slackness of his life, disappointed them. He was much devoted to magnificence of building, and works of all kinds, though in other respects rather frugal, and was a lover of antiquity and arts." Prince Henry was indefatigable in his desire to learn and be virtuous, which made his early death the more tragic. These laudable qualities necessarily made him somewhat priggish. So distasteful did he find natural human expletives that he kept a box for fines from members of his household each time they swore. But the service he did to the arts in a pathetically short life should make us overlook the somewhat chilling nature of his piety. At the age of fifteen he had purchased the valuable Fitzalan library from Nonesuch Palace on the death of John, Lord Lumley. It is due to him that the books, which are now in the British Museum, were not dispersed. At his palace at Richmond he laid out gardens and built fountains, and having appointed his new surveyor, he at once commanded him to build a gallery at Whitehall for his collection of pictures. Few of these have been identified, but his own portrait by Gheeraerts, with Lord Essex at the kill of a staghunt, and the "Youth looking through a leaded Window" attributed to the school of Cremona, both now at Hampton Court, were among them.

Nothing by way of creative architecture seems to have been carried out by Inigo in the service of the Prince, and nothing by him in the ordinary run of repair work survives. The picture gallery at Whitehall was probably never begun, and the "piling, planking and brickworks for the three islands at Richmond", the construction of stairs and buildings and the conveyance there of water through pipes, all to the previous plan of Solomon de Caux, were of a secondary nature. The monthly account books for payments of wages, materials and work at Richmond, St. James's and Woodstock Palaces for the Prince of Wales were subscribed by Inigo Jones and, amongst others, Thomas Baldwin and Francis Carter. The names of these two men are constantly met with in state documents relating to building activity during our

30

period. Thomas Baldwin had been appointed in 1611 Comptroller of the Works to the Prince of Wales, a post he afterwards held for Kings James and Charles, at a salary of £120 10s. 0d. per annum until the year of his death in 1641. All his life he worked closely with Inigo, repeatedly signing with him reports on the royal buildings, submitting estimates for repairs, and supervising the operations of his superior. He was a man of high position in his profession, and very probably himself designed buildings of which as yet no records have been found. Francis Carter [1] (not to be confused with Edward Carter, who may have been his son, since he seems to have been active at a rather later date and died in 1653), originally a carpenter, was in earlier days responsible for the great hall roof and wainscot at Trinity College, Cambridge. He was at the time of Jones's and Baldwin's appointments made Clerk of the Works to Prince Henry (he was to enjoy a similar post for his life-time under King James), at a fee of 2s. 6d. a day, including Sundays, only 6d. a day less than the Surveyor's.

We next hear of Jones in September of this year attending a philosophical feast which caused some stir at the time because of the gargantuan quantity of wine which was consumed and the amount of verse it occasioned. The feast was given at the Mitre in Fleet Street by Thomas Coryat to celebrate the publication of his *Crudities*, an extraordinary hotchpotch of a book of travels across Europe which comprises many entertaining and illuminating observations upon the cities he visited. Coryat walked the entire way home from Venice to the English Channel and on his safe return hung up his shoes in Odcombe church in Somerset, of which his father was rector, by way of commemorating the excursion. He had made his friends contribute panegyric verses for publication in the *Crudities*. One of the contributors was Inigo Jones, and the first stanza of his poem began thus:

> Odd is the Combe from whence this cock did come
> That crowed in Venice 'gainst the skinless Jews,
> Who gave him th' entertainment of Tom Drum;
> Yet he undaunted slipt into the Stews
> For learning's cause; and in his Attic rage
> Trod a tough hen of thirty years of age. [2]

Evidently the eccentric Coryat took in good part these and several ensuing stanzas rather more facetious than poetic, and composed at the expense of his reputation for serious living. In return Coryat generously described Inigo in Latin verse as:

> Nec indoctus, nec profanus
> Ignatius architectus.

In November of 1612 Prince Henry died tragically of typhoid fever, whereupon the office of Surveyor suddenly lapsed. In spite of this unexpected check to his career Jones was too busy to repine for long. Previous arrangements for the impending

[1] There is a portrait of Francis Carter by Dobson at Blenheim Palace.
[2] The remaining stanzas all but one were published in Allan Cunningham's *Life of Inigo Jones*, 1831.

marriage of Princess Elizabeth to the Count Palatine were not discontinued. They included in honour of the union two masques, one written by Thomas Campion, the other by George Chapman. Both were accordingly produced by the late Prince of Wales's Surveyor on two consecutive nights in the middle of the ensuing February. The first, commissioned by the King, was held in the Banqueting House. The second, given as a gesture of loyalty by the Inns of Court, was likewise held at Whitehall. Campion recorded of his masque: "I suppose few have ever seen more neat artifice than Master Inigo Jones showed in contriving [the motion of the stars], who in all the rest of the workmanship which belonged to the whole invention showed extraordinary industry and skill." Chapman was still more satisfied with his own, which started with a procession from the house of the Master of the Rolls in Chancery Lane all the way down the Strand to Whitehall. He described it as "a show at all parts so novel, conceitful and glorious, as hath not in this land been ever before beheld". Moreover, he proclaimed that "it was invented and fashioned, with the ground and special structure of the whole work by our Kingdom's most artful and ingenious architect, Inigo Jones"—yet, as far as we know, the artful and ingenious architect had built nothing to his own design in stone, brick or mortar. In connection with Chapman's masque one of Inigo's sisters is for the first and only time referred to—possibly as lending a helping hand in the proceedings. After a payment to Inigo there is in the Inns of Court accounts an item of £10 to "Mrs. Johnes for her brother Mr. Inigo Johnes".

On the 27th April 1613 Jones was promised the reversion of the office of Surveyor-General of the King's Works and Buildings, at the time still held by the ageing Simon Basill. Thus the most coveted office in the realm for a person of Inigo's talent and ambition was fairly within his grasp. The opportunity arose for him once again to travel abroad, and since there were no duties to prevent him taking it he went, as John Webb correctly stated, soon after Prince Henry's death.

This foreign tour, which lasted nearly two years, is the only one of which any written particulars survive, sketchy though they be. Mr. Gotch pieced together in his painstaking manner the itinerary of the tour from notes, often dated, which Inigo made in the margin of his copy of Palladio's *Quattro Libri* and from the correspondence of Lord and Lady Arundel. For it was definitely at their expense and in their company that Jones travelled across Italy at this time. On the 10th April Lord and Lady Arundel had left London as the escorts of the newly wedded Princess Elizabeth and her bridegroom to their future home at Heidelberg. There the distinguished escorts stayed for a while, leaving on 14th June, vià Strasburg and Basle, for Italy. Inigo may not have accompanied them to Heidelberg, but was probably with them when on 1st July they reached Milan, whence the greater number of their attendants were sent back to England. A week later Sir Dudley Carleton, ambassador in Venice, wrote that Arundel "had Inigo Jones in his train who will be of best use to him, by reason of his language and experience in these parts". Inigo Jones will have been engaged to advise them on the purchase of pictures and sculpture, and to point out to them the chief antiquities and noblest buildings in the various cities they visited, most of which were by now familiar to him. Beyond these agreeable duties to a patron so intelligent and cultivated as Arundel, Inigo was free to do as he pleased. He does not seem to have been with the Arundels all the time, and occasionally went off at will on his own business. This undoubtedly was to visit all those places mentioned by Palladio in his book, in the margin of which he wrote down comments. He also had with him his sketchbook [1]—now preserved in the library at Chatsworth—in which he made quick jottings of figures and heads from drawings and pictures of the renaissance masters.

By 23rd September Inigo was in Vicenza, where he made a drawing and recorded a long description [2] of the Teatro Olimpico. The next day he visited the famous Villa Rotonda, commenting upon its solidity and the expense that must have been incurred upon the terrace walls. In January of 1614 he was in Rome, where he compared all Palladio's plans and designs with the ruins themselves. He gave a list of twenty-six temples in and around Rome, and included among them Bramante's comparatively modern tempietto in the cloister garth of S. Pietro in Montorio, where he deplored the use of pilasters on the cella and the consequent necessity of making the door too small. While he was in Rome he sorrowfully recorded that the Pope was pulling down the great hall of the Basilica of Constantine [3] in order to set up the last of its columns for a figure of Our Lady before the church of Sta. Maria Maggiore. Apart from some short excursions from the city he remained there until March, studying and measuring antique remains and sketching the draperies of classical sculpture. The current guide-books for visitors to Rome in those days were still Palladio's, and there is evidence that Inigo greatly relied upon them. [4]

From March to May Jones was at Naples with the Arundels. By the middle of the latter month he was back in Rome making careful measurements of the Pantheon and noting down "more than is in Palladio". This great and most complete monument of the Romans impressed him more than any other, and was, as we shall see, to influence his own buildings in many particulars. (Eleven years later an acquaintance named William Smith, a painter of burnished work, was to tell him that Pope Urban VIII removed the brass beams of the portico to melt them for ordnance, and that he had witnessed the vandalism being perpetrated. [5]) In July Inigo was in Venice by himself; and on 1st August recorded that he talked to Scamozzi, who had convinced him on some point of a discussion about vaulting. He evidently saw a good deal of the old architect, whom he did not much like. When advancing a theory of

---

[1] A few facsimile copies were printed for the 6th Duke of Devonshire.

[2] W. G. Keith, *A Theatre Project by Inigo Jones*, *Burlington Magazine*, Vol. XXXI, 1917.

[3] He called it the Temple of Nerva Traiano.

[4] They were *L' Antichità di Roma* (1554) and *Le Descritione de le Chiese*.

[5] On several occasions Inigo was to lament the spoliation of Roman ruins by irresponsible Popes, of whom perhaps the Barberini was the worst offender. "All the good of the ancients will be utterly ruined ere long *questo Papa e poeta*" is one complaint, and Arundel was a sympathizer who wrote him letters in the same strain.

his own that the ancients put modillions on the frieze of a very high cornice in order to accentuate its features, Scamozzi flatly contradicted him. "This secret Scamozi being purblind understood not", Inigo commented irritably. "Scamotzio errs", he noted about some other technical point. He resented his "ignorance and malice" and thought he claimed to be the author of theories which Palladio had really originated. Nevertheless Inigo learnt much from Scamozzi, made a special journey to see his Villa Molini, and acquired four of his drawings. After a second visit to Vicenza, to restudy the palaces of Palladio, he rejoined the Arundels. The party then set their steps slowly homeward by way of Genoa. There Inigo observed some of the palaces which had so deeply influenced Rubens; and he made the following interesting generalization about their planning. "At Genoa they use most commonly to have two [entrances] one at each end, and it doth well for each apartment hath his loggia to walk in the morning or to make one roddy [sic] in the summer, without troubling the hall, but on the outside one is more graceful for bringing a frontispiece in the midst which is the greatest ornament a house can have." [1] After Genoa the party travelled down the Roman road along the Riviera. We can picture the cumbersome procession of packhorses and mules, bearing the carefully crated treasures and luggage which had not previously been despatched by sea from Ostia or Leghorn. No carriages, we must remember, could pass along that sometimes steep and always narrow track. Lady Arundel, no doubt wrapped in a heavy ermine-lined mantle if the mistral was blowing, would be carried in a litter behind her husband, that deeply reflective nobleman riding ahead. Behind her would be her women, jogging uncomfortably on pillions over the rough surface. Inigo, we may imagine, would for ever be in the rear, halting at intervals to relate the wild acanthus leaves to the foliage of the Corinthian capital, and examine whatever scrap of Roman carving he might espy thrown up by the wayside. Slowly they would dip along the shore under the ochreous rocks; then mount the foothills through the olive groves and the umbrella pines until they reached the great monument at La Turbia, which Augustus had erected to commemorate his triumph over the savage Alpine tribes and to mark the ancient boundary between Italy and Gaul. Thence they passed into Provence and stopped at Arles and Nîmes, where Inigo made notes against Palladio's woodcut of the Maison Carrée, and scrutinized the Temple of Diana. Of this monument he possessed a plan and section drawing by Palladio. They halted at the Pont du Gard, which Inigo sketched, and of which he admired the huge stone scantlings, laid without cement or mortar. It may have been on this return journey that he visited the Château de Chambord and took careful note of the famous double staircase. "They are but two to ascend and the newel hath a wall with windows cut out but this it seems was discoursed [sic] to Palladio and he invented of himself these stairs."

According to a dated note which was written retrospectively, the party was home

[1] This note is typical of Jones's difficulty in expressing himself clearly. Most of his sentences are cryptic and have to be re-read to be properly understood.

by 18th January 1615. That year was to bring further changes to Inigo Jones's fortunes. The death of Simon Basill caused his accession to the office of Surveyor-General of the King's Works and Buildings. The leisurely journeys to the Continent were now over. The days and weeks measuring up temples in the Roman Forum,[1] visiting villas along the Brenta, and copying the classical masters in the galleries of Italian noblemen, were at an end. The long submission to a self-imposed discipline of study had been fulfilled. A second and greater opportunity had arrived for the no longer youthful artist to do justice to his trained talent for architectural design. By now his interests had already shifted—to quote his own words—"more particularly" to architecture.

*     *     *

There is little doubt that during the brief period he served Prince Henry, Inigo Jones instilled into him an artistic as opposed to an iconographical appreciation of pictures. There is no doubt that he did the same service for Lord Arundel, who until Charles I and the Duke of Buckingham outpaced him, owned by far the largest collection of pictures in England. Arundel had begun to scour Europe for works of art when a young man of twenty-three on his first continental tour to the Netherlands, France and Italy in 1609. During the 1613–15 tour he was chiefly looking for pictures by Titian and Giorgione and seeking to establish friendly relations with British diplomats, like Sir Dudley Carleton at Venice, or purely business ones with paid agents like Edward Norgate [2] and William Petty. These men were to find for him in the ensuing years rare manuscripts, coins, marbles, statuary and whatever works of art as well as pictures they could obtain at reasonable prices. That Inigo conducted business for Arundel with these overseas agents we gather from a letter written from the Earl to his wife in the summer after their return to England: "I make no question but Mr. Jones will soon speak with Mr. Oldborough and have under his hand some certainty of his disbursements and employment in Rome, considering his Mr. I am sure Mr. Jones will, in his bargain with Cimandio,[3] include that picture of his father and uncle which hangs amongst the rest." And two years later, when Arundel was obliged to accompany King James on a progress to Scotland, he directed a consignment of twelve pictures he was expecting by sea to be delivered to Inigo Jones. On the Earl's return the two men examined the pictures together, after which Jones was given £200 with which to pay the agent who had bought them.

In similar ways Charles I was to make use of the surveyor's expert knowledge of works of art. Royal commands were issued that Jones should from time to time put in order the Kings' collection of medals and rearrange his collection of coins. It seems that the surveyor had full access to the royal collections whenever he wished,

[1] For *Coelum Britannicum* Jones made a composite sketch of monuments in the Foro Romano.

[2] Edward Norgate (d. 1650) was an illuminator and heraldic painter who became Blue-mantle Pursuivant and Windsor Herald. He was employed by Charles I as well as Lord Arundel as foreign agent to buy pictures.

[3] Presumably a Roman selling his family portraits.

and Joachim Sandraert tells how "the King's famous architect" on his own authority once conducted him into the royal cabinet and showed him a book of Holbein's designs. When in January 1636 Charles received a gift of pictures from the wily Secretary of State to the Vatican, Cardinal Barberini, who had first ascertained what would be most acceptable to a royal collector with supposed Romish leanings, he immediately sent for Inigo Jones. According to Gregorio Panzini, the Papal Agent to the Queen, Jones was accounted "a great connoisseur". Panzini wrote to the Cardinal that when the pictures were unpacked Jones, the very moment he saw them, "greatly approved of them, and in order to be able to study them better threw off his coat, put on his eye-glasses, took a candle and, together with the King, began to examine them very closely. They found them entirely satisfactory . . . the King liked particularly those by Leonardo, Andrea del Sarto and Giulio Romano." There is an interesting sequel to this story which gives an insight into Inigo's character, opinionated and at times a trifle absurd. "The King's architect, Jones", Panzini resumed, "believes that the picture by Leonardo is the portrait of a certain Venetian, Ginevra Benci, and he concludes it from the G and B inscribed on her breast.[1] As he is very conceited and boastful he often repeats this idea of his to demonstrate his great knowledge of painting. As the King had removed the names of the painters, which I had fixed to each picture, he also boasts of having attributed almost all the pictures correctly. He greatly exaggerates their beauty, and says that they are pictures to be kept in a special room with gilded and jewelled frames. . . ."[2] Inigo may have boasted of his knowledge, but it was probably superior to that of any of his contemporaries, including Arundel and the King. His enthusiasm, exaggerated as it may have appeared, was absolutely sincere. Lord Maltravers, Arundel's son, writing to William Petty that same month, told him that the King's surveyor was simply "mad to see" a very important consignment of Neapolitan pictures which Petty had just shipped to England. On another occasion Sir Balthazar Gerbier remarked that Inigo almost went down on his knees to beseech the Duke of Buckingham for a Titian which he had set his heart on obtaining for the King.

\*       \*       \*

If for the moment we disregard Inigo Jones's copious masque designs for figures and scenery, does there exist a single picture in oils, whether portrait or landscape, that can be ascribed to him with certainty? It is true that at Albury Park there is a finished portrait (attributed to him on no apparent authority) of Clifford, 5th Earl of Cumberland, who wears a falling collar, his hair down to his shoulders and whose left hand holds an order hung on a ribbon from his neck. The arrogant and slightly self-conscious tilt of the young man's head coincides with the unconciliatory pose that Inigo himself invariably adopted as a sitter. At Chatsworth there hangs a landscape of men hawking, one of them on horseback, round an opening or quarry. The

[1] If Barberini's gift to Charles I really was a Leonardo, then the portrait may have been the Lichtenstein Ginevra Benci, now in the National Gallery; it has no initials but shows signs of having been cut at the bottom.

[2] R. Wittkower, "Inigo Jones, Puritanissimo Fiero", *Burlington Magazine*, February 1948.

4    Sketch by Inigo Jones for Scene II, "The City of Sleep", of Sir William Davenant's
masque, *Luminalia,* 1638

5    Sketch by Inigo Jones for Scene I, "Night", of Sir William Davenant's masque,
*Luminalia,* 1638

6    Drawing by Inigo Jones in his Sketch Book and adapted by him from a
figure in the Martyrdom of St. Lawrence by Bacio Bandinelli

background is indifferently painted; the figures on the other hand are good, and the horse very spirited and baroque. The rider's pose—he is holding out his rein in his right hand—and the horse's action, bear some relation to Rubens' equestrian portrait of Francisco, Duke of Lerma, painted in 1603. Indeed the whole composition owes its derivation either to Rubens or Vandyke. Lord Burlington, who acquired the picture, attributed it to Inigo Jones, but on whose authority is not known.

At least three self-drawings by Jones survive—in pen and ink, and chalk (12), The pen-and-ink self-drawing, now in the Royal Institute of British Architects was done between the ages of forty-five and fifty. It shows a handsome head—the skull particularly ovoid—a long straight nose, an aggressive mouth, and strikingly searching eyes, deep-set beneath low eyebrows. The remarkably free and sure sweep of Inigo's pencil strokes suggests that he achieved rapid likenesses. His head and figure sketches are no less accomplished than his landscape sketches, and both, curiously enough, are far more compelling than his architectural drawings. For Inigo Jones was first an artist and only subsequently an architect. On this account his buildings, although derivative from Italian sources, are redeemed from dry pedantry, and infused with a vigorous pictorial element. The valuable little sketchbook at Chatsworth contains only a few architectural drawings made to accompany working memoranda. The bulk of the pages contain notes with sketches of drapery taken from antique figures, emperors, soldiers and women. Special emphasis is laid upon the folds of their garments. These, Jones explains, must be deep in the middle and thin at the top and bottom. Experimental folds made from paper models are not commended. He gives directions how to draw the outlines of children and arrive at the true proportions of their bodies. In this connection he quotes Caravaggio, and refers to a wooden frieze of putti which he possesses to illustrate his meaning. The remainder of the sketches are not done from life, but are copies or variants of drawings by the renaissance masters, of whom Raphael, Michelangelo, Agostino Caracci and Parmigianino appealed to him pre-eminently. For the *Masque of Queens* Jones's drawing of Homer is practically a copy of Raphael's Homer in the Parnassus stanza of the Vatican: this suggests that he had made a study of that artist during a visit to Rome before 1609. The beautiful drawing (6) in his sketchbook of a naked youth drawing a sword is copied directly from a figure in the Martyrdom of St. Lawrence by Baccio Bandinelli.[1]

Messrs. Simpson and Bell, in their descriptive catalogue of the masque drawings, claim that the style of Jones's figure drawings during and after the visit to Italy in 1613–14 is noticeably influenced by Guercino, whom he will have met in the small northern town of Cento in Emilia. Their claim is fortified by the presence among the Chatsworth drawings of a sketch by Jones of a head inscribed "Guerchino da Chinto". It is of a young man—Guercino was seventeen years Jones's junior—with full hair parted in the middle and falling thickly to cheek level. They also affect to

[1] This is Miss Joan Sumner Smith's identification. See *Burlington Magazine*, July 1952.

see in Jones's earlier landscape drawings the romantic and meticulous approach to nature of Adam Elsheimer (Lord Arundel owned two paintings by this exquisite artist), and in his later mountain and woodland scenes the influence of the masters of the Venetian and Bolognese schools. There are surely better grounds for supposing that he was influenced by the precise technique of that little master of the roadside, the Frenchman, Jacques Callot. Musketeers, pedlars, gipsies and every variety of vagabond life were victims to the pencil of this boy, who at the age of twelve had run away from home and attached himself to a destitute troop of Bohemians bound for Florence. Mr. Sitwell points out that Jones must have come across Callot, either along the roads with his companions, the strolling players, or in Florence after he had been appointed engraver to the Grand Duke of Tuscany and had introduced his stock of characters to the court scene painters, Giulio and Alfonso Parigi. It is quite obvious that many of Jones's figures for ante-masques,[1] the baboons, mountebanks, tooth-drawers, corncutters and dwarfs, owed their paternity to Callot's nomadic acquaintances. In the masque *Love's Triumph through Callipolis* (1631) the figures of the glorious boastful lover, and indeed the other lovers, are taken practically straight from Callot. It is equally obvious that several of Jones's sets for masques were derived from Giulio Parigi's scenes, to which this extremely imaginative artist imparted the sense of open sea or country within the confined area of his architecturally treated proscenia. For the *Masque of Queens* Jones borrowed, as already indicated, from Parigi's intermezzi in *Il Giudizio di Paridi* a number of ideas, such as the structure of the House of Fame; and for *Tempe Restored* (1632) he even copied, with only slight omissions, the setting of the Garden of Calypso.

By the time the masque of *Florimene* was performed at Whitehall on New Year's Eve of 1636 the nature of Jones's landscapes had become noticeably more English. The transition is not altogether surprising. After twenty-one years his memories of Italian landscape began to fade before the gentle northern contours so persistently before his eyes. Jones's standing scene for the Isle of Delos in *Florimene* depicts a glade in an English park with estate cottages on either side. The winter scene, in the first intermezzo,[2] of leafless trees before a cottage with a smoking chimney rather suggests the purlieus of a Buckinghamshire hamlet than the pastoral slopes of a Greek island. Even so the classical scenery never entirely deserted his retentive memory, especially when street architecture was represented. In his drawing for Davenant's *Britannia Triumphans,* two years later, of a setting which he called "English houses of the old and new forms . . . and a far off prospect of the City of London and the river of Thames" the features of the houses, in spite of their pointed gables, are classical, and the grouping of the two rows decidedly Tuscan. All the same one should be cautious before dogmatically attributing the style of a man of Jones's catholic

[1] The ante-masque was used to introduce the various disreputable characters, the better to show off the heroic characters in the masque proper.
[2] The intermezzo, or intermedium, took place between acts. It was the opportunity of the scene artist to produce magnificent spectacles, often quite unrelated to the main drama.

tastes to particular influences. On the whole his designs were original and his adaptations stamped with his own strongly individual treatment. His architectural scenes especially owe less to the influence of others than to direct observation.

Mr. Sitwell has called Inigo Jones the first and greatest English artist of theatrical scenery. The bold claim cannot easily be disputed, although we are necessarily on weak ground in assessing this most ephemeral of the arts. If only a handful of Inigo Jones's drawings had survived just to cover, say, one of the later and maturer masques—for example, the *Luminalia* or *Festival of Light* (4, 5)—their evidence of his greatness in this particular art would be enough. Nothing could be conceived more expressive of somnolence than Inigo's sketch for the City of Sleep (4), its fantastic towers and spires and distant hillocks poised on the segment of a rainbow: nothing more deeply moving than the pen-and-ink wash of the first scene of night, a still sheet of water in which a low, full moon is reflected and to which a clearing between tall, sombre trees leads down a sloping lawn. Upon the thumbed and creased sheets of paper the splashes of distemper made by the scene-painters over three hundred years ago are a perpetual reminder of the vanished splendours to which these sketches gave rise.

*      *      *

The technical achievement of Inigo Jones in theatrical production was no less remarkable than the artistic. Webb wrote of his masques: "For the variety of scenes, machines, habits, and well ordering of them, in the judgement of all foreign ambassadors and strangers, they excelled whatever of that kind was presented in any other court of Christendom besides." It is only fair to interpolate that the foreign ambassadors were on the whole more guarded in their praises than Webb would have us believe and the French, needless to say, the most critical, in spite of the fact that their own country could not as yet hold a candle to Jones's masques.[1] Yet Webb's eulogy of his master's achievement was thoroughly justified, in that no theatrical spectacles more elaborate than the English court masques had been seen in Europe since the Florentine productions of the preceding century:[2] moreover, the contemporary intermezzi, staged between operatic acts by the Parigi, did not eclipse in splendour their counterparts at Whitehall. In England Inigo Jones had positively revolutionized the dramatic scene. Nothing like his stage machinery had been supposed practicable by his untravelled compatriots. We must remember that as recently as 1576 the first theatre in England was built by James Burbage in Moorfields. Known as the "Theater", it was without precedent, shaped like an amphitheatre, and roofless. Although the private stage in Italy at this date was of far more advanced form, the London "Theater" was the first organized public stage in

---

[1] We have the French Ambassadors' somewhat captious opinions of the *Masque of Queens* (1609) and of *Time Vindicated to Himself and to His Honours* (1623).

[2] Of which the *Mascherata della Genealogia Degli Dei*, performed at Florence in 1565 to designs by Vasari, was the most celebrated.

renaissance Europe. In this respect England can claim once again to be a pioneer of democratic amenity. She was incidentally the first nation to introduce the system of superimposed galleries. These were not all provided with seats, it is true, but stools with cushions could be hired by the more luxurious playgoers. Until Inigo Jones's time movable scenery was very little used since the stage projected into the auditorium. An occasional isolated tree-stump to suggest a forest might be placed at one corner of the stage, or a trestle with trencher on it to simulate a banquet at another, with the title of each scene painted on a board and hung up alongside. These stage props of the sparsest kind would of course remain throughout the whole performance, and the actors merely assemble themselves close to the appropriate symbol of each scene. It was left to Inigo Jones to introduce his startling innovations from what he had seen during his Italian travels. The French theatre had at this time no ideas to offer him, for until the end of the seventeenth century it was to retain the old-fashioned arrangement of the auditorium practically surrounded by a standing pit. On the contrary, the court masques under the first two Stuarts at Whitehall considerably influenced the later magnificent festivals organized for Louis XIV at Versailles.

Inigo evidently identified himself with Palladio in his ambition to produce masques on a scale of formidable architectural dimensions. There exist inserted in Jones's copy of the *Quattro Libri* a drawing and a plan by him for a stage, based on the Teatro Olimpico at Vicenza which was begun by Palladio at the close of his life and finished by Scamozzi. Instead of the five perspectives carried out by Scamozzi, Inigo in his design gave but one under a wide arch. A marginal note shows that far from his scheme being less developed than Scamozzi's, it was intended to provide by means of movable curtains and wings a greater variety of scenery than was allowed by the unchanging perspectives at Vicenza. In other words Inigo adopted the classical formula of the theatre, first laid down by Vitruvius and amplified by Serlio, Palladio and others, as a basis on which to construct the scenic requirements of his imagination. He somehow acquired and brought back from Italy Palladio's first designs for the Teatro Olimpico, which he kept constantly before him as he developed his theme.

Until the approach of the Civil War put an abrupt term to all organized spectacles, the development of Inigo Jones's theatrical art can systematically be traced over thirty-five years. The marvel is that one man managed to produce so many revolutionary changes in a single art, let alone architecture as well.[1] In the *Masque of Blackness,* produced for Queen Anne in 1605, he made two technical innovations. The first was, quite simply, the use of a painted stage curtain depicting a forest landscape with huntsmen, which was either let fall to the ground or drawn aside in two folds to disclose the second innovation. This was a complete sea-scene. Never before in England had a single scene been used in place of several distinct symbols simultaneously presented. The seascape remained throughout the masque, and all the acts took place before it. Although in *Blackness* one scene only was pre-

1 His dual achievement can be paralleled, not surpassed, by Bernini.

sented, by the time of *Florimene* and the *Royal Slave* [1] at Oxford in the sixteen-thirties six and eight changes of scenery respectively were contrived. In the *Hue and Cry after Cupid,* in honour of Lord Haddington's marriage, Jones brought about a further perfection of stage setting in the first use of the proscenium, or ornamental border, which was made to surround the curtain and stage like a picture frame, an idea he had learnt from Baldassare Peruzzi. In the masque *Hymenaei* Jones introduced perhaps his greatest novelty of all in the use of turning machinery, called by Ben Jonson the *machina versatilis.* This enabled eight masquers to sit in a globe of the world, seemingly suspended in the air, which, on being turned round, displayed them to the audience. Whether Jones invented the device we do not know. Stephen Harrison, in his *Arches of Triumph erected for the entry of James I to London,* in 1603, had illustrated an arch, called by him Cosmos Neos, over which he placed a globe made to revolve slowly by means of four persons concealed in the rear. Inigo may have seen the illustration, or even the actual arch, which perhaps gave him the idea. It was evidently a popular one, and Alfonso Parigi copied Jones's suspended globe trick in the performance of the *Nozze degli Dei* at Florence in 1637. Finally Jones perfected in *Hymenaei* a scenic system which was both practical and effective. This was known as the Vitruvian system, which the Italian renaissance stage had first adopted. It comprised triangular turning frames, or *periaktoi,* enabling rapid and easy changes of scenes in the wings. Jones's first presentation of the system had been made in Christ Church hall at Oxford in 1605. It did not prove popular, and the innovation of his "rare devices" was for a time completely overlooked.

In the *Masque of Queens* the Italian element was more pronounced than in any of Inigo's previous masques, not only in the fearful hell scenes and the architecture of the House of Fame, but in the brilliant lighting effects. By an ingenious system of translucent glasses filled with water the reflection from hundreds of candles and rushlights flickered over the spangled dresses of the performers. The friezes were filled with lights of all colours of the rainbow, which in Jonson's words were "like emeralds, rubies, sapphires, carbuncles, etc., the reflex of which, with other lights placed in the concave upon the masquers' habits, was full of glory". In *Luminalia,* one of the last masques, the lights were still more carefully trained on the performers, and in the night scene wonderfully subdued by means of oiled papers. Finally, in Davenant's *Salmacida Spolia,* performed in 1640 just before the Puritan edict put an end to all court pageantry, the height of Inigo's stagecraft and the culmination of his scenery was reached. In the words of its producers the objects of this masque were "by all means to reduce tempestuous and turbulent natures into a sweet calm of civil concord". Alas for this pious aspiration in the face of the impending calamities! Ground plans for the elaborate scene-shifting in *Salmacida*

---

[1] "The interludes thereof were represented with as much variety of scenes and motions as the great wit of Inigo Jones (well skilled in setting out a court mask to the best advantage) could extend unto." Anthony à Wood, *Athenae Oxonienses,* 1691.

*Spolia* exist.[1] Here we see Jones's developed system of side shutters and back shutters set in grooves so that they could with the minimum of difficulty be rolled backwards and forwards on runners. At the sides were cogged windlasses and ropes with which to raise and lower the clouds. The strange spectacle of a cloud descending and enveloping the Genius of the three Kingdoms (in this last masque the King and Queen took part), then gently lifting him up to the heavens again, "gave great cause of admiration, but especially how so huge a machine, and of that great height, could come from under the stage, which was but six foot high". Were there, we wonder, no spectators on the occasion who foresaw the significance of that cloud's action upon their doomed sovereign?

Yet in spite of the perfection of Jones's stagecraft at court, the public theatre in England throughout the seventeenth century remained practically unaffected by it. Luckily, however, John Webb had a hand in the last masque produced by Inigo, and he was not the man to allow anything that redounded to his master's credit to pass away neglected or unrecorded. In conjunction with the author of *Salmacida Spolia*, the admirable disciple years later—and surprisingly enough during the Commonwealth by special permission of the Protector—produced the first English opera, *The Siege of Rhodes*, making full use of the movable scenery and *periaktoi* introduced by Jones. Never before had women in England appeared on the public stage. The warm reception of the opera was immediate, and the wonderful spectacle loudly acclaimed. Many more years were allowed to pass before scenery of such excellence was produced again. But the performance of the *Siege of Rhodes* was not forgotten, since it marked the transference of the wonders of the masque stage to the public theatre. Furthermore, owing to John Webb's piety, the drawings for *Salmacida Spolia* and so many of Inigo's later masques were preserved, and have come down to us in this undeserving twentieth century.

[1] Lansdowne MSS. 1171, British Museum.

CHAPTER TWO

# INIGO JONES—
# CHARACTER AND STATUS

THE partnership of Ben Jonson and Inigo Jones, which opened so auspiciously with *The Queen's Masque of Blackness* in 1605, was destined not to endure. Here were two men of the same age, of similar humble parentage, both artists of genius and high ambition, patronized simultaneously by a new dynasty which was anxious to give them unlimited scope provided they worked together jointly and harmoniously. Then, after a period of remarkable successes, their relations deteriorated, and led to a violent explosion and a sequel of vitriolic recrimination. Much has been written about the causes of the quarrel, Jonson's fierce and adolescent jealousy, Jones's overbearing arrogance, the poet's superior learning and the architect's superior artistry; the inferior wisdom of the one, the inferior education of the other—all of which explanations are doubtless well considered and sound, but entirely beside the point. The trouble was that each was vigorously responsive to the compelling demands of his own calling, and naturally unprepared to cede anything to the equally strong claim of his rival's.

The fact was that Jonson took the intellectual content of his masques more seriously than anyone else did. He was convinced that what he termed the "soul" of the masque was something of infinite value. By this he meant the complex mythological arguments which he dressed in verse to be recited by simple lords and ladies, to whom and the spectators the masque was merely the pageantry of an evening. The plot, seemingly unprofound, and the poetry of these masques were his "invention", and as such outweighed any other consideration. He gravely resented—it is only fair to say from the very beginning of the partnership—the prevailing tendency to hold in higher respect the decoration and mere mechanics of the show. "Painting and carpentry", he complained in bitter irony, "are the soul of masque." Poetry had become the handmaid to gilded cloth and deal boards. So

> Pack with your peddling poetry to the stage,
> This is the money-got mechanic age.

As the applause won by his partner became louder and louder, so did his resentment mount from irritation to contempt, then to intense dislike. These emotions were

45

embittered by his conviction of the other's unworthiness and, above all, lack of learning. Jones, for his part, stoutly declined to admit the superiority of poetry to dramatic production, which he refused to recognize as a mechanical art of only fleeting importance. In his view his scenic effects were of permanent significance, since they were the offspring of Architecture, which he held to be the goddess of the liberal arts. Furthermore he was on the defensive, because in his day in England the visual arts generally were not yet admitted to the same high plane as literature. He was not a little over-sensitive to Jonson's satires directed at this "engineer" and "architectonicus professor", who "is or would be the main Dominus—do All in the work". And here Jonson had touched upon Jones's Achilles heel, which was undoubtedly an unfortunate tendency to bombast.

Jonson's wrath was evidently seething long before it exploded, for William Drummond of Hawthornden records that the poet on a visit to him in Scotland in 1618 reviled the architect and told him that he had "said to Prince Charles, of Inigo Jones, that when he wanted to express the greatest villain in the world, he would call him an Inigo". He was, he assured Drummond, "an arrant knave, and I avouch it". This was strong language to use about a partner in conversation with their employer's son, especially when that son was the heir to the throne. It was not relished by the Prince of Wales. Yet the partnership continued to function until the final break came in 1631 with the publication of *Love's Triumph through Callipolis,* on the title-page of which Jonson put his own name before Jones's. Jones foolishly took immediate umbrage and was very angry, and the King, now Charles I, took his part. This did not prevent Jonson from pouring forth a spate of venomous and damaging satire, which only recoiled upon himself. Inigo, he asserted, was a snob, for ever referring to the pedigrees of his well-born acquaintances and the degrees of their gentility. "I have upon my rule here the just *perportions* of a knight or squire . . . down to headborough or tithingman, or meanest minister of the peace" he is made to say in the *Tale of a Tub.* He mispronounces the simplest English words and mis-quotes his Latin. He is absurdly addicted to certain over-used words like "feasible" and "conduce". He dresses far too splendidly for his station in life, wears doublets of velvet and embroidered caps. Above all he brooks no correction, suffers no other person's talents but his own to be praised, and "must be sole inventor", not only architect, scene-painter and stage producer, but in fields where he cannot possibly hope to succeed, music master and even poet as well. An intimate friend[1] sent Jonson a line or two of warning—"I heard you lately censured at court that you have lighted too foul upon Sir Inigo, and that you write with a porcupine's quill dipt in too much gall", and advised him, if he could not retract what he had written, at least to "repress any more copies of the satire on the royal architect; for, to deal plainly with you, you have lost some ground at court by it: and as I hear, from a good hand, the King, who hath so great a judgement in poetry, as in all others things else, is not well pleased therewith. Dispense with this." The sting in this well-meant

[1] James Howell, author and diplomat.

7    Inigo Jones in his old age. A study by William Dobson for the finished portrait in Chiswick House. (This portrait came from Treowen Court, Monmouth)

8    Santa Susanna, Rome. Façade by Carlo Maderna built shortly before Inigo Jones's visit to Rome in 1614

letter lay in the implication that since the King was a great judge of poetry Jonson, who was his poet laureate, had better have a care of his position. The result was that Jonson never wrote another masque for the court and Jones had his triumph in thenceforth collaborating with minor poets who were content to subordinate their art to his.

If we take account of Ben Jonson's tempestuous nature we can easily sympathize with his feelings of disappointment and jealousy. He was utterly and rather touchingly sincere in his sense of the wrong that had been done to poetry and himself by the man who, once a promising artist and his friend, had turned out a mountebank and a fraud—for that is what he undoubtedly believed Inigo to be. But it is difficult at this distance to understand, without other evidence, the imputation of dishonesty levelled by Ben at Inigo. He kept on repeating it. "Not ten fires," he exclaims in reference to the one that destroyed the Banqueting House at Whitehall, "nor a parliament can with all remonstrance, make an honest man" of the architect of its successor. No references by other disinterested persons to this grave charge exist, and the only hint that the accuser gives us is that Inigo re-used old material in his masque scenes for which he was paid more than once. Jones retaliated as best he could to Jonson's quick-firing satires with heavy epigrams. "To his false friend Mr. Ben Jonson", he indited one, and said truly enough:

> thou hast writ
> Of good and bad things not with equal wit:
> The reason is, or may be quickly shown
> The good's translation, but the ill's thine own.

He complained how he had for years put up with Ben's interminable, boring stories out of friendship, drunk with him to excess out of sheer good fellowship, and even preferred his company to that of great lords—an admission from Inigo that meant a good deal more than it would have from most people. All he had received in return was ingratitude and deceit. He then finished with a couplet, not ungenerously worded and rather aggrieved than vindictive:

> From henceforth this repute dwell with thee then—
> The best of poets, but the worst of men.

We are left to conclude that in the quarrel most blame attaches to Jonson, and that Jones was rather bewildered by the whole affair. But then we do not know enough of Inigo's personality to judge how intolerably his conceit exasperated his contemporaries without himself being faintly aware of the fact.

If we look at the portraits of Inigo, other than the self-drawings (which are remarkably sparing of the tiresome trait), we cannot fail to detect strongly in evidence that air of self-importance which so particularly annoyed Ben Jonson. In the National Portrait Gallery version, which is a contemporary copy of the Vandyke expressly painted for Webb, afterwards sold to Sir Robert Walpole and now in Russia, Inigo is about sixty of years of age. He wears a velvet skull cap from which flamboyant rays of strong wavy chestnut hair spring like streamers from an electric ventilator. The eyes are wide, protuberant and staring, and the mouth, being firmly shut, is shown to be underjawed. The whole head is tilted upwards in an aggressive and self-important pose that is distinctly unprepossessing. In the Dobson portrait at Chiswick [1] Inigo is by now an old man of over seventy and his hair and beard are grey. The features have already softened and the face is calmer and more resigned. Yet it is clear as day that the subject before us is a person who knows his worth and will not leave us in any doubt of it. The most pleasing of the portraits is the drawing by Vandyke in red chalk which was given to Lord Burlington by the 4th Duke of Devonshire and has now found its way back to Chatsworth. Inigo holds loosely in his right hand a sheet of paper which has given him matter for deep reflection. His eyes are focused, under falling brows, upon the distance, and he has forgotten for the moment to strike an attitude. We can here study the real man because he is unselfconscious and absorbed. There is the vast expanse of brow, crowned by a banded cap from which the hair this time is falling in a natural and easy manner: the extremely handsome nose, long and finely moulded: the lips slightly parted, on the point of expressing an opinion that will, when it comes, be forceful and considered. About the whole face there is an air of slight perplexity and deep thought which conveys inner humility and greatness.

John Webb, who knew him better than any man, categorically affirmed that Inigo was "neither arrogant, nor ambitious", words which, coming from his apprentice and deputy for close on a quarter of a century, cannot lightly be dismissed. Certainly his relations with his assistants and inferiors, who might well have had reason for resentment and jealousy, were invariably cordial. He appears to have treated them fairly, and given them a free hand once he had proved their worth. Several were made beneficiaries by his will. Vertue tells us he heard that Jones was generous to other artists. He must have been easy-going and open-handed over money matters, for he cheerfully went unpaid for his great work at St. Paul's Cathedral, and endured long arrears of pay on other occasions without complaint. When the Office of Works announced that they could not afford to pay his workmen, Jones voluntarily surrendered his own salary until their wages were met. To his own people, then, who had learnt how to handle him and moreover come to revere his great gifts and determination to get his way for the sole sake of his duty or his art, he may not have appeared arrogant or ambitious. But there is evidence that he seemed so to strangers who were unlucky enough to cross his path. The humble inn-keeper who was peremptorily commanded by the King's surveyor to demolish his inn because it encroached upon the garden of a person of good quality; the mean woman who was summarily told to fill in the pond in which she was wont to water her diseased horses and thereby pollute the King's drinking water; and the still meaner woman whom he had put in the stocks for escaping from a sealed plague-house, in

---

[1] A sketch, even freer and finer than the finished portrait at Chiswick Villa, came from Treowen Court, Monmouth, for sale at Messrs. Spink's in the summer of 1952 (7).

order to pray in the Abbey, and thus infecting the congregation; these people on the other hand one and all deemed him arrogant and autocratic. There were, too, the celebrated cases of the parishioners of St. Michael-le-Querne, Cheapside, and St. Gregory's. In the first Inigo, as a member of the Royal Commission for Buildings, forced a man to demolish his shop in order to make room for additions which he thought suitable to the church. The parishioners wanted to build the additions in their own way, and only won their battle by persistently pretending to mislay the surveyor-general's plans. The second case portended a more serious outcome. At the time of reconstructing St. Paul's Cathedral, Inigo, after giving the matter very careful consideration, ordered the parishioners of St. Gregory's to demolish their church, which was endangering the foundations of the cathedral. The parishioners would not have been quite so indignant if the surveyor had not a short while ago pronounced that there was no such need. The matter rankled deeply, and in 1641 Inigo was cited to appear before the House of Lords. There it was disclosed that he had actually started to demolish the church and positively threatened, if the parishioners would not complete the process, to have the pews and galleries sawn down and the furnishings thrown into the street. The surveyor wished, so the parishioners proclaimed, to be "sole monarch" and had displayed a most domineering temper towards them. Jones put up a spirited defence and denied the charges brought against him. The case seems to have been brought to no conclusion. It was probably deferred because of the political troubles.

\* \* \*

The early biographers of Inigo Jones persistently claimed that he was a Roman Catholic, and implied that the Italian style of his architecture was largely derived from Catholic sympathies. The legend was first started by Vertue, who was told by Wren that Inigo died at Somerset House a papist. Somerset House had been the palace of Charles's French Queen, and her chapel there one of the legitimate centres for Catholic worship. The legend was strengthened by the capture of the architect in the Civil War at Lord Winchester's seat, Basing House, in Hampshire, a papist as well as royalist stronghold. The place was sheltering, amongst others, Hollar, the Bohemian, and Faithorne, the English engraver, and Robinson, the actor, all prominent Roman Catholics, when it was besieged by Cromwell's forces. At six o'clock on an October morning in 1645 the house capitulated. Robinson was killed for mocking the soldiers, but the others were spared and ignominiously taken prisoner. "There was the famous Surveyor", a parliamentary broadsheet gleefully proclaimed, "and great enemy to St. Gregory, Innico Jones, who was carried away in a blanket, having lost his clothes." Another broadsheet referred to him ironically as the "contriver of scenes for the queen's dancing-barn". But the biographers never stopped to explain why, if he was born and died a Catholic, he was baptized and buried in Protestant churches; nor how within so short a time after the penalizing laws against Catholics passed in consequence of the Gunpowder Plot, a man of

Jones's small influence would have found employment in the Prince of Wales's household and then of the King's; nor how he was elected a Member of Parliament in 1621,[1] and a Justice of the Peace for Westminster seven years later. On the other hand it was not unusual in those unstable times for intellectual persons to change their religion, usually for reasons of expediency. Lord Arundel, the leading Catholic layman, whose father, grandfather and great-grandfather had been condemned to death for the faith, and forfeited their titles and estates, apostatized. Ben Jonson, who was a convert, did likewise, and the ultimate expression of Scepticism was Lord Herbert of Cherbury's dying remark, when offered the last sacrament, that if there were good in anything it was in that, and at all events it could do his soul no harm.

If therefore we have no record that Inigo Jones was a secret or even temporizing Catholic, his political sympathies were presumably with the High Church Erastianism of Archbishop Laud and Charles I. The interesting discovery of Dr. Wittkower [2] that in 1636 he was called "puritanissimo fiero" by the papal legate, Gregorio Panzini, in a letter addressed to the Propaganda in Rome, and described by the Superior of the Queen's Capuchins "as one of those Puritans or people without religion", does not necessarily imply that he was an enemy to the Church of Rome. The term Puritan was in the seventeenth century applied indiscriminately by royalists and Catholics to prominent persons not of their persuasion. The word had a political as well as a religious significance. In 1616 the Venetian Ambassador wrote home that William Herbert, Lord Pembroke, who at the time held the office of Lord Chamberlain, was "head of the Puritans", simply because he opposed the foreign policy of James I and Buckingham. The charge was of course totally remote from the truth. Jones's loyalty to the Crown was as consistent as his patron, Pembroke's. A passing cynicism about religion,[3] especially if Jones had previously been a convert like his former friend and contemporary Jonson, would be quite enough to provoke the offensive charge from two highly placed emissaries of the Pope.

*     *     *

It is natural to inquire at this stage what were the formative influences upon Inigo's architecture, which resembled nothing hitherto seen in England. Little is known of Jones's foreign travels outside Italy, and nothing at all of the impressions made upon him by buildings in Denmark and the Netherlands—if indeed he ever visited these lands. He has recorded the scantiest observations upon architecture in France. In none of his buildings are Scandinavian, Flemish or even French influences discernible. That reduces the search for sources of influence to Italy. And there, the

[1] He was elected member for Shoreham borough vice Sir John Leedes, Kt., who was expelled from the House on 16th February 1621. Parliament was dissolved 8th February 1622. There is no evidence in Notestein's index that Jones spoke in Parliament.

[2] R. Wittkower, "Inigo Jones, Puritanissimo Fiero," *Burlington Magazine*, February 1948.

[3] Jones however prefaced his will in the conventional phraseology of his times: "I commend my soul to Almighty God hoping by the death and passion of my Saviour Jesus Christ to have remission of my sins."

world's richest centre of classical and renaissance prototypes, we can safely do an immense amount of elimination.

To begin with, we look for prominent buildings which had just arisen or were in process of arising in those cities which Jones is known to have visited. Which, for instance, were the newest churches and palaces that this highly observant and susceptible man may have seen as he wandered about Rome in 1614? On the edge of the Quirinal Hill, in what is now known as the Via Venti Settembre, are two churches, balancing one another, dedicated respectively to Sta. Susanna (8) and Sta. Maria della Vittoria. The façades of both churches are in the heavy counter-Reformation style which followed the mannerist style of Michelangelo's dramatic invention and preceded the highly fanciful and lively rococo contours with which, later in the seventeenth century, Bernini and Borromini were to surprise the sombre streets and squares of Rome. The façade of Sta. Susanna was added to Carlo Maderna's recent nave by G. B. Soria in 1603, and that of Sta. Maria della Vittoria built two years later by Maderna himself. Neither of these rather constricted elevations, tightly packed with fussy, stodgy detail, can have appealed to Inigo's taste for free planes and sparse ornament. If he ever made any notes upon the two churches they have not survived. Yet he may well have had their elevations at the back of his mind, when he recorded in his sketchbook his objections to the form of decorative treatment which characterizes them. "In all inventions of capricious ornaments", he wrote, "one must first design the ground, or the thing plain, as it is for use, and on that vary it, adorn it. Compose it with decorum according to the use and the order it is of...." Whereupon he proceeded to deplore the evil of heaping capricious ornaments upon façades at the expense of their design, and to blame the man chiefly responsible for it. "And to say true all these composed ornaments the which proceed out of the abundance of designers and were brought in by Michelangelo and his followers in my opinion do not well in solid Architecture and the facciate of houses, but in garden loggias stucco or ornaments of chimney [pieces] or in the inner parts of houses these compositions are of necessity to be used." Then in the following famous words—brief slapdash jottings though they are—he sums up his principles of what is fitting in architecture. "For as outwardly every wise man carrieth a gravity in public places, where there is nothing else looked for, yet inwardly hath his imaginacy set on fire, and sometimes licentiously flying out as nature herself doth oftentimes extravagantly, to delight, amaze us, sometimes move us to laughter, sometimes to contemplation and horror, so in architecture the outward ornaments ought to be solid, proportionable according to the rules, masculine and unaffected." These pronouncements are interesting in that they are directed not only against the prevailing exponents of the baroque in Italy, but against the contemporary Jacobeans at home.

Other recent churches which Inigo must surely have studied in Rome are Maderna's more satisfactory façade of Sta. Francesca Romana, rebuilt at the southern end of the Forum for Pope Paul V in 1613 (its medieval campanile features in Jones's composite sketch of the Forum for the masque *Coelum Britannicum*); S. Lorenzo in Miranda, rebuilt in 1602 within the prostyle of the Temple of Antoninus and Faustina (it also features in the same sketch); and the north front of the Lateran basilica. The twin steeples [1] of this front date from 1560, and Domenico Fontana's faultless portico from 1586. They are products of the developed Italian renaissance and Inigo will have preferred them to any Roman church architecture of his own day. He must also have seen Fontana's Lateran palace, which contemporaries considered remarkable for its unbroken, astylar façade.

When we come to Venice and the surrounding district of Veneto, we are on far more promising ground for seeking the sources of Inigo Jones's architectural inspirations. He was clearly not interested in the Gothic filigree of the Doges' Palace, the Lombardesque porphyry discs of Sta. Maria dei Miracoli, or even the horizontal masses of Sansovino's palaces. It was architecture of a still later phase of the Renaissance that appealed to Jones's sense of classical propriety. His surviving sketches and notes plainly indicate that he looked to Palladio as his principal teacher and guide. And it was not Venice itself, where Palladio's buildings are confined to a few famous churches, which Jones made his main field of studies, but firstly Vicenza, and secondly the banks of the Brenta and the lush, watered plains of Veneto, where Palladio's palaces and villas have become part of that beautifully ordered landscape. Inigo Jones visited these palaces and villas one by one, and to them we shall look in due course for the major influences upon his own work.

In addition to the famous copy of the *Quattro Libri*, Inigo somehow acquired in Italy a large number of original drawings by Palladio.[2] Whenever he noticed any variations from them in the finished engravings of the book he made a note against them in the margin. At least forty-six original versions of the drawings illustrated were owned and identified by him. With such veneration did he regard Palladio that he even recorded a conversation with one of his old masons in Vicenza, who pointed out to him two capitals on the Palazzo Thiene carved by the master's own hands. Yet Inigo in no sense slavishly followed Palladio. On the contrary he freely dissented from him whenever he believed him to be mistaken in fact or theory, writing in the margin the terse words "not to be imitated". Particularly was this the case whenever the Italian adhered too dogmatically to the tenets of Vitruvius, whose pedantry often made Jones remonstrate. "Methinks that Vitruvius might as well prefer the grammarian to the philosopher as the mathematician to the architect", he noted in his copy of Vitruvius.[3] Indeed, the mistake Palladio made was to overlook the limitations of this doctrinaire Roman scholar, who flourished at the beginning of the reign of Augustus Caesar and consequently never lived to witness the great age of imperial architecture. Vitruvius's doctrines embodied late Hellenistic principles of

---

[1] These feature in another scene for *Coelum Britannicum* where they rise above a curious Tuscan Gothic structure with crocketed gables. It somewhat resembles Sta. Maria della Spina, the chapel on the left bank of the Arno at Pisa.

[2] Many of these are now at Chatsworth.

[3] Vitruvius's *I Dieci Libri Dell'Architectura*, 1567, Inigo Jones's annotated copy at Chatsworth.

architecture, for he was totally ignorant of early Greek buildings, about which his rash statements betray that his information was second-hand.[1] Wherein then does the value of his teaching consist? It consists mainly in technical information about building methods during the limited period between Alexander and Augustus; and in the establishment of the rule of the module,[2] which assures the proportions of an architectural unit. Upon the foundation of the module Vitruvius constructed his principles of architecture, namely order, arrangement, eurhythmy (by which he implied beauty and fitness), symmetry, propriety and economy of embellishment. These principles he elaborated in long passages which are fascinating and surprisingly unboring to read. It is Vitruvius's renaissance followers who are often so boring in their reiteration of the uses of the classical orders and in their over-emphasis of those of his doctrines which do not really matter.

Palladio, in adopting Vitruvius's principles, evolved the more advanced notion that pure architecture was applied mathematics and dependent for its abstract beauties upon ''the correspondence of the whole to the parts'', just as the human figure, to reflect the divine image of God, had to be perfectly balanced and proportioned.[3] He elaborated the most abstruse rules of harmonic progression to attain architectural perfection, in identifying musical with architectural ratios. Inigo Jones imbibed the neo-Platonic teaching of Palladio, that the architect is an intellectual whose creations symbolize the almost supernatural images conceived in his mind. He learnt from him to regard as interdependent the units of a building, whose interior plan as well as exterior surface must be strictly proportioned. He, too, saw architecture in terms of the human-figure analogy, inherited from Vitruvius. ''As in design'', he wrote, almost paraphrasing Palladio, ''first one studies the parts of the body of man as eyes, noses, mouths, ears and so . . . one comes to put them together to make a whole figure. So in architecture one must study the parts as lodges, entrances, halls, chambers, stairs, doors, windows, and then adorn them with columns, cornices, sfondati, statues, paintings . . .'', and he continued to unfold a fascinating string of legitimate ornaments. Where he differed from Palladio and certainly Vitruvius was in his implication that these columns, cornices, etc., might be adventitious ornaments, and not in the words of the former ''all members necessary for the [structural] accomplishment of the building''. He reaffirmed Palladio's seven most beautiful shapes for a room, viz.: ''The fairest manner of rooms are 7, round, square, diagonal proportion [i.e. the diagonal of a square for the length of a room], a

---

[1] For instance he had an absurd theory that the Greeks put empty vessels under theatre seats so as to amplify the voices from the stage. ''If it is asked in what theatre these vessels have been used'', he writes vaguely, ''we cannot point to any in Rome itself, but only to those in the districts of Italy and in a good many Greek states.''

[2] The module is the divisor upon which all the other measurements of a classical building depend. In modern times it was first reassessed by Vignola in his *Cinque Ordini d'Architettura*, 1563, as half the diameter of the column at its greatest thickness.

[3] See R. Wittkower's recondite articles on the ''Principles of Palladio's Architecture'', *Warburg Institute Journal*, 1944

square and a third, a square and a half, a square and two-thirds or two squares.'' From these formulae he deduced why he had for so long admired the Temple of Jupiter in Rome. It was simply because its plan was based on a series of circles and its proportions were determined by dividing the largest diameter into six parts and then recombining them.

Many of Inigo's notes are mere paraphrases, often in the briefest form, of Palladio's Italian text. Others are memoranda for his own purposes, one of which may well have been to compile a book on architecture, since the words ''See my note book on Architecture'' are constantly repeated. But throughout these jottings there is a marked absence of pedantic deductions and a reluctance to dogmatize, not shared by Vitruvius and Palladio. Jones's latitude is shown in several passages where he gives more than one opinion and recommends that a sound judgment must decide which is most appropriate to the particular argument at issue. ''That which is done by reason and is gracious though it vary from the usual way is good and to be followed'', he writes about a novel manner of treating the Corinthian capital. ''The liberty of composing with reason is not taken away'', he writes again in his odd manner of phraseology, ''but who follows the best of the ancients cannot much err''. And the summary of his philosophy lies in these words: ''To vary is good but not to part from the precepts of the art.''

\*     \*     \*

On the evidence of the notes it is hard to believe that Inigo Jones, imbued as he was with classical culture, ever built in the so-called Elizabethan or Jacobean styles. It is tempting nevertheless to trace the early development of his architectural style in the sketches of buildings he made for masque scenery. Thus, in his rough sketch for the House of Fame in the *Masque of Queens* (1609) we have in a sense the earliest of his architectural drawings (10). It is of a hexagonal structure in two stages. The lower stage, crowned by an architrave supported by caryatids, has on its central front an opening with winged victories in the spandrels; and on the two flanking fronts windows with panels of bas-reliefs over them. The three visible fronts of the upper stage have trifoliated arches. The whole affair is an imposition of Gothic detail upon a classical background. A cancelled design for this masque depicts a castellated gateway having a portcullis, flanked by twin towers containing cruciform arrow-slits. This design we are inclined to describe as medieval. But it no more suggests a real medieval structure than Horace Walpole's Strawberry Hill conveys the true rust of the Barons' wars. For *Oberon the Faery Prince,* a masque in honour of Prince Henry performed in 1611, Jones made several drawings of Oberon's Palace which are certainly more Jacobean in character than any others. The original sketch for the front of the palace, on which Inigo wrote the most precise measurements of every detail, shows an airy battlemented structure with bartizans at the corners and slits for crossbows, a huge doorway with terms supporting a broken pediment, a central cupola and two rather Puginesque chimneys. The composition

10 "The House of Fame". Drawing by Inigo Jones for Ben Jonson's *Masque of Queens*, 1609, showing Gothic and classical architectural influences

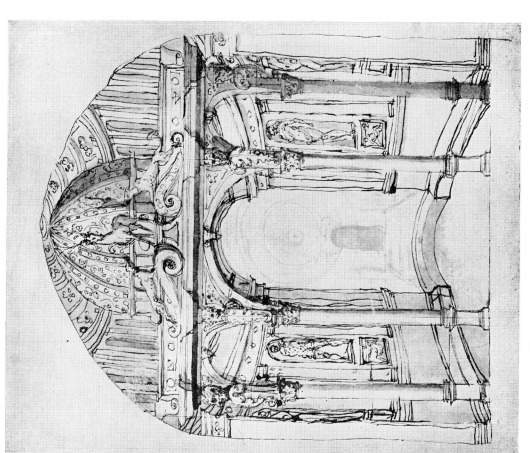

9 Scene probably connected with Ben Jonson's Masque *Oberon*, 1611. Drawing by Inigo Jones showing early essay at classical architectural design

11   Drawing by Inigo Jones of his Catafalque for King James I, 1625

vaguely recalls the keep of Bolsover Castle which was being built by John Smithson at this very time. Two other drawings for the palace show a screen upon tenuous columns, with a central pediment whereon hounds bay at a stag—a conceit which he may have observed at the Château d'Anet, when he was in France eighteen months previously, or merely adopted from de l'Orme's book in which it features (9).

Yet nowhere in his voluminous but disconnected memoranda does Inigo convey a hint that he had ever built in or countenanced the manner of his English contemporaries. Consequently the frequent attributions made to him, by Horace Walpole and nineteenth-century writers, of houses in the Jacobean style, especially those dating from 1614, can be dismissed. The remarkably few buildings that can with documentary proof be called his are all specimens of his neo-classicism. Finally, in judging whether a private house in the classical style could be of his design one should always inquire whether the client was a person who moved in court circles. Unless he was a highly placed official who enjoyed the royal favour he would stand little chance of engaging the services of the King's Surveyor of Works.

What, for instance, did John Webb have to say about Inigo Jones's style? He wrote as follows: "... . I must tell you that what was truly meant by the art of design was scarcely known in this kingdom until he under the protection of his late sacred Majesty [Charles I] and that famous Maecenas of arts the Rt. Honble Thomas Earl of Arundel and Surrey brought it in use and esteem among us here." Webb's meaning is clear. Inigo Jones, under the patronage of these august persons—and without reference to patrons, who supplied the money, it was indelicate to attribute innovations solely to the artist—was the first Englishman to introduce form into architecture. Webb uses Inigo's own favourite word, "design", which so excited the mockery of Ben Jonson. Yet Arundel was not in this connection a passive patron who merely paid and basked in the adulation which the efforts of a hard-worked subordinate had earned for him. James Howell, in a letter written during the Earl's life-time, remarked of him that he, "observing the uniform and regular way of stone structure up and down Italy, hath introduced that form of building to London and Westminster and elsewhere, which, though distasteful at first, as all innovations are, yet they find now the commodity, firmness and beauty thereof, the three main principles of building". Howell, in his reference to the three current principles of building, was more or less quoting Sir Henry Wotton's well-known conditions: commodity, firmness and delight.[1] He was hardly exaggerating the Earl's claims, because Arundel had in 1618 been made the most prominent member—we would say chairman—of the commission to restrict houses from arising on new foundations within two miles of the city of London. The commission, on which Jones likewise served, became of immense importance after it was reformed in 1625. Not only did it prevent the encroachment of new houses upon open spaces: it promoted a high standard of building materials, and encouraged the use of brick in place of lath and

[1] Sir Henry Wotton, *The Elements of Architecture*, 1624.
[2] Sir Edward Walker, *Life of Lord Arundel*, 1651.

timber. It introduced the method of Flemish bonding, which eventually led to the beautiful gauged and rubbed brickwork, to be perfected by Wren's workmen. It demanded certain order and system in the design of street houses which necessitated some attempt at town-planning. The regular layout of squares, beginning with Lincoln's Inn Fields and Covent Garden, to Inigo Jones's planning, was the outcome of the commission's authority. Arundel's right-hand man, servant and monitor, who from the first inculcated in him an understanding of the classical culture and who now conceived and carried out these important reforms, was of course the King's surveyor.

The tragedy is that Inigo Jones, during his long term as surveyor to James I and Charles I, built so little. It was due to the two Kings being severely curtailed by Parliament from spending out of national funds on public monuments. The royal masques were another matter, since they were private performances, for the most part paid out of the sovereign's own resources or those of his courtiers. So were the King's personal collections of pictures and works of art. If vast official undertakings, like the Whitehall Palace scheme, had to remain dreams on paper, ecclesiastical and domestic projects on the grand scale were momentarily over. Church building had lapsed with the Reformation and was not seriously to revive until after the Great Fire of London. On the completion of the Knoles, Audley Ends and Hatfields—signs of the Tudor nobility's urge to establish themselves in the provinces—there was a lull until the Commonwealth magnates started building themselves seats. But during the tranquil years from the end of James I's reign until the Civil War, when an abrupt halt was called to all forms of private spending, few great houses were needed.

The astonishing thing is that, in spite of his restricted opportunities for architectural expression, Jones's reputation stood so high in the opinion of his contemporaries. Webb possibly allowed his hero-worship to exaggerate when he wrote: ''It was Vox Europae that named Inigo Jones [''the Vitruvius of all Christendom'' ], being much more than at home, famous in remote parts, where he lived many years, designed many works and discovered many antiquities, before unknown, with general applause. . . . Mr. Jones was generally learned, eminent for architecture, a great geometrician, and in designing with his pen (as Sir Anthony Vandyke used to say) not to be equalled by whatever great masters in his time, for boldness, softness, sweetness and sureness of his touches''; and when he called him the most famous architect of his age. Yet, like all Webb's statements, these deserve a fair hearing. There was some truth in his reproach that Jones was more esteemed abroad than in England, where his innovations did not in his lifetime always command full recognition, because they were not properly understood. We know that in Italy he consorted with artists like Guercino, Callot and Scamozzi, who were his peers. Rubens, Jordaens and Vandyke, who knew him and even worked with him in England, were qualified to assess his importance in relation to European art. They doubtless spread his renown in the Low Countries. As to Webb's assertion that Inigo ''designed many works and discovered many antiquities" abroad, his meaning surely is that he drew many buildings and revealed to his countrymen the importance of many ancient monuments through his researches and measurements. Within a decade after his death Inigo's status began to be more thoroughly appreciated by his countrymen. "Worthily reckoned among the most excellent architects this nation ever bred and a general scholar", is the concession Dr. Charleton made to his memory in the text of his *Stoneheng restored to the Danes,* a book published in 1662 to refute Jones's ludicrous claim that this monument was built by the Roman Britons in honour of the sun god Caelus. And, as an instance of his name being identified with good architecture, there is a passage in a letter written by Brian Duppa, Bishop of Salisbury, to his friend Sir Justinian Isham, only seven years after Jones's death: "There be few Inigos to raise up material buildings, but rational and moral buildings will meet with greater difficulties." [1]

Inigo Jones has been compared to Brunelleschi on the score that both men weaned their countries from the Gothic fashion of building and introduced a new style based on the methods of ancient Rome. To a limited extent only is the comparison permissible. Brunelleschi's task was far easier and he achieved more striking results because he found the Roman tradition only moribund and not by any means dead in Italy. Italy had never forgotten even in her darkest periods the classical source of her culture. Her lands throughout the Middle Ages were still strewn with the remnants of antiquity and often her medieval builders and sculptors, like the Pisani, copied, as they thought faithfully, from the classical fragments around them. In England of course the classical link had long ago been entirely severed. Inigo Jones was introducing a novel style of architecture to which English craftsmen were unaccustomed, in spite of spasmodic Tudor dalliance with renaissance decorative motifs. And without trained craftsmen the greatest architectural genius can accomplish little. Inigo Jones was badly served in this respect. Seldom do his buildings achieve high decorative quality or finish. Their design is always better than their execution. It was in vain that he preached Palladian proportion to ears which, if not deaf, were not yet attuned to hear. Inigo necessarily brought into practice the renaissance system of working drawings. Previously English craftsmen had contributed their own decorative features according to the ancient patterns inherited from their forbears. But proportion demanded that every feature should be reproduced strictly to scale as the master-architect designed it. The hazards of this new system were that until native workmen acquired sufficient training they produced indifferent buildings even to the designs of a good architect. For example, Inigo's design of the hall at the Queen's House, Greenwich, is quite comparable in excellence with Brunelleschi's design of the interior of the Capella Pazzi at Florence. Unfortunately the work of Thomas James and Richard Durkin, carvers of the King's ship, *The Sovereign of the Seas,* is not as sensitive as that of Donatello and Desiderio. The ceiling ribs and balusters of the hall gallery in the Queen's House are coarsely

[1] Quoted with the permission of Sir Gyles Isham, Bt.

carved. The medallions on the frieze of the Capella Pazzi are, on the contrary, little works of art. But if Jones was seriously handicapped by inexperienced craftsmen, Wren half a century later was able to profit from their remarkably swift improvement in the interval.

Mr. Herbert Horne's comparison of Jones with his compatriot Milton is rather more pertinent. Although the architect was thirty-six years the poet's senior, he was more representative of the pragmatical seventeenth century than of the visionary sixteenth century to which he belonged by birth and upbringing. For instance, he possessed none of the spontaneous lyric quality which makes his nearer contemporary Shakespeare a child of the impetuous, romantic Elizabethan era. He had the painstaking, syntactical temperament of the artist, a gift he shared with Milton. For Milton in returning to the correct traditions of antiquity, tidied up the loose ends of the English language left by the Elizabethan poets and set exacting standards of versification. Inigo Jones did a similar service for architecture and in his own we have a forewarning of the severely grand, minatory and organ note of Milton's poetry.

12. INIGO JONES: A SELF-PORTRAIT

*From a drawing at Chatsworth*

# CHAPTER THREE

# INIGO JONES—
# DOCUMENTED BUILDINGS

IN September 1615 Simon Basill died and at once the post of Surveyor-General of the King's Works and Buildings, the reversion of which had been promised to Inigo Jones two years before, was faithfully granted him. He was now a middle-aged man of forty-two. The emoluments he derived from the important new post were 8s. a day for his entertainment, 2s. 8d. a day for riding and travelling expenses,[1] and £80 a year for what was described as his "recompense of avails", or salary. The regular income amounted to an enviable £275 a year, but payment was often several years behindhand. In addition, the surveyor expected to receive extra payment for all special work of building and decoration beyond the routine duties connected with his office. He was also granted every All Saints' Day a parcel of stuff for his livery cloak, or uniform of office, to be worn at state functions. The routine duties which made the job no sinecure may best be understood by a perusal of the State Papers and Declared Accounts, wherein they are set forth. They consisted of constant reports upon such things as water supply and sanitation, public nuisances of all kinds, street encroachments, overcrowding and the disregard of building regulations within the City of London; an unending amount of repairs to the many royal palaces scattered up and down the country;[2] and preparation of noblemen's houses where the court was to stay during the royal progresses.

The adoption of these duties, which were to last him until the outbreak of the Civil War, when Inigo was an old man, makes a definite landmark in his career. Up till now the man we have been considering was the student of classical antiquities, the artist and masque designer. The new surveyor-general was not by any means to shed these rôles, but henceforth to assume another, by which he is best known to posterity. The architect emerges. And because the buildings of Inigo Jones are the prototypes of that English classical architecture which flourished throughout the eighteenth century and did not entirely disappear until the middle of the nineteenth,

---

[1] Inigo's travelling days varied from 20 to 131 in the year.

[2] The Declared Accounts in the Public Record Office for James 1's and Charles 1's reigns cover work done at some twenty-five royal houses.

they are of immense individual importance. Of the twenty or more buildings which Jones is known to have designed, eight partly survive today. Of the eight, four may still be seen more or less in the condition in which the architect left them.

1 *House for Lord Arundel at Greenwich* and *Arundel House in the Strand, 1615–17*

Inigo Jones's relations with Lord Arundel remained very close long after his return to London from the continental tour and even after his appointment to the surveyor-generalship. It might in the first place have been through Arundel's influence that the post was assured him, for it did not always happen, as we shall see with the luckless John Webb, that appointments held in reversion were confirmed by fickle monarchs. In a sense Inigo stayed in Arundel's service, for he continued to act as his agent in the purchase of pictures and works of art. Lord Arundel, in a letter to his wife from Wilton, had written on 30th July 1615: "Upon Thursday next the king dineth at Wilton, by which time my Lord of Pembroke hopes Mr. Jones will be come hither. I tell him I hope he will, but I cannot promise, because I spake not with him of it, when I came out of town." All that summer they were in touch, and the following extract from another letter from the Earl to his lady written after Inigo's royal appointment in the autumn shows what duties were expected of him. After giving directions to Lady Arundel how he wanted gilt leather fitted as skirting to some rooms in his house at Greenwich, Lord Arundel said: "I pray let Mr. Jones set the wainscot partition in hand for the low gallery, and let the organ be removed into the lower dining-chamber."

Nothing more is known of Inigo's work for the Earl's house at Greenwich, but two years later he was making drawings[1] for doorways at Arundel House in the Strand. He probably only contributed a few features to this great house of the Howard family, which stood between Essex House and Somerset House. Henry Peacham says that Arundel began to assemble his great collections at Arundel House in 1614. The famous sculpture and picture galleries, with their open views into the garden, wherein the Earl and the Countess were painted by van Somer in 1618, may have been added by Inigo Jones, who would best have known what his patron's requirements amounted to. That the whole house was not rebuilt by him at this time is more or less proved by some notes in the Palladio volume. In one margin Jones wrote: "an excellent invention of a cimatio see for this invention the architrave at Ar. House Greek but the carving in the cavetto is otherwise"; and in another: "the architrave at Ar. House which I think was of the temple of Minerva at Smirna by reason of the gorgons heads in the metopes of the frieze". Inigo had not visited Greece or Smyrna, and even if he had designed the Greek architrave at Arundel House would surely not have been in any doubts about the inspiration behind it.

2 *Newmarket, Cambridgeshire: royal lodging, brewhouse, stable and kennels, 1616–23*

From 1616 till 1623 payments are made for alterations and additions to the royal

[1] In the library of the Royal Institute of British Architects, London.

manor house at Newmarket. A new lodging for the King is the first item in the accounts and Thomas Stiles, who was to work in the royal service until the death of Charles I, was one of the masons employed. "A fair lodge and new stable" for the great horses, a dog house for the King's hounds and a brewhouse appear in succession. Edmond, or Edward Kynnesman, or Kinsman, mason, worked with Thomas Stiles on the brewhouse, which, the accounts tell us, had an architrave at both gable ends. Nothing, however, of these works remains. A plan and elevation signed by Jones for a brewhouse exist. The elevation is a dull and purely utilitarian affair.

Jones's earliest signed and dated architectural drawing belongs to the year 1616. It is indifferently done in pen-and-ink wash, and is of a central porch in three storeys under a pediment, which frames a heraldic cartouche. There is nothing to connect this fairly developed classical design with the Newmarket additions.

## 3  *Oatlands Palace, Surrey, 1616–17*

Fairly extensive works were begun in 1616 for Queen Anne at the royal palace of Oatlands in Surrey. This year Jones built a silkworm room, and the next "a great arched doorcase", or gateway, for which enormous and seemingly unnecessary pains were taken. Two sketches exist of a very rough sort in Jones's hand, one for each face of the gateway. Built into an outer garden wall, the straightforward pedimented structure with inverted scroll-supports is related to a design for a gate in Sebastian Serlio's *Architectura*.[1] It is shown in the background of van Somer's well-known portrait of Queen Anne holding five whippets on a leash. The Declared Accounts give detailed descriptions of how the expenses were incurred. Robert Stickles was paid for setting out on the spot the work for the masons to follow; Edward Kynnesman, mason, who apparently did most of the rough work, "for squaring, working and setting of Caen stone for part of a great gate at Oatlands House being wrought up the jambs three foot in breadth apiece and two foot di thick, the gate being twelve foot high and seven foot broad between the jambs, having on each side Doric columns cut rustic with a frontispiece and a square table of marble set over the same . . ."; Thomas Stiles, master mason, for riding all the way from St. Albans expressly to finish the gate; Edward Basill [2] (perhaps a son of the late surveyor), clerk of the works, for looking to the materials and keeping a day book; Arnold Gonerson [3] for "his extraordinary pains", unspecified, and Henry Hearne [4] for his pains in keeping the accounts. Two lesser gateways were added by Jones afterwards, and as late as 1636 he was busy with some vaulting and a new chimneypiece in the palace. The following year he made a sketch of a landscape to be painted in oil on the open wall of a garden house. The great gateway was demolished about 1860.

[1] The first five books published 1559.
[2] Edward Basill figures as clerk of works in the royal service until 1636 when he probably died.
[3] Arnold Gonerson was perhaps a quarry owner. He is paid for supplying freestone by sea to King's Lynn for Sir Roger Townshend at Raynham in 1621. Townshend described him as a mason.
[4] Henry Hearne acted as clerk of works for the Crown from 1615 until 1637.

We now come to the earliest building of Inigo Jones to have survived, in spite of a number of vicissitudes in the eighteenth and nineteenth centuries which made a mockery of the architect's original composition (14). In 1708 the sills of the ground-floor windows were lowered and sash frames substituted for mullions and transoms. A hundred years later the house was divided into five tenements, with disastrous consequences to ceilings, fireplaces and internal decoration.[1] Fortunately the injuries it sustained have been repaired, and the alterations eliminated: the building has been very ably restored to its seventeenth-century condition by the Ministry of Works. It is of very great—perhaps of the very greatest—importance in the history of our domestic architecture, since it is the first absolutely classical example to have been begun in England.

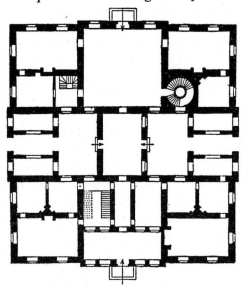

13. The Queen's House: Plan

The Queen's House arose indirectly out of a minor tragedy. Anne of Denmark, hunting one day in the park at Theobalds, aimed at a buck and shot, alas! Jewel, James I's favourite hound; "at which", we are not surprised to learn, the King "stormed exceedingly awhile". But that enigmatic monarch, if not strictly uxorious was fundamentally well disposed towards his spouse. He quickly recovered his natural good temper and next day sent her in token of forgiveness a diamond valued at £2,000, as a legacy from his dead dog. He also included, as a gesture of his affection, a grant of Greenwich Park in jointure. The Queen waited a year or two before commissioning Inigo Jones to replace an old gatehouse, which stood upon the edge of the garden of Greenwich Palace, with something more elegant to enable her to cross the public Deptford–Woolwich highway, into the park dryshod. Building was accordingly begun in October 1616, but ceased in 1618, a year before the Queen's death. It was not resumed until the next reign in 1629 for Henrietta Maria, to whom Charles I had given the property, and was not finished until 1635. Some of the wainscot was still being carved the following year, and even in 1637 work indoors was in process while canvases were put up to keep the sunshine off the Queen's windows.

The first reference to the building is found in a letter written on 22nd June 1617 by John Chamberlain to his friend Sir Dudley Carleton, then Ambassador at The

1 We owe it to Queen Mary II's respect for the name of Inigo Jones that the Queen's House was not demolished when Greenwich Palace was being rebuilt. Hawksmoor made designs to improve it at a later date and these were rejected.

14    The Queen's House, Greenwich: the South Front

*Architect: Inigo Jones, 1616–35*

15   The Queen's House, Greenwich: the Galleried Hall, 1630–35

*Architect: Inigo Jones*

Hague. "The Queen removed on Tuesday from Greenwich to Oatlands and the Prince to Richmond: she is building somewhat at Greenwich which must be finished this summer. It is said to be some curious device of Inigo Jones, and will cost above £4,000. . . ."

Once named the House of Delight, the building was meant by its architect to be rather more than a glorified bridge connecting the palace garden with the park. In fact it became a royal plaything and, like the later Petit Trianon, a lavishly decorated retreat, where the Queen could retire from the rigours of court life and amuse herself at pretending to be just an ordinary lady. In designing it Inigo Jones had in mind the casino or Villa di Papa Giulio built outside the northern gate at Rome by Vignola and Ammanati for Pope Julius III's recreation. Among a series of preliminary sketches are three for a house designed upon a hemicycle like the Pope's casino. Others show a central block surmounted by a domed lantern and joined at its four corners by four square pavilions containing stairwells. But these essays were abandoned in favour of the existing design, for which two models were prepared and approved. For his designs and models the architect received payment, as well as for "taking down the old house over the park gate there, as in digging the foundation of the new buildings, making of cellars, and bringing up the brick walls of the said new buildings . . .". For seventy-seven days, ending 30th June 1617, Inigo Jones was paid at the rate of 6s. 8d. a day; again from 1st August to 30th November and again from January to April of the next year at the same rate. These payments were additional to his salary as surveyor-general.

The "curious device" of Inigo Jones was of course so described by Chamberlain on account of its site athwart a main road, and its Italian planning and façades which in England were absolute novelties. Until John Webb, after the Restoration, filled in the centres of the east and west sides over the roadway so as to make them uninterrupted elevations (117 ft. in length) and the building a solid rectangle, the Queen's House had consisted of two blocks (115 ft. long) connected on the first floor by one central bridge room only. The building resembled in fact two Italian palaces facing each other across a narrow thoroughfare. The planning of both blocks was strictly proportioned. The old Elizabethan great hall and screens passage having been abandoned, a saloon on the central axis was substituted, with lesser rooms and stairways grouped around it in absolute symmetry. The façades were naturally the most startling innovation to Jacobean eyes, for they were studiedly based on Italian prototypes,[1] and—what is particularly significant—prototypes which were *not* Palladian.

Of the origin of the façades Inigo Jones gives a hint in the notes of his Palladio volume, where he says that he visited Scamozzi's Villa Molini near Padua, built in 1597, and repeated some of its features in the Queen's House.[2] In a comment upon

[1] Since the outside walls had only reached *piano nobile* level by 1632 the Queen's House was not the first Italian building to be seen in a finished state by our countrymen. The first was the Banqueting House.

[2] W. Grant Keith, *R.I.B.A. Journal*, August 1937.

balustrades between columns, he notes that where the top of the pedestals of the columns "be no higher than the floor of the portico and then the rail of the parapet or leaning must be let into the body of the column as I did at Greenwich in the portico towards the park and as I have seen at ponte della Cagnia near padoa in a villa of clarimo Molin"—a departure, as it happens, from Palladio's practice. To a large extent Inigo adapted Scamozzi's design to the south or park front at Greenwich, merely ignoring the pediment of the portico, the sloping roof and large lantern of the Villa Molini. He borrowed the rusticated basement storey, the windows of the basement and *piano nobile* and the central recessed portico. For the north, or garden front, Inigo was largely inspired by the Villa Medici at Poggio a Caiano [1] near Florence, built in 1485 by Giuliano da San Gallo for Lorenzo il Magnifico. Inigo used the same but greatly modified arrangement of a terrace substructure (omitting the vaulted colonnade beneath) and beautiful curved perron approaching it.[2] He further-more derived the idea of linking his two blocks from the wasp-waisted plan of the Villa Medici, using only a narrow bridge room for the Queen's House in place of the double cube of the other, whose scale is altogether larger. The material he chose was brick, faced with rusticated stone to first-floor level, plastered and limewashed above. On this account the Queen's House was long known as the White House.

Whereas the proportions of the larger rooms are a square and two-thirds, Inigo made the saloon, or hall, being the principal of them all, a cube of 40 ft. (15). Its proportions are absolute because the compartmented ceiling is flat. The massive corniced beams are of carved pinewood; the flats are enriched with a guilloche, and the frieze with a wave-mould; all are painted in green and gold. The same moulds appear on the Banqueting House ceiling and, until the house was gutted by fire in 1912, appeared upon some of the principal ceilings of Lees Court, Kent. The panels of the Queen's House ceiling were originally filled with canvases by Orazio Genti-leschi [3] of Pisa and his daughter Artemesia, depicting the Arts of Peace, which were taken down and removed to Marlborough House by Sarah, Duchess of Marlborough. Around the hall a gallery is carried upon vast cantilever scrolls, likewise richly carved. The surprisingly thin-waisted balusters are turned and not moulded. Their original white—now faded to grey—and gold colour scheme has been restored by the removal of twenty-four over-coats of paint. The wainscot in the hall may have been the work of Thomas James, Richard Durkin, and Zachary Tailer, carvers, and George Cary, painter and gilder.[4] There was a sharp exchange of letters in 1637 between Inigo Jones and the Navy Commissioners, who had pressed the first two men, previously exempted, into carving Peter Pett's great three-decker, *The Sovereign of the Seas*. The beautiful floor in black and grey marble, which follows the

[1] R. Wittkower, *British Art and the Mediterranean*, 1948.

[2] Robert Adam made use of this curved stairway at Kedleston and Osterley.

[3] Gentileschi came to England in 1626. He introduced to this country the style of Italian decorative painting first made popular by Raphael and Giulio Romano.

[4] Durkin is known to have carved two great picture frames, Tailer ten wooden pedestals for statues and Cary to have painted and gilded five picture frames for the house.

pattern of the ceiling, was laid by Nicholas Stone. His nephew, Charles Stoakes, claimed that between the years 1636–9 Stone, "appointed by Mr. Surveyor", did make the "fine mosaic pavement and geometrical stairs and many other works" in the Queen's House with the help of his cousin Gabriel Stacy. The "geometrical stairs" means the curved tulip staircase with wrought-iron balusters which adjoins the hall to the north-east.[1]

The hall gallery gives access to the two principal apartments reserved for the Queen's use upstairs. They face the palace and river. On the west is her bedroom, with a rather feeble gold-painted cornice. The large rectangular flat of the ceiling originally contained a panel by Giulio Romano, which has been replaced by a poor composition of Aurora accompanied by Zephyrs dispersing the shades of night, by, it is said, Thornhill. The cove of the ceiling still retains some early arabesques, masks, scrolls and fleurs-de-lis by Orazio Gentileschi. To the east of the gallery is the Queen's cabinet with ceiling of pine. A blue pigment background sets off the gilded carving by John and Mathias Christmas, who also, to the architect's intense annoyance, were in the middle of their work called away to decorate *The Sovereign of the Seas*. The acanthus scrolls of the frieze link up the fleurs-de-lis of France with ciphered cartouches. In 1639–40 Sir Balthazar Gerbier, who was in Antwerp, negotiated on Jones's behalf with Jakob Jordaens for painted panels on canvas to fill the ceiling and walls of the Queen's cabinet. Eight canvases were supplied, set up and inventoried. In 1808 they were removed, and their whereabouts since have never been discovered. Inigo had wished Rubens to be commissioned, but his charges were considered too expensive, and before a settlement could be made a letter from Gerbier announced his death. When Jordaens consented to provide the panels Inigo gave Gerbier detailed instructions as to how he wanted them painted. The subject was to be the story of Cupid and Psyche. "The faces of the women", he wrote, must be made "as beautiful as may be, the figures gracious and svelta." Care must be taken by the artist to consider how the light from the windows would strike the paintings once they were set in place.

When Henrietta Maria returned at the Restoration as Queen Mother, accommodation for her at the Queen's House was found inadequate. We have seen how John Webb thereupon enlarged his master's building by dexterously adding two end bridge rooms to the open centres of the western and eastern sides. No architect could have been chosen more ready to treat Inigo Jones's little masterpiece with sympathy. Webb employed upon his new ceilings John Grove, who in 1662 had become Master Plasterer and was later to work for Wren on some of the city churches.

5   *Holyroodhouse, Edinburgh*, 1617

Fourteen years after his succession to the English throne James decided to pay a

---

[1] This hall, with flat compartmented ceiling and gallery carried on brackets, was copied on a larger scale by the Palladian Leoni a hundred years later at Moor Park, where the craftsmanship is noticeably more refined than at Greenwich. Kent likewise copied it at Wakefield Lodge.

first visit to his native kingdom. A magnificent progress to Scotland was staged in July 1617 to impress his needy subjects in that barren and sadly impoverished country. In the royal suite were the Earl of Arundel and the reigning favourite, the Marquess of Buckingham, whose ostentatious and extravagant equipage, instead of pleasing, merely shocked the dour Scotsmen. A gossipy letter from John Chamberlain to Sir Dudley Carleton stated that many things had been sent ahead from London to Edinburgh, including two organs and other furniture for a chapel, for which Inigo Jones was responsible. Nicholas Stone recorded in his note-book that he was sent at this time to Edinburgh, where he undertook to do wainscot work in the King's closet and chapel and upon the organ. Since Jones did not accompany the progress, Stone will have carried out the work on the surveyor's behalf and at his dictation from London. There are payments to Inigo Jones about this time for much riding and travelling to the sundry royal palaces, so possibly he had already made a preliminary journey to the Scottish capital before July.

This year Jones drew detailed plans for a new Star Chamber "which the King would fain have built, if there were money",[1] which there was not. Consequently the chamber was not built and the King had to rest satisfied with repairs to the existing one. But the surveyor's unexecuted elevation, preserved in Worcester College library, Oxford, is of great interest. It is an ambitious and absolutely Palladian design, conceived before that for the Banqueting House. Its character must have struck the King and the officials who looked it over as something quite revolutionary. The façade derived straight from the palaces at Vicenza. Wholly rusticated, it was divided into seven bays with a central pediment over four Corinthian columns. Its window surrounds were heavily blocked in that fashion which a hundred years later was associated with the name of James Gibbs.

## 6   *Whitehall, work for Lord Buckingham, 1618*

At this date George Villiers, whose wealth and power were still on the increase, had not yet been granted a separate London establishment. James in fact could not bear him to be out of his sight for any length of time. In 1618 Inigo Jones was paid for "working, framing, rearing and finishing the Marquess of Buckingham and Mr. John Murray [Keeper of the Privy Purse and later created Earl of Annandale] their new lodgings towards the Privy Garden" at Whitehall. These lodgings were in part of the old rambling palace along the river side, and Jones's work amounted to little more than hasty alterations and the design of a ceiling for the Marquess's dining-room. At a later date John de Critz,[2] the King's serjeant-painter, decorated the walls of the various rooms with grotesques. In the compass chamber he did a painting of two flower-pots in stone colour, with flowers in them, over the chimneypiece. The cornice of the chimneypiece he pricked out in blue. The accounts rather pointedly

[1] John Chamberlain to Sir Dudley Carleton, 22nd June 1617.
[2] John Decreete, or de Critz, b. 1555, d. 1641, was serjeant-painter from 1605 till his death. He was paid for an immense amount of specified taskwork at practically every royal palace.

specify that the King provided all the timber and materials, whereas Buckingham merely paid for the workmanship. At every palace where the King was wont to stay over long periods, lodgings for the favourite were prepared next his own.

Inigo had been in London in January for the performance of the masque *Pleasure Reconciled to Virtue*—it was accounted a failure and was the last masque for some years to come. In the spring he may have made a hurried visit to Rome. A rough sketch, undoubtedly by his hand, of a fountain, inscribed "ffontane di Giovanni Maggi Romano Roma, 1618", is difficult to explain, if Jones had not drawn it on the site. He is next heard of in October eating grapes and peaches with Lord Arundel in Ware Park.

### 7 Queen Anne's Hearse, 1619

In March 1619 Queen Anne died and Inigo Jones, if he had a heart, must surely have mourned this frank, generous woman who spoke her mind to all and sundry, loved artists, and relished every opportunity for artistic display. She possessed humour and tolerance. She seldom chided her unsatisfactory husband, did not resent his unconventional peccadilloes, and loyally came to his aid whenever he made a fool of himself. She let him go his way and she went her own uncomplaining. Many husbands would consider her a model wife, were it not for one incorrigible, uncontrollable failing—reckless extravagance.

Her funeral, however, was a posthumous exception to this venial failing. Eyewitnesses grumbled that it "made but a poor show", a state of affairs the Queen would have intensely disliked. Another wrote that it "was but a drawling tedious sight". Only the spectacle of her hearse was applauded and this was acknowledged to be "the fairest and stateliest that I think was ever seen", by that ubiquitous gossip, John Chamberlain. If her widower felt constrained to stint her memory at her obsequies, her old protégé, the King's surveyor, evidently did not, for the hearse was his contribution. Furthermore he was properly paid for it. There exists a sketch by Inigo for a catafalque for a Queen—undoubtedly Queen Anne's—a thronelike structure, its canopy and scrolling crests supported on terminal figures. Within it the seated figure of the Queen holds orb and sceptre. Maximilian Colt, the monumental sculptor, worked the capitals and much of the ornament, including the leaves of the lead oak-tree made to grow out of the top of the canopy.

### 8 The Banqueting House, Whitehall, 1619–22

On the 12th January 1619 some workmen, repairing scenery for a masque, allowed it to catch alight and the fire quickly spreading soon burnt the Banqueting House at Whitehall to the ground. The fire destroyed all the records in the Signet Office and the books of the Council, and was only prevented from setting the whole Whitehall Palace ablaze by the timely energies of the Lord Chamberlain, William Lord Pembroke, and his brother Philip Lord Montgomery. They organized a fire-brigade, got water from the Thames and pulled down old inflammable buildings around the palace. But their efforts did not prevent the London rabble, always attracted by disasters, from breaking into the palace and pilfering whatever they could lay their hands on, including the King's bed. The City of London generously offered to rebuild the hall and the King, acquiescing, gave it in return the liberties of the White and Black Friars and Great St. Bartholomew. By 19th April Inigo Jones had prepared designs for a new building which he and his colleagues, Thomas Baldwin, William Portington,[1] Francis Carter and George Meale[2] submitted with an estimate for £9,850. As it turned out, the estimate was over £5,000 on the low side. On 1st June work was begun and on 27th of the same month Inigo Jones was paid upon the Council's warrant for a model of the proposed building.

At Chatsworth there are two drawings in Jones's hand showing the Banqueting House much as it is at present, namely a Palladian palace of two storeys over a basement, and in seven bays, the three centre ones projecting. The more finished of the two drawings was carried out, except for the richly filled pediment, the high roof, and the reclining Michelangelesque figures over the windows—the lack of which features is much to be regretted. The plan which accompanies both drawings and one of the drawings allow for a low wing at either end. But they too were omitted. These wings would also have been an improvement for practical reasons (the finished hall had no internal staircase), as well as for architectural balance. There are two other drawings by Jones for details, one dated 1619, of a great door, which does not exist, the other of a window, which can be identified with those windows along the upper storey. It is easy to trace the sources from which Inigo pieced together this integrally Vicenzan composition (1). For example the voussoirs of the basement windows, the first-floor pedimented windows with their three central balconies, and the broken entablature over the columns derive from Palladio's Palazzo Iseppo de' Porti; the carved frieze of masks and ribboned swags from the Palazzo Thiene;[3] and the unfortunate continuous balustrade from the Palazzo Barbarano. The whole composition was, unlike the Queen's House, essentially a Palladian exercise, and not any less successful on that account.

Inigo did not entirely depart from the style of the Banqueting House's predecessor, to judge from the only record there is of it, a plan and measured elevation of its basement storey made by John Smithson soon after it was built. This basement was rusticated and pierced with small square windows, like the existing basement. The plan, moreover, shows an unsatisfactory internal arrangement which made James I very indignant when he rode from Windsor in September 1607 to see how his new Banqueting House was progressing. The State Papers relate that when the King came inside the hall he could scarcely see out because of the columns which

---

[1] William Portington, King's master carpenter, probably died 1628–9 when he was succeeded by Ralph Brice.

[2] George Meale, clerk of the works at the royal palaces until the middle 1630's.

[3] Where the frieze was not carried out—an indication that Jones worked from the plates in Palladio's book rather than from studies of the originals.

had been set up before the windows, of all places, "and he is nothing pleased with his lord architect for that device". Who can the lord architect have been in the year 1607 when Inigo Jones was probably in Italy? He was certainly an amateur, to have placed classical columns in front of windows, and yet, judging by Smithson's drawing, someone who had travelled to Italy. Perhaps, since he took such pains to try and save it, Lord Pembroke had been the lord architect.

Work on the new Banqueting House went forward at a great rate and no expenses were spared. In the accounts are special charges for a new pier off the Isle of Portland [1] for shipping the stone all the way to Whitehall, and for a cartway from the quarry, three-quarters of a mile distant, to the pier. The architect brooked no delays or obstructions from workmen or contractors. On 15th July 1620 he complained in a letter: "For the works of the banqueting-house, it seems there is no thing made ready for the second order of pillars and cornice, the which will amount unto at the least 400 tons" of stone. He insisted that the stone must be forthcoming, "for if this work is not finished this year, His Majesty as you know cannot be satisfied".[2] On 17th August Inigo, who was then lodging at Arundel House, wrote to his absent host: "The banqueting-house goeth on now well, though the going of the masons away have been a great hindrance to it",—this was a constant grievance of sixteenth- and seventeenth-century architects—and he begged Arundel to "show some exemplary punishment causing them to be sent up as malefactors, it will deter the rest from ever doing the like". Nevertheless Sir Symonds D'Ewes, who was up from the country at this date, happened to observe in passing the stately new Banqueting House then in building. By 31st March following the work was finished.

The purpose of the Banqueting House was primarily, as its name implies, for feasting, and a painting by Gerard Honthorst exists of Charles I and his Queen dining there in public, while attentive footmen serve endless dishes and little spaniels frisk about the floor. Pepys watched Charles II soon after his restoration touch for the King's Evil there, and Evelyn, describing the last Sunday of that monarch's life, drew a warning parallel between the magnificence of the scene and what was so soon to follow. "I can never forget", the moralist recorded with no little relish, "the inexpressible luxury and profaneness . . . a French boy singing love songs in that glorious gallery", while the King toyed with his concubines. Then all was over, for death suddenly claimed the chief participant in the sybaritic scene. The Banqueting House was also used for all sorts of ceremonial occasions, the reception by the sovereign of foreign ambassadors, and the hearing of addresses and petitions, as well as for masques. But it has always proved unlucky in its uses. The room was impossible to heat—there are not even fireplaces—the acoustics were appalling and the smoke from the torches blackened the King's pictures, so the performance in it of winter masques had to be discontinued by Charles I. After the fire which destroyed

[1] The inhabitants of Portland cleared the harbour of rock at low tide one Sunday afternoon in return for beer.
[2] Letter to an unknown recipient—see Hodgkin MSS.

Whitehall Palace in 1698 it was turned into a chapel, and finally after endless vicissitudes and in default of a better use, the worst possible was found for it by Queen Victoria, who lent it to the Royal United Service Institution for their museum. And so in this twentieth century, when successive governments complain that in all London there is no suitable accommodation for the entertainment of foreign notabilities, England's grandest feasting room, built by one of her greatest architects, is unprocurable for the very purpose for which it was designed.

The Banqueting House has never been spared criticism for aesthetic as well as practical shortcomings. Sir Balthazar Gerbier, that jealous and rancorous man, inveighed against the columns of the frontispiece, which he fancied were too heavy and threatened to pull down the walls on the heads of passers-by. The pilasters by contrast looked to him "like things patched or glued against a wall". These were silly criticisms actuated by malice. On the contrary there is a certain meagreness about the façade—noticed by James Fergusson—as though the architect had not been allowed to make use of all the embellishments he intended. The central pediment of Jones's drawings would have crowned the massive elevation better than the too small balusters on their too deep base, but the engaged columns and pilasters are perfectly proportioned to the wall surface. Furthermore the air of austerity about the façade must have been greatly diminished by the different coloured stones originally used: golden yellow Northamptonshire for the base, grey Oxfordshire and Yorkshire for the *piano nobile*, and glistening white Portland for the attic storey. These materials were worked by Nicholas Stone [1] at the rate of 4s. 10d. a day, and the way in which he made the length and breadth of the courses fall into place between the windows is beyond all praise. Unfortunately, the whole of the ornamental stonework, including the upper frieze and capitals, had to be refaced, first by Soane in 1829 and later in the nineteenth century—for such is the corrosive effect of London soot—by Barry.

Soane was obliged to carry out drastic renovations of the roof. He also made slight changes in the decoration of the hall itself. This immense apartment, 110 ft. long, 55 ft. broad and 55 ft. high, is a double cube, partly surrounded at upper floor level by a balustraded gallery. It is undeniably impressive, but even if we try to discount the forest of ungainly show cases, which utterly break our line of vision, and the ignoble match-boarding on the walls, taken even into the window reveals, we are struck by a certain frigidity. When the hall was first built the frigidity was enhanced by the fact that all the windows on the west side were blocked and unglazed.[2] To overcome it various proposals were put forward for covering the naked walls. One approved by Charles I was that Vandyke should paint them with scenes illustrating the history of the Order of the Garter; but the artist evidently shrank from so

[1] Other eminent carvers at work on the Banqueting House were William Cuer, the King's master mason, 1620–2, and Zachary Tailer, 1634–5.

[2] Hence a window had to be unblocked to enable Charles I to walk through to the scaffold. Count Magalotti in 1669 said that drops of the King's blood were still to be seen on the window threshold and however often washed away, would reappear.

16 Covent Garden: Doorway of Inigo Jones's still surviving within North Arcade, 1631

7 Chiswick House: Gateway built by nigo Jones, 1621, for Beaufort House, Chelsea, and re-erected by Lord Burlington, 1740

18 "The Queen's Chapel" at Marlborough House, London. Built by Inigo Jones, 1623–6. The east-end furnishings date from Charles II's reign. (From an early nineteenth-century print)

formidable a command and somehow managed to elude it. Another was to have them covered with tapestries—made by the newly established Mortlake factory—from the Raphael cartoons, which Charles had bought on the advice of Rubens. According to Henry Peacham, tapestries from Raphael's History of St. Paul used to hang on the walls before the Rubens ceiling was fixed in position, and Count Magalotti noticed that the upper walls were covered with tapestry in 1669. Unfortunately the frigidity is not mitigated by the recent repainting of the hall—columns, walls and ceiling—a uniform battleship grey-green with gold parcelling. John de Critz's original colour-scheme was a stony white, "the ground thereof picked in with fair bise" (blue) and gold. The window-frames and doors were painted a timber colour, and the shutters a variety of hues. As a background to the magnificent Rubens panels, lately freed from layers of discoloured varnish and re-stored to their glowing tones,[1] the new ground colour selected is, to say the least, unsuitable.

In 1629–30 Rubens was on a visit to this country as ambassador from Madrid to conclude peace between England and Spain. It was then that Charles I finally persuaded him to fill the nine panels of the Banqueting House ceiling. The subject chosen was the celebration of the good government of James I and that homely and easy-going monarch's glorious apotheosis. Sketches were submitted to Charles by the painter after his return to Antwerp and approved. By August 1634 the nine canvasses were finished, with the help of Jordaens,[2] and only an attack of gout prevented Rubens personally bringing them to England. In December of the following year they were shipped over and the King, in paying £3,000 for them, expressed himself well satisfied, as indeed he might be.

The subject was doubtless suggested to Rubens by Veronese's "Apotheosis of Venice" in the Doges' Palace at Venice. The Whitehall ceiling was one of the great artistic triumphs of Charles's reign. It gave the English a first taste for decorative painting on the grand scale, and was emulated with lesser success by native painters—Streater at Swakeleys, and Thornhill at Greenwich Palace.[3]

9    *Chiswick House, gateway,* 1621

There is a careful drawing by Jones of a simple gateway entitled "for the M. of the Wardes at Chelsea 1621". The Master of the Court of Wardes was Lionel Cranfield, later created Earl of Middlesex, and his residence was Beaufort House, Chelsea, once the home of St. Thomas More. Cranfield, who had been one of Coryat's guests at his famous feast and an intimate of Inigo, was also Chief Commissioner of the Navy. A man of brilliant financial brain, he diligently checked waste and

[1] In the course of their history the Rubens' panels have been repaired and cleaned six times, first by William Kent. The last occasion was in 1950.

[2] Vertue heard this from Kneller who as a boy learnt it in Antwerp from old artists known to both Rubens and Jordaens.

[3] At Powis Castle the Fleming, Lanscroon, adopted the Veronese apotheosis theme, over the great staircase.

prevented unnecessary expenditure of public money; for these services he was to be impeached by Parliament and unfairly condemned for corrupt practices.

In Kip's view of Beaufort House the gateway is shown behind the house, leading into the fields to the north. When the house was demolished in 1740 the gate was given by Sir Hans Sloane, its owner, to Lord Burlington who piously re-erected it as a garden ornament at Chiswick Villa (17) and got Pope to compose the following lines for a tablet.

> Oh, Gate, how cam'st thou here?
> I was brought from Chelsea last year
> Battered with wind and weather.
> Inigo Jones put me together,
>   Sir Hans Sloane
>   Let me alone
> Burlington brought me hither.

The gateway is of pure Palladian design and the carving sharp and exact. Engaged Doric columns support an entablature with pediment. The triglyphs of the frieze are perfectly spaced and lie perpendicularly over the columns according to Jones's repeated direction. The short flanking walls are capped with balls on pedestals, somewhat reminiscent of the crests of Palladio's flanking walls to S. Giorgio Maggiore at Venice. (There are several attractive gateways of slightly later date to be found up and down the country whose unexpected classicism at first sight suggests the hand of Inigo Jones. Photographs of them compared with one of the Chiswick gateway will probably determine whether the first impression was justified.)

10  *New Hall, Essex: alterations, 1622*

This enormous palace, of which today one-tenth survives to form a country house of no mean dimensions, was bought by the Duke of Buckingham. What precise alterations Buckingham carried out are unknown, for they altogether disappeared in 1737. At first Buckingham employed the King's surveyor to work for him, and on 5th September 1622 John Chamberlain in a letter to Sir Dudley Carleton wrote that New Hall "is now altering and translating, according to the modern fashion, by the direction of Inigo Jones, the King's Surveyor". But Inigo was apparently superseded in Buckingham's graces by Balthazar Gerbier, who had entered the Duke's service in 1616. In 1624 Gerbier was giving orders for a model to be made of New Hall, which suggests that he was by then in charge of the work. Gerbier, who was a close friend of Rubens, introduced him to Buckingham: he then bought for his patron £10,000 worth of pictures and works of art from the great painter's collection. In the gardens of New Hall were set up Roman heads and Bologna's group of Cain and Abel which had belonged to Rubens. Gerbier told Buckingham that if he were given time "de miner tout doucement", he would fill New Hall with such works of art that foreigners would visit it in processions, and certainly the Duke's treasures, so rapidly amassed, were the wonder of his contemporaries. Nevertheless, Jones continued to submit designs to Buckingham and in the year of the favourite's death made a beautiful coloured drawing of a ceiling either for New Hall or, less probably, for York House in the Strand.

11  *Theobalds Palace, Hertfordshire: a stable, 1623, and banqueting house, 1624*

During the lonely summer of 1623 King James was mourning the absence of his beloved Baby Charles and Dog Steenie on their ill-advised expedition to Spain. His only solace was an enduring interest in hunting and horses. The surveyor-general was made to build a new stable for him at his favourite palace of Theobalds; though why that should be necessary is a mystery, for a plan of the pre-existing stables, made only five years before by John Smithson, shows that they already accommodated ninety-nine horses. On 16th August Inigo Jones wrote that he had visited Theobalds a few days ago, and that his new stable would be finished in three weeks' time.

In the accounts for 1625–6 are payments for a new pavilion, built at the far end of the park for the old King to rest and sleep in. From the description given, the room was of classical design. It had two large window-cases of Portland stone on either side a doorway, approached by a pair of stairs. The cornice was of Purbeck and Oxfordshire stones. The flat lead roof was meant to be walked upon. A seat was contrived within the pavilion with elbows for the monarch's special ease. The window-frames, door and seat were painted green by John de Critz, the serjeant-painter. At the same time the park paling, the bridge and ironwork were painted the same colour. The gardens were replanted with pear, cherry and apricot trees, whose roots were carefully turfed over: the beds were filled with strawberries and sweetbriers. It was at Theobalds that James chose to spend the greater part of his last years and at Theobalds that he died.

12  *Marlborough House Chapel, 1623-6*

All this year great preparations were being made in England by reluctant officials to welcome—if that is the right word for the anticipated reception of a bride so horribly unpopular—the little Infanta of Spain. A deputation of peers was sent to Southampton to receive her. With them went Inigo Jones to arrange pageants and shows. It was on this occasion that he had conferred upon him the freedom of the City of Southampton.

The Infanta of course never came. The result was that the Prince of Wales and Buckingham were given by the populace a rapturous welcome, which would surely have been moderated if the daughter of the Inquisition had accompanied them. But before the outcome was foreseen, arrangements were put in hand for her lodgings at Denmark (soon to be renamed Somerset) House and St. James's, where new chapels were to be built, "for which order is taken with the surveyor, Inigo Jones, to have them done out of hand and yet with great state and costliness". On 16th May the foundation stone of the Queen's Chapel, as it was called, at St. James's, was laid. The Spanish Ambassador was present and "made a cross on the first stone, laid it in mortar, made a prayer in French, that God would dispose of that foundation to His glory and the good of the church and universal good of all Christians". He then gave £80 to the workmen. The building had not gone far when it was learnt that the chapel would not be wanted after all. However, work upon it was soon resumed, this time for the benefit of a French Catholic bride. On Holy Thursday of 1626 Henrietta Maria walked with her ladies all the way from Denmark House to see the chapel which was just about fit for worship. During the Commonwealth it was stripped of most of its fittings, but after the Restoration mass was once more celebrated in it and Queen Catherine of Braganza drove through the park to attend a service there on 21st September 1662. Samuel Pepys watched her go, and such was his appreciation of good music that he used frequently to attend a worship he cordially disliked in order to listen to the singing. So many good Church of England men were attracted to the Queen's Chapel for the same reason that people began to murmur and complaints were made until the practice was stopped.

The Queen's Chapel is about the most complete memorial to Inigo Jones to survive (18). It is the least spoilt of all his buildings. Although certainly small and without aisles—it is a double cube 56 ft. long, 28 ft. broad and 28 ft. high—it well illustrates Jones's principle that a public edifice should be plain outside, lavish within. Count Magalotti, who attended mass there in 1669, was right in saying that "it cannot boast any exterior appearance or show". The west end of the chapel, which abuts upon the pavement of the street, is the only front with pretensions to ornament. It is constructed of brick and stone quoins finished, as the original accounts [1] state, with mortar "drawn like ashlar". The casement windows in solid frames have survived. The "great cornice round about the top of the chapel with two frontispieces" is still in place. So are the ten lions' heads of Portland stone, "to carry the water from the upper cornice". To the south of the chapel are the apartments in which used to lodge Queen Catherine's grand almoner and until very recently the late Queen Mary's prebendary.

The whole breadth of the west end of the chapel inside is taken up by the royal pew. Its three original openings to the nave have been restored since the war. When Magalotti attended mass in the chapel the middle opening was filled with a glass window at which he saw the Queen standing. Against the north wall of the pew is a fireplace, of which Inigo made a pencil sketch inscribed "chimneypiece in her Majesty's closet chapel at St. Jameses". It was painted white by Matthew Goodericke, a pupil of John de Critz. The east window is presumably the first Venetian window in England, and will have been taken by Jones, not from Palladio, but Scamozzi.[2]

The great barrel ceiling is a triumph of Inigo Jones's combination of simple motifs to achieve magnificence. And the triumph is not less spectacular because he

[1] In the Public Record Office, Declared Accounts E 351/3262–3.
[2] The so-called Venetian opening first appears as a single unit on the façade of SS. Annunziata at Arezzo, 1506 (by A. San Gallo) and at S. Eligio degli Orifici, Rome, 1509 (by Raphael). It is established all over Italy by the second half of the sixteenth century. Palladio used it as a repetitive motif, *vide* the Basilicana, Vicenza.

copied the ceiling design out of Palladio's book. When the Ministry of Works stripped off the layers of superfluous paint they found the coffers to be of pine, carved with great vigour. They had the whole ceiling repainted in the original colours, for which they found guidance in the early accounts. These recorded not only the carving in the ceiling coffers "with eggs, anchors, flowers and lacing work"—Roger Pratt noted that Jones here used rosettes and the guilloche mould in the correct Roman manner—but the painting of the majority of them in white, and the twenty-eight over the altar in gold. Thus the Ministry of Works spared no pains or skill in restoring this chapel, as far as was humanly possible, to the condition in which Inigo Jones left it more than three hundred years ago.

## 13   King James I's Hearse, 1625

In March 1625 James I, who had for some months been sorely distressed by gout and obliged to give up his favourite pastime, hunting, succumbed at Theobalds Palace.

If Inigo Jones's catafalque for Queen Anne was a success that for James I was a masterpiece (11). Again Chamberlain wrote to Carleton of "the hearse, likewise, being the fairest and best fashioned that hath been seen, wherein Inigo Jones, the surveyor, did his part". His part consisted of the design, and some structural features that showed his characteristic ingenuity. The particular scheme of a dome carried on columns may have been suggested by Bramante's famous tempietto in Rome, but the general idea was doubtless inspired by Domenico Fontana's gorgeous catafalque for the funeral of Pope Sixtus V. Inigo's dome was stuck with flags and the twelve figures standing upon the entablature below it held flags. The figures were sculptured by Hubert le Sueur. John Aubrey was told that Inigo with his own hands moulded in plaster of Paris the heads of the four caryatides which upheld the canopy, and clothed them in drapery of white callico, "which was very handsome and cheap", to look like white marble. Where exactly the caryatides stood is not quite clear, if Inigo's perspective drawing of the catafalque was faithfully followed. It may be that the detached figures on plinths are what Aubrey had in mind. The whole hearse was gaily painted by Matthew Goodericke and the wax effigy of the King was fashioned by Maximilian Colt, who made a rapid journey to Theobalds specially to mould the face after death.

## 14   Covent Garden Piazza and St. Paul's Church, 1631–8

Inigo Jones was more in the confidence of King Charles than of King James. Whereas the father's tastes were intellectual rather than artistic, the son's were the reverse. He did not inherit his father's love of learning so much as his mother's love of the arts. His accomplishments therein were the results of determined self-discipline. He was accounted the best dancer of his court. He was extremely musical, kept forty court musicians, and played the viola da gamba with more than mere proficiency. He drew well and used to take lessons from Vandyke in the artist's studio at Blackfriars—much to the scandal of the Puritans. So as well as being one of the great art connoisseurs of all time Charles was in some degree an executant and probably happier in the company of artists than of any others. He had a high opinion of his surveyor-general's abilities and invested his office with those autocratic powers which he unwisely considered indispensable to leaders. Soon after his succession he appointed a new commission to reduce the number of houses being built within the City of London. Of the fifty members of the commission any four, "whereof the Surveyor of our Works to be one", had the royal authority to decide when the allotment of ground was desirable, and to choose the site for the erection of every new house within the city boundaries.

During the first years of the new King's reign the reports to the Privy Council are filled with actions taken by the commission against offenders who had dared to dig foundations and even start new houses without permission. In many cases they were obliged to demolish what they had begun and were summarily committed to Newgate for their pains. Such uncongenial work kept the surveyor-general fully occupied. Apart from doing a drawing of a simple Tuscan archway for St. James's Park and another of a cupola with a clock face for Whitehall, both dated 1627, he seems to have had little time or opportunity for architecture until the next decade.

As a result of Lord Arundel's Commission of 1618 the square or piazza, as it was called, at Covent Garden was eventually laid out (19). It was the first geometrically planned town space to be designed in England and was the forerunner of the countless squares, crescents and circuses which in the eighteenth century were to transform London and make provincial cities, like Bath, Edinburgh and Cheltenham, into resorts of elegance and delight. The very word piazza declares the Italian origin of Covent Garden's new symmetry. John Evelyn, when at Leghorn in 1644, remarked in his diary that "the piazza is very fair and commodious and, with the church, whose four columns at the portico are of black marble polished, gave the first hint to the building both of the church and piazza in Covent Garden with us, though very imperfectly pursued"; and John Webb pointed to the same origin in his *Vindication of Stone Heng*. They may well have been correct, since both Lord Arundel and Jones must frequently have passed through Leghorn on their way to and from Rome. The legend that Jones built the church, actually the cathedral, of S. Francesco and the piazza at Leghorn is, however, utterly without foundation. The design of S. Francesco, completed in 1594 by Alessandro Pieroni, in the Doric order, with a pedimented façade and a projecting loggia of three bays upon coupled columns, bore the slenderest resemblance to St. Paul's Church, and was typical of its date and district.[1] The Place des Vosges in Paris will just as certainly have been seen by Arundel and Jones. Its four sides of uniform houses built upon continuous

[1] *The Guida Manuale di Livorno*, 1876, stated that Jones was "allievo di Giovanni Bologna". The *Enciclopedia Italiana* says that the Piazza d'Anne, at Leghorn, was by Jones. In fact it too was by Pieroni. Was Jones his pupil before Pieroni's death in 1607? Both cathedral and piazza at Leghorn were reduced to rubble in the last war.

arcades, may equally well have supplied the two commissioners with ideas for the square at Covent Garden.

No documents survive to tell how much Inigo personally contributed to the building of the piazza and its church, but Webb's reference to the church "built likewise with the porticoes about the piazza there by Mr. Jones" is good enough evidence—if any further were needed—that this Italian scheme was his. The novelty of the buildings excited the liveliest interest among the *cognoscenti* of the day and the King made a special visit to view the work in progress. But only the north and east sides of the piazza were completed. Colen Campbell's plate in *Vitruvius Britannicus* and Samuel Scott's oil-painting at Wilton (19) give a clear idea of what these sides looked like. The elevations were of two storeys over a rusticated arcade. The arcade, according to Sir Roger Pratt, was derived from Serlio. Horace Walpole thought the piazza nothing remarkable and the pilasters of the elevations homely, uncouth work. But to our eyes, accustomed to every derogation from architectural propriety, the proportions of the two fronts seem pleasing and exact. Little of Inigo's piazza is left today, and the remnants of the north-west arcade, and the corner house rebuilt for Admiral Lord Orford, are ghosts of the residences once fashionable in this romantic quarter of London. Under Lord Orford's house and facing east along the length of the arcade a fine original doorway has been left undisturbed (16). Its rusticated pilasters, Ionic capitals with festoons and elliptical pediment are typical of Inigo Jones's new classicism.

On the west side of the piazza Inigo placed his church of St. Paul's, with two flanking gateways connected by retaining walls (now disappeared). In 1638 the church was ready to be dedicated by Bishop Juxon. What we see today is barely the skeleton of Inigo's building. In 1688 the body of it and in 1727 the portico had practically to be rebuilt. Later the whole church was repaired by Lord Burlington. In 1795 it was burnt out and again rebuilt—the fronts in stone in place of the original brick—by Thomas Hardwick. In 1872 it was altered and in 1888 the turret was taken down while the red brick side walls were refaced and coloured. In the last war it was badly shaken by bombs.

Walpole thought the church, as he saw it, lacking in dignity and beauty. He attributed these defects to the parsimony of the Earl of Bedford by whom it was commissioned. Bedford told Inigo Jones that he could scarcely afford a barn, let alone a church: whereupon the architect retorted : "Then, my lord, you shall have the handsomest barn in England." Lord Burlington's group, on the other hand, greatly admired it and considered it one of the few buildings produced by the moderns to bear comparison with the works of the ancients. Their praise was inspired by archaeological rather than aesthetic sentiments. They saw in the massive Tuscan columns and overhanging eaves of the east portico the rules of Vitruvius obeyed to the letter. After taking careful measurements they calculated the height of the columns to be one-third the width of the temple; their thickness at the bottom to be one-seventh their height, and their thickness at the top three-quarters their thickness at the bottom. The central inter-columniation had been correctly made wider than the side ones. The eaves of the pediment projected to a distance one-third the length of the portico roof. Nowhere had the architect put a foot wrong and his every dimension was a proper interpretation of the module.

Few people today will experience these academic rhapsodies, and some, like Horace Walpole, may consider this much-altered church lacking beauty. There is perhaps something a trifle absurd about the blocked central door—owing to the orientation of the altar placed behind it—which makes the east portico meaningless. Thwarted by the seeming entrance we wander round to the west end. Here we come across a repetition of the east end, the same bold door (but unblocked) under a round window and two long windows at the sides. Yet where by the rules of common sense there ought to be a portico over the only entrance to the church, there is none.

Nevertheless the east end is not, as Walpole considered it, undignified or in any sense mean. It has the nobility of enduring strength. Nor is it without historic interest. St. Paul's church is the first building in England to have a classical portico with detached columns.

### 15 *Somerset House and Chapel, 1632–8*

When in 1623 the Infanta of Spain was expected to arrive as bride to Prince Charles, preparations were speedily made to house her in the old Tudor palace of Somerset House. Two years later the French Princess and her large retinue were installed there instead. Subsequently the surveyor-general and his men were called upon to make many alterations and improvements. Thus in 1626 John de Critz was "curiously" painting the ceiling of Henrietta Maria's closet with grotesques. He decorated the frieze with antique work made to frame panels of badges, gilded and shadowed. Two years later Matthew Goodericke was painting the ceiling of the Queen's cabinet with gilded foliage and the woodwork blue—evidently the Queen's favourite colour. Zachary Tailer was carving chimneypieces and door-cases in the same room with lace work and beads. About this time Goodericke and John James, carver, were moulding a number of deal picture frames, "of the larger sort", for the Queen. In 1631 Nicholas Stone agreed to work a chimneypiece in the Queen's bedchamber of white marble "according to directions" of Inigo Jones. The following year Jones drew a kind of fountain head (a "sestern" he called it) to go in the base-court for garden use, and in Stone's account book for 1636 his cousin Gabriel Stacy was paid for working such a cistern in black marble.

The chapel at Somerset House, which Jones started at the same time as the St. James's chapel, seems to have been discontinued for rather longer. It was resumed in 1632 and finished in 1636. On 17th September of the latter year the Superior of the Queen's Capuchins wrote to Rome a description of the opening ceremony. "The work was finished not without great difficulties: the architect who is one of those Puritans, or rather people without religion, worked unwillingly, however

19  Covent Garden, 1631–8. View of North Side, showing Church and part of East Side. Architect almost certainly Inigo Jones. (From a painting by Samuel Scott at Wilton House)

20  St. Paul's, Covent Garden, 1638. Architect: Inigo Jones. The church has been several times restored. (From an engraving by Thomas Malton)

21    Somerset House, London, showing classical block by Inigo Jones, *c.* 1636. (Detail of a painting by Samuel Scott)

22    Old St. Paul's Cathedral, showing Inigo Jones's refacing of West End and Portico, 1634–43. (From a drawing by Wenceslaus Hollar)

with the help of God and the artifices we have employed in hurrying him up by giving him presents from the Queen or by other means, this building has been completed, and is more beautiful, larger and grander than one could ever have hoped for.'' The chapel was long ago destroyed, but there is a fine sketch by Jones for a window to it, obviously suggested by the niches in the Pantheon. Isaac Ware, in his *Designs of Inigo Jones,* gives a plate of the altar-piece, which, if accurate,[1] shows what a lot Wren owed to Jones's inspirations. This altar-piece, unusually French in design, foreshadows those which were to appear in the post-Fire city churches. Ware also gives an elevation of a screen which has affinities with conventional Jacobean wainscot in its quasi-terminal figures under shell crests. For his work on the chapel Jones was paid, quite apart from the alleged gifts from the Queen and others, £1,050.

There are two drawings by John Webb for an extension to Somerset House, upon one of which he inscribed: ''Upright of the Palace at So. House 1638, not taken.'' The words ''not taken'' imply that the design was rejected, probably by the King. The upright is a noble and very ambitious affair on the monumental scale. The existence of Webb's drawings gives rise to the question: In what year did Jones build his front, which Sir William Chambers demolished in 1776? Jones made a drawing in 1636 for a chimneypiece, which Stone set up in the Queen's ''new closet''; and Edward Pierce, senior, was paid the same year for painting sundry picture frames a sad lute colour, and designing patterns of gilt leather for the ''new drawing-chamber'' and ''new privy chamber''. If these new apartments were behind Jones's front, then the front had presumably been finished a little time previously, say about 1635. Webb's rejected designs will have been for an extension to the palace and not a replacement of his master's front.

We know what this front was like from Campbell's plate, a picture by Samuel Scott (21) and a drawing done by Sir John Soane shortly before the building was pulled down. It consisted of a *piano nobile* and attic floor in five bays between Corinthian pilasters, coupled at the ends, all over a rusticated arcade. The composition was doubtless suggested to Inigo by the courtyard of the Palazzo Thiene. The same design was elaborated either by him or some close disciple on the front of Lindsey House in Lincoln's Inn Fields. By embracing the two floors within one order Inigo improved upon Palladio's design and produced a composition which for strength, simplicity and elegance could hardly be surpassed.[2]

16  *Chapman's Monument, St. Giles-in-the-Fields,* 1634.

When George Chapman, the old poet and translator of Homer, died in 1634 and was buried in the churchyard of St. Giles-in-the-Fields, he was greatly mourned.

[1] The altar was dismantled in 1647 for being Papistical. The Burlingtonians, Kent, Campbell and Ware, who edited and reissued volumes of drawings purporting to be Inigo Jones's designs, are not at all trustworthy. They sometimes altered and invented designs which they unashamedly attributed to their hero.

[2] Peter Harrison, the American architect, adapted Inigo Jones's Somerset House front to his Market Hall, Newport, Rhode Island, in 1761, where it is given seven instead of the original five bays.

Inigo Jones, whom Chapman had termed "our only learned architect", raised a monument over his grave on the south side of the church. It has lately been removed for safety into the body of the church. It is not an object of beauty, but its survival gives it interest. It is shaped, rather surprisingly for Inigo Jones but in deference to the Homeric deceased, like a Greek altar stone with acroteria at the two corners, and is much worn. The inscription which has at least once been renewed now speaks out loud and bold, as follows: "Georgius Chapman poeta 1634 Ignatius Jones Architectus Regius ob honorem Bonarum literarum familiari suo hoc mon DSPC".

### 17   Winchester Cathedral Screen, 1634–8

Between 1634 and 1638 a choir screen in Winchester Cathedral was erected to a design by Jones, adapted probably from a woodcut in Serlio's book for a triumphal arch at Verona (24). It was a classical device with a central opening under a pediment surmounted by reclining figures. On either side of the opening were Pantheon-like niches between pilasters. They were filled with the figures of James I and Charles I, which, when the screen was destroyed in 1820, were placed on either side of the west door, where they still stand. They were modelled by the French Huguenot sculptor, Hubert le Sueur, with whom a contract was made by the architect. Two rough sketches for the statues were drawn by Jones for le Sueur's benefit and dated 17th June 1638. Jones's instructions were that the figures must be cast in brass, and be 5 ft. 8 in. high. For his services the sculptor was to receive £340. The faces of the two monarchs are expressionless and the bodies formalized.

### 18   St. Paul's Cathedral, 1634–43

Old St. Paul's Cathedral had been from time immemorial a financial embarassment. It was always requiring attention. If it was not falling down or catching fire then its spire was struck by lightning and there arose the unavoidable problem how to find the money to set it right again. In Queen Elizabeth's reign nothing was done to the structure at all and in that of her successor, when money was even scarcer, every effort was made to defer repairs for as long as possible. At last matters became so serious, and the squalor and decay of the ancient fabric so disgraceful, that in November 1620 James I set up a Royal Commission to investigate what steps need be taken. The commission included Sir Baptist Hicks, a rich mercer and money-lender, John Chamberlain, the letter-writer, Pembroke and Arundel, the two peers invariably associated with artistic and aesthetic causes, and the surveyor-general. Subscriptions were raised—no doubt a large contribution was expected from Hicks, lately made a baronet—but little was done, and much of the stone fetched from Portland by the Bishop of London was appropriated by Buckingham to build his watergate and other garden refinements at York House. Before the commission was set up Jones, in the course of his duties for the Commission on Buildings established two years before, was obviously concerned about the condition of the cathedral. In his letter to Lord Arundel of 17th August 1620 he had written: "The plan of all the encroachments about Paul's is fully finished. I hear that the masons do begin to make up that part of the east end which they have demolished, not well—but with uneven courses of stone. I am now going to the Mr. of the Wards [this was his friend, Lionel Cranfield] to tell him of it." Inigo Jones was not the man to overlook unsatisfactory workmanship, even if it was not directly his own concern.

Eight years were to elapse before a Bishop of dynamic energies was appointed to the see of London. This was William Laud, who in 1631 was responsible for a new commission being formed whose recommendations he was determined should be adopted. Inigo Jones was not made a member of this commission, but was employed by it. He was asked to report on "what disgrace or other inconvenience" St. Gregory's church and some adjoining houses were likely to have on the "cathedral church when it shall be repaired and reduced to the ancient dignity" it held of old, and directed to begin repairs at the south-east end and proceed westwards. As already mentioned, he first reported that St. Gregory's was causing no mischief to the cathedral foundations and then, to the parishioners' intense chagrin, changed his mind. In 1634 Inigo was formally appointed surveyor of the fabric of St. Paul's, a post he agreed to undertake without payment in connection "with so good a work". He was allowed to nominate a substitute and chose Edward Carter [1] who at a salary of 5s. a day was to remain deputy-surveyor until his death in 1653. Work was not to be started until there should be £10,000 "ready in [the] bank". Subscriptions this time poured in—the merchant, Sir Paul Pindar, was a particularly generous subscriber—and the first four stones of the new work were laid by the Archbishop of Canterbury, as Laud had now become, the Secretary of State (Sir Francis Windebank), the Dean of Arches (Sir Henry Marten) and the Surveyor (Inigo Jones). At first the surveyor sought to obtain marble from Ireland for his building material. This proving impracticable, stone was once more fetched from Portland and when the ships and mariners carrying it were pressed by the Admiralty, representations had only to be referred to the Archbishop who had the nuisance promptly stopped. Two hundred and forty-four loads of oak were sailed from Hampshire for the repairs. Here there was trouble of a different sort which was not resolved so simply. The Hampshire J.P.s resolutely refused to charge the carriage of the timber to the ships to the county's expense, as was usual when material for the King's use was transported over long distances. So in order not to delay the carriage the expenses had to be borne by the cathedral funds.

It is greatly to the credit of Inigo Jones that he held St. Paul's in veneration. "So great and noble a work", was his opinion of the old cathedral, for the sake of the foundations of which his reconsidered judgment induced him to sacrifice whatever surrounding buildings were a threat. His opinion was in strong contrast to that

---

[1] In September 1643 Edward Carter was by ordinance of both Houses of Parliament nominated Surveyor of H.M. Works in the place of Inigo Jones at a salary of £300 p.a. "in full of all fees, wages, diet, boat-hire, riding, and all other profits and allowances whatsoever . . ." He was buried in St. Paul's Church, Covent Garden. His successor was John Embree, former sergeant-plumber.

of John Evelyn, who was uncompromising in his contempt for Gothic churches, which he termed "heavy, dark, melancholy and monkish piles", and "mountains of stone, vast and gigantic buildings indeed; but not worthy the name of architecture". When the question arose after the Fire of London whether to save as much as possible of the Gothic remains of St. Paul's or build afresh, Evelyn expressed himself strongly against "patching it up anyhow", and voted for an entire rebuilding on classical lines. Jones, on the other hand, did his utmost to save the old fabric, however unsympathetic some may deem the methods he adopted. Although his work on St. Paul's altogether disappeared after the Great Fire his drawings and Hollar's engravings have survived upon which we may pass judgment. They make it difficult for us to agree wholeheartedly with Webb's view that the alterations at St. Paul's constituted one of Jones's chief claims to fame—if for the moment we except the west portico.

The sum of Jones's repair work was to encase the Gothic core of the south-west front, the west end and north-west front, that is to say from transept to transept, with a classical skin. He did not touch the inside. In the words of Webb, "he reduced the body of [the cathedral] from the steeple to the west end, into that order and uniformity we now behold"—this was written before 1666—"and all posterity will be grateful to Mr. Jones". Alas for these words of anticipation! Even if they had not been made nugatory by the Great Fire, it is questionable whether posterity would have been quite so appreciative of the work as Webb foretold. As it happened, when the ruins were properly examined after the fire the classical skin was found not to have been properly tied to the old work and so in any case would have had to be pulled down. Jones's original design for the west end, before the idea of a colonnade was entertained, is disappointing. It amounts to a weak interpretation of a quattrocento façade with a Venetian central gable and two cupolas added to the flanking towers. The subsequent decision to build the portico led to some modifications of this design, if Hollar's engravings of 1658 are to be trusted. The pilasters upon the façade were omitted. So was the central gable. The south-west front and transeptal elevations were not more meritorious than the intended west end. Inigo gave his windows rounded heads and deeply projecting entablatures, with cherubs' masks for keystones. The existing buttresses he converted into pilasters crowned with balls or obelisks. In the tympana of the west and transeptal fronts he put circular windows and made massive console scrolls of Italian quattrocento type link the upper with the lower stages. The interesting thing about these classical trimmings is that they are not at all Palladian.

The west portico, which was added as an afterthought, can never have blended satisfactorily with the inadequate classical face-lifting of the Gothic cathedral (22). It was none the less an extremely noble work which as a self-sufficing unit excited great commendation from Pratt, Evelyn and other contemporaries, and its demolition by Wren was never forgiven by his successors, the Burlingtonians. Webb was unstinting in his praise that Jones, "by adding that magnificent portico there, hath contracted the envy of all Christendom upon our nation, for a piece of architecture, not to be paralleled in these last ages of the world''. Count Magalotti, familiar with the masterpieces of his native Tuscany, looked at it in 1669 when it was still almost intact, and had nothing but admiration for it. He noticed that it was "ornamented with stones worked with great perfection and symmetry, according to the rules of the Corinthian order" and that the fluted columns rested "on well-proportioned bases". It was in fact a triumph of neo-classical architecture.

The entire expense of the portico was borne by Charles I as a pious memorial to his father. Its practical purpose was to serve as an ambulatory for the public who had for centuries been accustomed to treat the nave of St. Paul's as a place in which to meet, walk and do business. From time to time this practice was discontinued by order of the Dean and Chapter, but never for long. As early as 1602 John Chamberlain complained of an order "to shut the upper doors in Pauls in service time, whereby the old intercourse is clean changed and the traffic of news much decayed". Laud, however, was of opinion that the cathedral should serve a different purpose from that of commerce and gossip and put a stop to the abuse once and for all, not only during services but at other times. He held the unpopular notion that the cathedral had been built primarily for worship. The new portico therefore offered a wise solution, sanctioned moreover by classical precedent, for Jones himself had noted that: "The ancients used porticos for commodity of the people . . . and to give majesty to temple." Jones's several notes on temples and churches have an interesting bearing upon the form which his portico at Paul's finally assumed.

What examples of church porticos would Jones have seen? Those at the Lateran basilica [1] and St. Peter's. But each of these had intentionally been made part of the façade of its respective church. At St. Paul's Inigo was obliged to add to a façade already there. So he went for help back to the ancients and adopted the precedent of the Pantheon portico and some of the old basilican porticos, which differed from those of the moderns in that they were not integrated frontispieces. He calculated from a strict observance of the module that owing to the great width and height of the existing cathedral, his portico should have a depth of two columnar bays. In other words he chose the Roman "eustyle" temple front. According to Vitruvius, this disposition, whereby the intervals between the columns should be as wide as the greatest thickness of two columns and a quarter, and the middle interval only as wide as the greatest thickness of three columns, was meant to result in the most convenience (notably for a large concourse of people) and beauty. The eustyle front however left him with irregular spaces at the angles of his portico; but he solved the difficulty thus presented with ingenuity. At each angle he placed a pilastered pier close to the column, so as to make it appear doubled, thereby conveying to the composition a sense of strength as well as elegance. There were precedents in Palladio for this treatment, to which recourse was had upon the angles of the Villa Repeta

[1] Fontana's north portico: not of course Galilei's great west portico, which was added in the eighteenth century.

portico. The success of Jones's careful manipulations can be measured by the certainty that, had he spaced all his columns evenly, one would have fallen in the middle of the façade opposite the main entrance, an outcome illogical and ugly, and of course wholly unacceptable.

By 1639 the portico was being built, for in that year Edward Carter certified that three masons, Thomas James, Robert Moore and John Taylor, engaged on carving the capitals, were neglecting their duties "to the great prejudice thereof and the evil example of others". The first of these men had already worked for Jones at the Queen's House and two years previously was one of those pressed by the Navy Commissioners to decorate *The Sovereign of the Seas*. The master mason in charge was once again Nicholas Stone. By 1643 work on the cathedral was abruptly stopped by the outbreak of the Civil War. Except for a new steeple, the building was practically finished at a total cost up to date of £101,330. During the troubles the cathedral was used by Cromwell's troops for stables, and when the scaffolding in support of the roof was removed for firewood the choir vault fell in. The beautiful portico was converted into shops for seamstresses, with stairs ascending to lofts above. Le Sueur's statues of Kings James and Charles were thrown off the balustrade. After a chequered period of revival lasting barely twenty-three years, Old St. Paul's Cathedral met its fate in the Fire of London. Although the portico was left standing Wren, not unnaturally, felt unable to incorporate it in his new composition, which entailed a complete rebuilding of the cathedral from the ground upwards.

### 19   The Barber Surgeons' Hall, 1636

The Barber Surgeons' Hall in Monkwell Street was entirely obliterated in the bombing of the City of London during the last war. But long before that event Inigo Jones's work there was demolished. The theatre, considered by Horace Walpole his finest architectural achievement, had been repaired in 1730 by Lord Burlington at great expense, only to be pulled down in 1784. The greater part of the seventeenth-century remains followed suit in 1895.

The Barber Surgeons' Company took a long lease from the City Corporation, of a plot of land adjoining their premises, on which to build a theatre for anatomical operations and lectures, as well as a new court-room. An indenture, dated 16th May 1636, formerly in possession of the Company,[1] read as follows: "It is ordered with the general consent of the whole court here present that the theatre shall be proceeded in and built according to the plots drawn by His Majesty's Surveyor." A plan and designs for the theatre in Webb's hand are preserved at Worcester College. The plan is in the shape of an oval, with a pair of projecting turrets for stairs at one of the narrow ends. Between the turrets was a small portico on Tuscan columns and a central window under a broken pediment. The roof rose to a point on the outside. Isaac Ware [2] gave a section of the theatre showing four degrees of seats one above

[1] All the Company's archives were destroyed in the 1941 bombing.
[2] *Designs of Inigo Jones*, 1733.

the other. These were of cedar and adorned with figures of the seven liberal sciences, the twelve signs of the Zodiac and a bust of Charles I. The coved ceiling was painted with the constellations of the heavens.

The court-room, which may also have been Inigo's work, was entered by a classical doorway with a bust of the architect in the pediment. The plaster ceiling was decorated with a large oval panel and rococo foliage in the spandrels. In the centre of the panel a raised octagonal cupola, like that formerly in the drawing-room of Ashburnham House, gave light to the room.

The accounts show items of expenditure of 11s. to one Mr. Mason [1] who drew the plot for the theatre, 13s. 9d. to a Mr. Wilson,[2] mason, for measuring in the theatre, 11s. to others for the same purpose; and 11s. 6d., "when Mr. Inigo Jones the King's Surveyor came to view the background". Was this last payment for entertainment of the august visitor? On other occasions the Company's officers were obliged to visit the architect, no doubt at his office in Scotland Yard, and 7s. 1d. was "spent by water at times when we went to Mr. Surveyor about the theatre".

*     *     *

Towards the end of his life, even before the clouds of the Civil War were gathering, Inigo's architectural activities tended to slacken. The number of buildings to which we can point as definitely his became scarcer, although the number of those which indirectly owed their character to his influence naturally increased. Sketches in Inigo's hand, and a finished upright finely drawn with ruler and compass in Webb's, show that the surveyor was hoping to erect a gate at Temple Bar between the years 1636 and 1638. The model, derived from Jones's Roman studies, followed the Triumphal Arch of Constantine, which dates from the early fourth century A.D. when Roman architectural design had passed its zenith. It is curious that Inigo should have found inspiration in this heavy, uninspired block.[3] He took great pains over versions of the circular panels for which he made several sketches of figures—always drawn by him with greater freedom than purely architectural subjects. The gateway was not built and it was left to Wren to provide the famous Temple Bar which now stands at Theobalds Park. There exists also a sketch done about this time "for friezes at Wimbledon, part of relieve, part painted". At Wimbledon Henrietta Maria had lately bought the manor-house of the Cecils and Nicholas Stone was working there as late as 1641, very probably under the surveyor-general's direction. But after 1640 the State Papers give no further information about Jones's official duties. One of the last was to estimate for taking down parts of the parapets and pinnacles of the Tower of London, then in danger of collapsing. The King's affairs were entering a perilous stage and the political horizon was perceptibly darkening. On 2nd September 1640

[1] Possibly William Mason, mason, who worked for the Crown at the Tower of London, 1625–6 and 1632–3.

[2] Possibly Henry Wilson, mason at Whitehall, 1631–2, and at the Tower, 1633–4.

[3] Nicholas Stone, jun., in his diary (1639), greatly admired the Arch of Constantine and the reliefs, which he considered the best in Rome.

an ordinance of both Houses of Parliament suppressed the performance of all public plays and so brought about the end of pageantry. In December of the following year Inigo went through the disagreeable experience of appearing before the House of Lords to answer grave charges brought against him by the parishioners of St. Gregory's. He was also implicated with others the same month in a brawl in Whitehall between some citizens and gentlemen of the Court. It is easy to guess on which side the surveyor's sympathies were enlisted.

On 28th July 1642 we hear of Inigo Jones at Beverley, in Yorkshire, with the King, for on that day Charles gave him a receipt for the loan of £500. It was never repaid him and as late as 1668 John Webb, as his principal executor, was still trying to claim it from Charles II.

Webb had been left behind in London to act as deputy-surveyor and to safeguard his master's interests in Scotland Yard.[1] But these duties did not last him long. The following year Jones was superceded as surveyor by Edward Carter, who was to remain until his death high in Cromwell's favour. In fact Jones and Webb, who did brave and dangerous service in carrying papers from London to the King's quarters, were recognized as uncompromising royalists. After his capture at Basing House, Inigo suffered the sequestration of his whole estate. The exorbitant penalty was remitted on his making application to Parliament, and in view of his age and his not having taken up arms he was instead fined more than a thousand pounds. His losses must have been severe, for a raid was made on his London premises and some waggons, presumably full of his belongings, were seized at his house. Nevertheless, Inigo was not financially ruined, for Vertue recorded that he had, with Nicholas Stone, at the outbreak of the war taken the precaution of burying their ready money first in Scotland Yard and then, for fear lest informers had spied upon them, again for greater safety in Lambeth Marshes.

## 20 *Wilton House, Wiltshire, 1649–53*

Inigo's connection with Wilton had been a long one, and if he travelled with his early patron William Lord Pembroke in Italy in 1601, will have extended over half a century. In 1615 Lord Arundel wrote to his wife from Wilton that Lord Pembroke desired Inigo to go there immediately to meet King James. In 1620 he was summoned there by the King, who commanded him to investigate the ruins of Stonehenge. After the death of William Lord Pembroke in 1630 his brother and successor Philip continued the family association with the surveyor, and when in 1647 a serious fire destroyed most of Wilton there was still time to extend the hereditary patronage to a commission.

Philip, 4th Earl of Pembroke and 1st Earl of Montgomery, was a far less amiable character than his elder brother. His early rise to fortune was due to the "comeliness of his person", which, with his passion for hunting, according to Lord Clarendon, rendered him "the first who drew the King's eyes towards him with affection".

1 Where Jones had his lodgings and office.

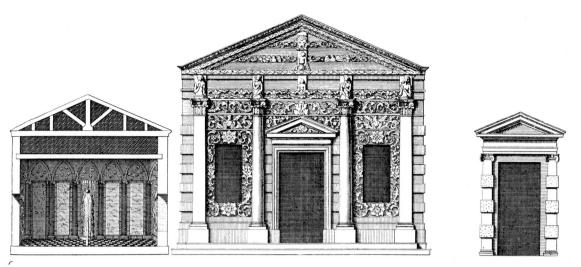

23   Wilton Park, Wiltshire: the Grotto, an astonishing façade of sculptured stonework.
(From C. Campbell's *Vitruvius Britannicus*, 1717)

24   Winchester Cathedral: Choir Screen, designed by Inigo Jones, 1638. Removed,
1820. (From J. Vardy's *Some Designs of Inigo Jones*, 1744)

25   Wilton House, Wiltshire: the centre of the South Front, built by Inigo Jones, 1649

The result was that at the early age of twenty-one he was created by the susceptible James, Earl of Montgomery. But he never took the trouble even to feign a return of affection or gratitude to his good-natured benefactor and so his reign as favourite was a short one. Philip Herbert was of a violent disposition, choleric and foul-mouthed. He quarrelled with everyone, and his loyalties were, to say the least, ambiguous. He voted against Strafford in 1641, thus deeply offending Charles I, who accordingly dismissed him from the important office of Lord Chamberlain. There-upon he joined the Parliamentarians, for whom however he made no effort to dis-guise his contempt. Yet before the Civil War he had entertained Charles I in several summers at Wilton, which of all places the King was said to love most in England. Lord Montgomery, although an ill-bred and unlearned man, liked pictures and architecture. After the King he was Vandyke's greatest patron and, with the King's encouragement and interest, spent much time and money on improvements to the garden and house at Wilton.

The sequence and authorship of the works at Wilton before the fire of 1647 are confused and difficult to disentangle. Sometime in the 'thirties, after his succession, Earl Philip employed Isaac de Caux to lay out a huge formal garden with elaborate water-works, which stretched to a length of 800 ft. to the south and south-east of the house across the river Nadder. The layout of these gardens has entirely disappeared. They were formed of countless fussy little beds of unrewarding effects, to judge from the plates in de Caux's book on his Wilton improvements. If, as John Aubrey stated, King Charles persuaded Earl Philip to make the gardens, then he probably introduced de Caux, who years before had with his brother Solomon laid out the grounds at Hatfield for Lord Salisbury, worked at Richmond Palace for Prince Henry and in 1623–5 constructed rock, encrusted with shells, under the Banqueting House for King James.[1] Isaac de Caux, who described himself as engineer, architect and native of Dieppe, was to publish in 1644 a book[2] of designs intended to crown a life-time's invention of water-works, ingenious and dramatic. Nothing seemed too fantastic for his invention. One diagram in the book shows a lead nightingale on a branch and explains how by means of air and water pressure a whistle through its mouth is contrived. Another presents Galatea in a cockleshell drawn across a stretch of water by two mechanical dolphins; another a water organ which blows a trumpet at midday worked by the heat of the sun—when there is any—on the water; and another a statue of a man through whose mouth is emitted a noise, strange to relate, as of harp strings breaking. It is therefore natural to assume that Isaac de Caux had a hand in contriving the famous grotto (23) shown at the east end of the garden behind a pool in Richard Wilson's painting now in the house at Wilton. Celia Fiennes, who was typical of the seventeenth century for her interest in all phenomena natural or artificial, gave a description of the wonders contained within the grotto. "A sluice

[1] "Isaac Decois for making a rock in the vault under the Banqueting House, finding all materials, viz.: rock stuff, shells, carriage and workmanship, £20." Declared Accounts E 351/3257–9.

[2] Entitled *Nouvelle invention de lever l'eau plus hault que sa source avec quelques machines mouvantes par le moyen de l'eau et un discours de la conduite d'y celle.*

99

spouts water up to wet the strangers", she noted with obvious relish of this naive and favourite prank, and, in addition, "figures at each corner of the room that can weep water on the beholders . . . and a shower of rain made to descend from a coronet on the ceiling." These devices were of course very droll, but in one room there was another which was pretty as well. Some water pipes actually made the melody of nightingales. Freak jets and jeux d'esprit were extremely popular with the aristocracy. At a place called Goldwell, near Enstone in Oxfordshire, Thomas Bushell devised a similar grot which has disappeared, and at Chatsworth the weeping willow tree of lead still thrives in the grounds.

26.Wilton House: the Stables.    *From a drawing by Inigo Triggs*

The façade of the Wilton grotto exists, but not in its original position. It was long ago removed to another part of the gardens where it now serves as the front of a small house. It is one of the most extraordinary façades of the century. Count Magalotti, who saw it, described it as "rough cast with pumice stone and cockle-shells", and this is the first impression it conveys. In reality it is a wall of Chilmark stone completely covered with intricate carving practically in the round. The carving consists of flowing rococo patterns and female busts with long falling hair set on capitals. The flavour of this strange front is rather northern than Italian, although Colen Campbell, who illustrated it, implied that the busts derived from Florence.[1] This is unlikely. Vertue, who aptly called the grotto "a fountain with Basso rilievo and water stone work", attributed it to Nicholas Stone, junior; and Charles Stoakes wrote that Nicholas Stone, senior, designed as well as built many curious works for Wilton. Now in the elder Stone's account book are payments recorded in 1637 for work done by "Mr. Decans appointment", and again in 1639, for delivering a white marble cornice in six pieces "by appointment of Mr. de Caus", all for Lord Pembroke. From these records we may conclude that Stone the elder probably built the grotto, and other garden ornaments at Wilton, to the design and under the direction of Isaac de Caux, who was after all an architect as well as an engineer.[2]

[1] *Vitruvius Britannicus,* Vol. II. Perhaps Campbell meant from France.

[2] Isaac de Caux almost certainly constructed the even more elaborate grotto, which forms part of Woburn Abbey, in 1626–30. Its ceilings and walls are lined with the insides of shells. The patterns—notably the draped mascherons—are decidedly French.

Aubrey, who was a Wiltshire man and a friend of Lord Pembroke, ascribed to de Caux the beautiful stables lying to the south of the house (26). The design of the two end pavilions—connected by a low colonnade—each with a steep roof, lucarne window behind a balustrade and œil-de-bœuf panels over casement windows is unlike that of any known building of Inigo Jones. On the contrary, the distinct French character is precisely what we should expect of de Caux, and Aubrey's information is probably correct.

Aubrey again is very emphatic in stating that Pembroke began to rebuild the house at Wilton in 1649 "with the advice of Inigo Jones; but he being then very old, could not be there in person, but left it to Mr. Webb". And this no doubt is exactly what did happen. Inigo was by now seventy-six years old and life had lately been treating him harshly. It is surprising that he should have consented at all to work in the year of the King's death for a man who in his eyes must have betrayed their master, for at the very end Earl Philip had once again come to terms with Parliament. Perhaps the two men were never attached to each other; and in the Wilton copy of the architect's *Stoneheng* the Earl's son was to write in the margin with a touch of asperity that "Iniquity" Jones had derived £16,000 a year—a gross exaggeration—merely for keeping in repair the King's houses. If, however, Webb carried out the new work at Wilton it is equally certain that the inspiration of it was Inigo's. This we conclude from the drawings of which a number exist. Some of the more finished are in the polished hand of Webb, but six in wash, for ceilings, and six in pen and ink, for doors in the staterooms, are in Jones's hand, and signed and annotated partly by him and partly by Webb.[1] Nearly all the drawings are for apartments that no longer exist: for as well as rebuilding the south front, which survives, Jones and Webb rebuilt the three other fronts (only leaving the mid-sixteenth-century east frontispiece intact) and reconstituted most of the interior. The beautiful ceilings which feature in the drawings for the great stair, the cabinet room, the Countess of Carnarvon's bedchamber and withdrawing-room, the Countess of Pembroke's bedchamber and the passage-room into the garden, all disappeared in the drastic demolition of the north and west fronts by James Wyatt in 1801.

The great south front of Wilton is one of the glories of English renaissance architecture, and its composition determined the form of numerous Palladian buildings and country houses of the eighteenth century, like the Horse Guards, Holkham, Euston, Hagley and Croome. Yet the Wilton composition of basement, *piano nobile* and attic storey is of the utmost simplicity, omits the orders altogether and has already developed a character far more English than Italian. It bears less resemblance to a Vicenzan palace than does the Banqueting House, or to a Vicentine villa than does the Queen's House. The long front is only broken in the centre (25) by a noble Venetian window under classical figures, seated on either side an

[1] The Wilton drawings are very scattered. They are in the Radcliffe Camera, Oxford; Worcester College Library, Oxford; the R.I.B.A. Library, London. The most recent were discovered at Wilton by the present Lord Herbert, and are kept there.

escutcheon and coronet. It is tied together by a continuous balustraded parapet, in the middle of which a winged Victory perches nonchalantly on a ball. The front is flanked by tall corner projections, dictated to Inigo by towers that already existed on the Tudor house—projections to be repeated by the Burlingtonian architects almost as obligatory motifs. Thus this famous and familiar composition was to some extent derived from an accident.

The seven rooms of the south front survive practically as Jones and Webb left them, and form a group of great academic importance as well as incomparable beauty. Of them the double and single cube rooms are certainly the most famous seventeenth-century apartments in all England. The proportions of the double cube (27) are 60 ft. by 30 ft. by 30 ft., and it is curious that in this room, so dependent for effect upon regular dimensions, the architect permitted the fireplace not to be central on the main wall.[1] Campbell and subsequent draftsmen, as though shocked by a negligence on the part of their revered master, deliberately glossed over this defect by showing the plan of the double cube to be symmetrical in their plates and thus improving upon Jones by a cheat. Jones must of course have been fully aware of what he was doing and possibly a pre-existing chimney-breast necessitated the anomaly. Nevertheless the illusion of symmetry is marvellously maintained in spite of the architecture of the main wall not centralizing with the design of the ceiling.

The floor of the double cube is of wide oak boards that have acquired a silky canary gloss through centuries of polish. The walls are panelled with wide pine boards butted together and covered with plaster to a thickness of half an inch. Originally painted white, they have now faded to ivory faintly filmed with green; the enrichments are dulled gold. Between the Vandyke portraits in their contemporary frames are bold beribboned drops of fruit and vegetables in carved oak. Beautiful as is the design of the drops, their carving is noticeably inferior to carving done later in the century by Wren's craftsmen. On the east wall the immense, tabernacle-like door-case in the Corinthian order is comparable, notwithstanding its material, wood, to Palladio's and Scamozzi's marble door-cases in the Doges' Palace, in Venice, which will have inspired it. The reclining figures on the broken pediment add elegance, and the proud escutcheon dignity, to the noble composition. The doors, with deep acanthus leaf mould to the panels and circular plaques, suggest a French rather than Italian provenance. The cove of the ceiling was painted by Edward Pierce, senior, in arabesques and cartouches to frame Lord Pembroke's arms and motto; and the great oval panel by Emanuel de Critz [2] to simulate a rotunda open to the sky. The white marble chimneypiece, with its bold scrolls and swags, is, like the great door-case of Venetian design rather than "after the best French

1 In the north-east room next the Queen's cabinet at Greenwich, Jones was guilty of carelessly relating the plaster ceiling to the fireplace and so causing asymmetry.

2 Emanuel de Critz, 1605–65, son of John de Critz, the old serjeant-painter, painted the portrait of John Tradescant in the Ashmolean, Oxford.

manner'', as John Evelyn considered all the Wilton chimneypieces to be. The gilt overmantel in the form of an aedicule, before which stand figures of Bacchus and Pomona, determines the character of this superb apartment in which the highly sumptuous decoration is entirely subservient to the architecture.

The single cube is a little less sumptuous than its larger neighbour, and the wall decoration is different. Instead of the large fruit and vegetable drops, carved draperies are suspended beneath great trusses and rectangular panels of scrollwork. The device of crossed palm branches is, however, repeated. The cove of the ceiling is painted with arabesques and the cypher PM by the eighteenth-century Andien de Clermont; but the central allegorical canvas by Giuseppe Cesari is part of the original scheme. The dado panels are painted by Thomas de Critz[1] with enchanting little scenes from Sir Philip Sidney's *Arcadia*. Again, the spacing of the windows does not coincide with the chimney wall opposite and the resulting asymmetry is more apparent than in the double cube. The last of the Inigo Jones rooms and the least satisfactory is the hunting room. The repetition of the fireplace as a dado device is more curious than beautiful. The inset panels of hunting scenes, in one of which Earl Philip appears on horse-back, and in another, men shoot partridges under ''stalking-cows'', are by Pierce.

Neither Earl Philip nor Inigo Jones lived to see the rebuilding of Wilton finished. Lord Pembroke died in 1650, and his son allowed the great work to continue uninterrupted. It is not likely that Jones directed the operations after this event. He was very old and left all his business affairs in the capable hands of Webb. On 22nd July of this year he made his will, in which he described himself to be ''in perfect health of mind but weak in body''. Indeed the rather fretful notes which he was still in the habit of transmitting to the pages of his cherished Palladio volume bear out the phrase. No longer did he jot down those rapid but carefully considered memoranda on architecture. Instead, upon the end page he recorded prescriptions and remedies given him by his friends to parry the advancing ailments of old age. Lady Pembroke told him of an approved medicine for stone in the kidneys, and Lord Huntingdon gave him directions for purging the head by smoking under a cloth. Colds were evidently a recurring nuisance, and to sneeze by tickling the nose with a feather before meals proved efficacious. Not all the prescriptions, however, date from the last years of his life, and melancholy was apparently a trouble of thirty-six long years' standing. Against such onslaughts he had written: ''Copulation must be utterly eschewed for that thereby the best blood of a man is wasted and natural strength enfeebled. . . . To kimb the head often, to sing, use music. To sleep somewhat longer than ordinary'', are instead sound principles. For stomach troubles he advocated little meat, regular motions, and curiously enough ''to eat and drink claret wine extraordinary much at dinner''. And towards the end of his life his eyesight failed him.

[1] Thomas de Critz, d. 1676, was another son of John. He is described as painter in 1632 when paid ''for repairing a Holbein and picture of musicians by Titian'' for the King at Whitehall.

In 1651 he was once more occupying his old premises in Scotland Yard. On 21st June 1652 he died at Somerset House, "through grief", Webb wrote, "as is well known, for the fatal calamity of his dread master". To a man in his eightieth year who owed his life's prosperity and success to the munificent patronage of kings and courtiers, the drab patronage of Commonwealth magnates could have had little to offer. In spite of the forfeitures suffered through his loyalty to the Crown Inigo died a comparatively rich man. He left most of his money to Anne Jones,—his "kins-woman" he described her in the will—wife of John Webb, and their five children; £500 and half of his "wearing apparel" to Richard Gamon, clerk of the works at Somerset House and the Tower of London, who had married another kinswoman, Elizabeth Jones; and to several old friends and colleagues, who included John Damporte,[1] carpenter, and Henry Wickes, paymaster of the works. The residue was to be divided between his sole executor, who was John Webb, and two overseers of his will, Henry Cogan[2] and Henry Browne, both described as esquires. The poor of St. Martin's and St. Benet's parishes were not forgotten. Jones also provided £100 for his funeral expenses and £100 for a white marble monument. He was buried in the chancel of St. Benet's, Paul's Wharf, beside the graves of his father and mother, and the monument was duly erected. It consisted of a rectangular stone with an inscription on the front panel: at either end was a bas-relief of the Banqueting House and the portico of St. Paul's Cathedral. Between two obelisks rested his bust, which Edward Marshall, who may have sculptured it, snatched to safety before the disastrous flames of September 1666 could reach the church, and took to his own house in Fetter Lane.

[1] John Damporte, or Davenport, was a carpenter, who first appears working for the King in 1626. He was an expert at masque production under Jones and evidently a man of cheerful, facetious temperament who kept the workmen happy. By 1661 he was master carpenter.

[2] Henry Cogan, a small royalist squire of Kent, had been secretary to Sir Henry Wotton in Venice 1604–10. In 1654 Cogan translated a guide book to Rome.

# CHAPTER FOUR

# INIGO JONES—
# SOME ATTRIBUTED BUILDINGS

MANY improbable buildings are attributed to Inigo Jones on no documentary authority whatever. There is scarcely a county in England and Wales—or Scotland—in which some Jacobean house with, say, a window, gable or porch displaying a more or less regular use of the classical orders, or stranger still in which even some Georgian house, because its whole plan and proportions are strictly regular, has not been classified by over-zealous topographers as an Inigo Jones building. Frequently a casual investigation of date, style or original ownership will proclaim that the attribution must be entirely spurious. Sometimes it is most puzzling to make out why certain buildings, such for example as the lumpish brick tower of Staines church, the rustic stone bridge at Llanrwst over the Conway river, or the Scottish baronial turrets of Floors Castle, could ever have been mistaken for the work of an architect infused with the spirit of Vitruvius and Palladio. It is far easier to understand how the Georgian aedicular wainscot in the great hall at Knebworth, or the Roman front of Ebberston Hall, became confused with Jones's work of a century earlier, because Lord Burlington's school of architects deliberately revived the Jonesian style in reaction from the mannerism of Wren. Such confusions are the penalty in store for the reputation of a great artist whose life has not been chronicled by a contemporary.

If the majority of Jonesian attributions are unworthy of mention, a few deserve fair consideration. The buildings mentioned in this chapter all possess certain elements which make their attribution to Inigo Jones possible, if not always probable. Briefly, these elements are the advanced classical character of their design,[1] and the superior quality of their detail to that of contemporary work. They suggest that if Inigo was not personally responsible for the buildings, then someone else, either well versed in the antique principles of architecture, or closely acquainted with the surveyor's style, had designed them.

1    *Houghton Conquest House, Bedfordshire, 1615–21*

The ruins of this building, believed to be Bunyan's "House Beautiful", perched on

[1] The single exception to which this sentence does not apply is the chapel at Lincoln's Inn: see p. 109.

the escarpment of the "Hill Difficulty", are veiled in mystery.[1] The land on which the house stands, a mile north of Ampthill, was granted by James I to Mary, Dowager Countess of Pembroke, sister of Sir Philip Sidney and mother of Shakespeare's incomparable pair of brethren. Her sons' friendship for and patronage of Inigo Jones have been referred to in earlier chapters. About 1615, the year in which Inigo became the King's surveyor after his return from Italy, Lady Pembroke began to build. There are no records of the architect she employed. In plan Houghton House is E-shaped, without the old Elizabethan and Jacobean inner court, but axially disposed in the classical manner, common a generation later. Its outside appearance was originally like that of a small Blickling or Hatfield, in its walls of rose brick in English bond with stone dressings, its square corner towers, it curvilinear gables and tall clustered chimney shafts—in fact thoroughly Jacobean. No less Jacobean were the neo-classical touches in top-heavy pedimented doorways on the south porch and in the middle of the west front. These doorways clearly derived from woodcuts in Serlio's book, just as at Blickling similar doorways were taken from the same source by the surveyors Thomas Thorpe and Robert Lyminge. With the single exception of the axial planning—incidentally Horace Walpole termed it "the worst contrived dwelling I ever saw"—Houghton originally belonged to that Jacobean group of houses composed of tightly packed masses deriving from the French sixteenth-century châteaux which du Cerceau recorded in *Les Plus Excellents Bâstiments*.

Mary Lady Pembroke died in 1621, and her younger son, to whom she left the house, not wanting it, surrendered it to the Crown, which accordingly let it to the Bruce family. These events enable us to put the year 1621 as the latest date for the addition of the north and west frontispieces, since the latter bears on its entablature traces of the Sidney and Dudley crests. It is these two frontispieces which stylistically suggest the hand of Inigo Jones.[2]

There is little doubt that the two frontispieces or loggias (which are shown in their complete form in early engravings) were additions. Examination of the ruins has shown that straight joints exist between the red-brick structure and the stone loggias which were not bonded into it. Furthermore their character is essentially classical and Italian. The west frontispiece consisted of three superimposed stages of which the lowest, a portico of Doric columns and entablature survives in fair preservation (29). On the frieze between the triglyphs are carved the bear and ragged staff of the Dudleys (Lady Pembroke's mother's family) and the porcupine and pheon of the Sidneys (her father's family). The entasis of the columns and meticulous carving of the stonework are absolutely classical and correct. On the two upper stages balustrades were let into the columns in the very manner which Jones explains he copied from Scamozzi upon the south portico of the Queen's House. The north frontispiece was even more elaborate and the sources of its inspiration are interesting (28).

[1] Houghton Conquest House was unroofed and dismantled in 1794.
[2] Incidentally Inigo Jones was at Ampthill in 1621 preparing lodgings for a forthcoming royal progress that summer.

27    Wilton House, Wiltshire: the Double Cube Room (c. 1650) by Inigo Jones and John Webb; the ceiling painted by Edward Pierce and Emanuel de Critz

28  (*above*) Centrepiece of North Front. (From a drawing by Kimpton, 1785)

29  (*below*) Remains of Centrepiece of West Front. Additions
probably by Inigo Jones, *c.* 1620

Houghton Conquest, Bedfordshire

Professor A. E. Richardson first noticed a resemblance in the round-headed openings between engaged columns of the double portico (Doric below and Ionic above) to the superimposed stages in the courtyard of Palladio's Convento della Carità in Venice. Now we know from Jones's frequent notes that he was greatly impressed by this building of Palladio. The two portico stages of the north frontispiece were crowned by a third, composed of niches under a pedimented gable with scroll supports and obelisks on either side. This device is very commonly found on the façades of Roman churches of the late sixteenth century, such as the church of the Crociferi close to the Trevi fountain. It was also followed by Jones in an original design for the west front of St. Paul's Cathedral.

If 1621 was the last year in which these frontispieces could have been added to Houghton House we should remember that both the Queen's House and the Banqueting House were then still in process of building. It is therefore improbable that any English architect but Inigo Jones was capable of designing features so eminently classical: and considering his close connection with the Herbert family it is surely probable that Inigo Jones was the architect chosen by Lady Pembroke to add them to what John Aubrey described as her "curious house in Bedfordshire, called Houghton Lodge, near Ampthill". Aubrey went on to say: "The architects were sent for from Italy." That she employed Italians, either as architects or workmen, is unlikely. Far from lessening Inigo's claims Aubrey's words seem to strengthen them, for the surveyor-general was known to his contemporaries as a great traveller whose novel conceptions of architecture were derived from Italy.

## 2 Lincoln's Inn Chapel, London, 1618–23

In February 1613 Inigo Jones had produced Chapman's *Memorable Masque* for the Inns of Court. There was a payment to him that year by the Inns of Court of £100 "towards the works for the hall and street". Mr. Gotch thought the payment might have had no connection at all with the masque but have covered work on the hall screen. The masque was not held at Lincolns' Inn, it is true, but at Whitehall, whither the masquers went in a long procession from Chancery Lane. But the screen, for which £40 was paid to one Robert Lynton, in October 1624, is typical Jacobean joiner's work, of which there exist numerous examples in our university college halls. It bears little resemblance to the classical designs associated with Jones's style. However, on 25th November 1617 the Benchers of Lincoln's Inn ordered that materials to provide for a new chapel should be assembled. On 27th January of the following year the Black Books of the Inn record that "the consideration of a fit model for the chapel is commended to Mr. Indicho Jones, and Mr. Brooke, one of the Mrs. of the Bench is requested to move him concerning the same; and consideration is to be had of the recompense that shall be given to the said Mr. Indicho Jones for his pains therein". Christopher Brooke had been one of the select friends present at Coryat's Feast and to his account as a bencher the Inns of Court masque had been charged in 1613. A poet as well as a lawyer he mixed with artists and literary men and was doubtless held a suitable person to persuade his friend, who, as surveyor-general, could not be directly commissioned by the benchers to do work for them. There is no minute to state that Inigo Jones consented, nor does his name appear in the Black Books again. But there is nothing to indicate that he did not consent. In May 1618 £2,000 was voted for the cost of the chapel and in a November minute we read: "The model of the chapel agreed upon . . . the platform of the same model is appointed to be drawn by Clarke who hath undertaken the building of the said chapel." Now John Clarke (he died in 1624) was henceforth to be described in the Black Books as "freemason and workman of the chapel", but the fact that he acted as draftsman and possibly maker of the model as well as builder does not necessarily mean that the surveyor-general had not supplied the design. Nor does the fact that one, Otto Nicholson (the builder of the Oxford Carfax), was called upon to advise what manner of windows were most suitable, have the same implication. Moreover, Thomas Baldwin, the King's Comptroller of Works under Inigo Jones, with whom he repeatedly worked in close accord, seems to have supervised the chapel's erection. This he would surely not have done if Clarke the freemason had been its designer. After several delays the chapel was ready for consecration in 1623 and at the ceremony John Donne, another intimate friend of Inigo's, preached the sermon.

At first glance this ungracious building looks as though its designer might have been almost anyone else than the English Vitruvius. To begin with it was so badly built that by 1680 it was ruinous.[1] Wren then restored it and a century later James Wyatt, having pared the stonework and remodelled the mouldings, gave it a new roof. Finally in 1882 Lord Grimthorpe pulled down the west end, added a new western bay and gave the chapel the forlorn appearance that invariably resulted from his Gothic titivating of old buildings. Nothing of the seventeenth century remains inside the chapel today except an unimportant perforated screen at the back of the pews and some mutilated pew standards, which are not unlike those carved by Adam Browne[2] for Lambeth Palace chapel.

An eighteenth-century print[3] shows what the outside of the chapel looked like before Wyatt laid his hands upon it. It had heavy buttresses crowned with flaming urns on scale-capped finials, very much in the manner of Laud's ecclesiastical style of a decade later. The open undercroft or ambulatory looked exactly as it does now and it is this strangely contrived affair which retains its original character. Doric engaged columns form the piers which support the depressed Gothic arches. The vaulted roof ribs have Jacobean ovolo moulds. Many of the bosses at the intersections of the liernes are small heraldic cartouches; others are rosettes and foliage. The panels between the ribs are of late Perpendicular style.

[1] After the Fire of London it was found that Jones's additions to St. Paul's Cathedral had been insubstantially built.

[2] A John Browne was one of the joiners at work on Lincoln's Inn Chapel. Adam Browne worked under Inigo Jones, 1624–5. See footnote on p.152.

[3] Crace Collection, British Museum.

Vertue believed the chapel to have been built by Inigo Jones to prove that he could design in the Gothic style. Now there is at Chatsworth a drawing by Jones for the inside of a prison with just the characteristics of the chapel ambulatory—namely piers formed of clustered (Tuscan) columns supporting an elliptical vaulting. Inigo therefore could certainly design in this semi-Gothic style if he wanted to. But that he cared to build in it is unlikely. The benchers, being conservative sort of people, would probably have considered a chapel in any other style as unsuitable. So Christopher Brooke may well have persuaded his friend to sketch a design of the sort which he gladly left to his subordinates to carry out, modifying it as they went along.

## 3   Raynham Hall, Norfolk, 1619–22–37

Raynham Hall in the remote north-west of Norfolk presents several unsolved problems. In spite of the voluminous accounts kept of its building the master mind responsible for its design has not been revealed. Yet this great house, apart from its gables with rather oversize scrolls, which convey a recognizably Dutch flavour to the exterior, is so classical in plan and elevations that it is hard to suppose the owner and his band of local workmen were alone responsible for it. Sir Roger Townshend was for a short time Member of Parliament for Oxford, but in all respects a simple country gentleman who did not move in Whitehall circles. The fact that he was not attached to the Court and did not enjoy high office is perhaps an argument against the King's surveyor having designed his country house for him. But if Inigo Jones had nothing to do with Raynham, what other architect at this early date was capable of advising Sir Roger ?

The account books tell us that in the early part of 1619 an estate workman was already digging in the grounds "searching to find chalk". On 30th August a succinct note relates : "this week begin the building" of the house. Almost at once we learn that masons are working the freestone, and carpenters the oak moulds for the mullions and transoms of the windows. Locks and nails are bought at Fakenham market and Rudham fair, and John Baker, a blacksmith, comes over from Blickling, Sir Henry Hobart's vast seat in course of erection in the neighbourhood. There now appears the name of an important figure in the story of Raynham, one William Edge, described as a mason. Edge was a Raynham man, then thirty-five years old and presumably of little learning, for one would not suppose a Norfolk hamlet to provide a wide range of education. He lived till 1644, and up to Sir Roger's death six years before practically directed all the building operations. He also assisted in producing designs, for there are frequent items such as "to William Edge for 5 days in platting at 22d. p. die".

It appears that Sir Roger had the habit of fleeing from the bleak Norfolk landscape and the sweeping North Sea winds each winter. On 29th November of the year 1619 there is a record of payment of six weeks' wages to William Edge while in London with his master. This is interesting, for one immediately asks what was the purpose of the Raynham mason's visit and what new buildings did he see in the capital. He must almost certainly have watched the rapid progress of Inigo Jones's Banqueting House, which had been put in hand the previous January. In the following March Sir Roger applied for and was granted a licence to go abroad for three years so long as he did not include Rome in his itinerary. He did not avail himself of the full period's leave, but was abroad all that spring and summer. On 20th October the account books disclose payment "to Wm. Edge for xxviii weeks . . . Attending my Mr. in England and out of England at 6s the week viii$^{li}$ viij$^s$", when the master and his servant were apparently in the Netherlands. The reason why Edge was included in these travels must surely have been to enable him to study continental architecture. Unfortunately we are not told what cities they visited nor what buildings they looked at. But if Amsterdam was made an object of pilgrimage the new buildings of Lieven and Hendrik de Keyser (the last Nicholas Stone's master and father-in-law) will have attracted their notice. On 12th March 1621 Edge was paid wages for fifteen weeks in London again; and the rest of this year he was busy drawing and platting at Raynham. When he was living in Sir Roger's house and "dieting" there he received 1s. a day; when at his own home on the estate, in Sir Roger's absence, 11s. or 12s. a week.

In January 1622 the walls of Raynham Hall were rising, but the eventual appearance of the exterior was still undetermined. On the 15th Sir Roger noted that "it was thought fitting the lower hall windows should have frames of timber, and no mullions of stones put into them". This was a remarkable innovation, for the first buildings in England known to have wooden window-frames were the Queen's House and the Banqueting House.[1] Edge was instructing the carpenters and drawing patterns of moulds for the masons and bricklayers. Then a curious thing seems to have happened. Some untoward event necessitated the old foundations being taken up and new ones laid: and one of the freemasons, by name Thomas Moore, was paid for making the model of a new house. This sounds very drastic action to be recorded so light-heartedly and we cannot be sure whether the whole structure was indeed pulled down from top to bottom and an entirely new one begun all over again, or merely some annexe of the house. The accounts unfortunately are not specific on this point.

At any rate this same year Sir Roger began to keep what he headed "A book of remembrance concerning the buildings", which contains a number of memoranda upon practical matters. They show that by now Townshend had become deeply interested in architectural theories and doubtless well conversant in them. There occur jottings like the following: "That advice be had whether a flat roof or a steep roof be most convenient", and the answer (by whom supplied we are not told), "The flat roof is said to be most convenient." As it happened this advice was not followed at Raynham. Again: "That the upper square windows of the hall should have keystones of a foot and better in length put into the heads of them." There are in fact concealed keystones in the windows mentioned, but scarcely a foot in length.

[1] By 1731 the wooden casements at Raynham had been supplanted by sash windows.

"That there be passages left in the walls for the lead pipes." The lead downpipes, if these are what are referred to, pass down the outside walls and only pierce the great cornice. "That the great cornice on the front be covered with lead . . .", as it was, and is.

It may therefore be argued that, by the time Sir Roger began to keep the memoranda book, he had so far progressed in architectural knowledge that he felt ashamed of his early essay at building and so decided to pull down all that he and Edge had begun in 1619 and start afresh along more correct lines. The two must have learnt a good deal from their visits to London and the Continent within the past three years. This is borne out by a passage in an otherwise facetious letter written about forty years later to Sir Roger's second son, and eventual heir to Raynham, Horatio 1st Lord Townshend, by his neighbour, the distinguished architect, Sir Roger Pratt. In his letter dated 1663, Pratt, after a roundabout solicitation to become Lord Townshend's architect, paid tribute to the father's knowledge and skill in architecture. He wrote: "And Sir Roger bestowed his time to examine (as I have credibly heard) every inch accor. to Mathematics as he was able to do, witness his many Italian and French books of architecture." Even so, it is not from books that an amateur may learn everything, and besides, Sir Roger's travels apparently did not take him as far as Italy. Only there could he have directly learnt how to arrive at what is the Palladian plan of Raynham Hall: for as yet no country house existed in England (apart from the Queen's House, the building of which was very protracted) to which Sir Roger could go for a prototype.

The actual plan of Raynham (whether dating from 1619 or 1622 we are not sure) is a shrunk H, axial and symmetrical. Round the horizontally disposed hall and vertically disposed drawing-room on the central axis staircases and lesser rooms are ranged. If for a moment we try and forget the great curvilinear gables—possibly the outcome of Sir Roger's visit to Holland—and the rather mannerist superstructure of the west front, the elevations become almost Palladian. The material used, a pink brick laid in Flemish bond (and so an even earlier instance than the much-quoted one of Kew Palace), is admittedly not what we associate with the façades of Vicenzan palaces. But the stone frontispiece of the east elevation is instantly recognizable as Palladian (31). It has even been ascribed to William Kent, who added the west porch and altered most of the rooms in 1732. But this ascription is not correct, for there exist at Raynham two drawings which were made of the west and east elevations in anticipation of a visit of Charles II in 1671. The drawing of the east elevation shows the frontispiece almost exactly as it stands today. And there is no documentary evidence among the Raynham papers to suggest that the frontispiece was added because of the King's visit. It is true that the two rooms behind the frontispiece were redecorated by Kent and only the ceiling of the upper, or Belisarius Room, left untouched. It is easy enough to understand why. Whatever the rest of the room may have looked like the ceiling is precisely of that Inigo Jones style upon which Kent endeavoured to model his own work. It is divided into massive compartments of which the ribs are the same depth as the cornice. Its design closely resembles that of the saloon ceiling at Coleshill, which was built by Pratt. Moreover, the details of the plasterwork are identical. This resemblance gives rise to the question: was Pratt after all responsible for the ceiling of the Belisarius Room at Raynham? Did he work for Lord Townshend as he evidently wished to do in 1663 and even build the east frontispiece?

Sir Roger Townshend died on 1st January 1637 when, according to an inventory taken after his death, the house was unfurnished and so probably unfinished inside. Roger Pratt, again in the same letter from which we have already quoted, gives further useful information on this point. "Sir Roger [Townshend]", he tells the son, "left this house only decent and handsome as Augustus found Cleopatra after Mark Antony's death in her native beauty, which since your lordship hath finished and furnished with all possible ornaments." Sir Roger had been succeeded by his elder son, who reigned during the ten years which practically covered the period of the Civil War. The Townshends were ardent royalists and so were not likely to have done any more work to Raynham during the troubled times. Two years before the Restoration Horatio, who had succeeded his brother, was married. We know that in former centuries men were disposed to improve their ancestral homes upon occasions of marriage. Nevertheless there are three reasons for thinking that, in spite of the resemblance of the Belisarius Room ceiling to the saloon ceiling at Coleshill, it was not Roger Pratt who made structural alterations to Raynham. In the first place, Pratt made no mention in his very complete note-books [1] of having done any work at Raynham. In the second, he was not an exclusive Palladian and none of his buildings bears any relation to the style of the Raynham frontispiece. In the third place, he continued in his letter to Lord Townshend to write about the rooms at Raynham in a eulogistic vein, in which the most conceited architects—and Pratt was quite a modest one—do not write about their own works. The hall, for instance, he described as "the gallantest [room] I have seen . . . there was somewhat in it divine in the symmetry of proportions of length, height and breadth which was harmonious to the rational soul", and so on, in this high-flown strain.

There is a well-founded tradition that in his old age Inigo Jones paid several visits to Coleshill, where he gave particular advice to Pratt about ceilings.[2] If therefore Jones was the designer of the Coleshill saloon ceiling, is it very fantastic to suggest that Webb was the designer of the variant at Raynham, and that he carried it out for the first Lord Townshend just before the Restoration? The idea that William Edge, Thomas Moore or any other workman mentioned in Sir Roger Townshend's accounts was capable of supplying designs for the Belisarius Room ceiling, and above all for the east classical centrepiece, can be dismissed at once.[3] Only an artist of superior

---

[1] *Architecture of Sir Roger Pratt,* ed. R. T. Gunther, 1928.

[2] See p. 211.

[3] At the top of the house are two uncouth Jacobean chimneypieces that were probably the outcome of Edge's assiduous "platting".

powers could have made such noble designs. Webb was such an artist.[1] He was also an exclusive Palladian: and he is known to have done work for a number of royalist patrons in the east of England during the last years of the Commonwealth.

4  *Boston Manor, Brentford, 1622–3, and c. 1670 ?*

This house, so close to the capital, has always perplexed the scholars because it combines styles irreconcilably opposed to one another. In shape a compact rectangle, it has pointed gables, a porch and, within, ceilings and fireplaces, all of which are essentially Jacobean. The dates 1622 and 1623 appear on three rainwater heads and a plaster ceiling respectively. On the other hand all the window-cases, with their architraves and pediments, the cornice with pulvinated frieze over the second floor, and the niches in the gables, are irreproachably classical. It would be difficult to assign these features to any architect but Inigo Jones, if there were proof that they dated from these early years. But there is no proof whatever. In 1670 the house changed ownership, and the Clitherow family who acquired it certainly added outbuildings. They also added a fourth rainwater head to the west side which they dated 1670. We may assume therefore that in accordance with contemporary fashion, they applied the classical adjuncts to the outside of the house and otherwise left the structure—including the early rainwater heads—and interior decoration, as they found them.

5  *Castle Ashby, Northamptonshire, 1624–30*

The Compton family came into possession of Castle Ashby in Henry VII's reign, and in the third and fourth quarters of the sixteenth century built the greater part of the present house. William Lord Compton, having married at the very end of the century the daughter of a wealthy ex-Lord Mayor of London, was impelled on the death of his father-in-law still further to enlarge and embellish the already vast building. In fact his wife wrote to him in a very peremptory vein about this time: "Also my desire is that you pay all my debts, build Ashby house, and purchase lands, and lend no money (as you love God) to the Lord Chamberlain. . . ." Compton lived in great state, employed eighty-three household servants, four chaplains and three musicians, frequently entertained James I, and in 1618 was suitably raised to the earldom of Northampton.

The precise chronology of Lord Northampton's additions to Castle Ashby in the Jacobean style need not concern us here. When we come to the classical work, and notably the two-storeyed screen of Weldon stone thrown across the south front of the house, we take notice (30). In contrast to the conventional background, the screen is strikingly novel in style. Colen Campbell in his *Vitruvius Britannicus* (1720) emphatically attributed it to Inigo Jones and so did the county historian, John Bridges (*c.* 1720), who unlike Campbell is unusually reliable and accurate. Bridges also

[1] Tradition has for centuries claimed Inigo Jones as the architect Raynham. As early as 1731 Sir Thomas Robinson wrote to Lord Carlisle: "The greater part of the house was built by our master, Inigo Jones."

attributed the east front—now much altered and its lower arcade filled in—to Jones and claimed that several chimneypieces therein were made from his designs. This is somewhat strange, since a drawing made in 1719 for Bridges's impending history shows the east front in no classical dress, but of irregular Tudor form. Campbell not only gave a plate of the screen but another showing the two end wings, which it united, made classical so as to be in keeping with it. The wings were in fact never altered from their Tudor form, but since the plate presented them in a style that was certainly not early Georgian, but rather resembled some of Jones's and Webb's drawings for Whitehall Palace, it is possible that Campbell was not taking liberties. On the contrary he may actually have seen and transcribed some unexecuted drawings now lost to us, but then perhaps in his master Lord Burlington's collection. In the text of his book Campbell wrote that Jones's work at Castle Ashby was interrupted by the Civil War, when the Earl was killed fighting for the King. It is true that the 2nd Earl of Northampton was slain at the Battle of Hopton Heath in 1643, and there is no reason why Campbell's statement that in consequence all building had to be suspended need be disbelieved. But the south screen had been built for the 1st Earl, who died as long ago as 1630, since his escutcheon, not the son's, is placed in the pediment.

The screen or colonnade, although of far more advanced classical style, recalls Lyminge's connecting screen on the south front of Hatfield House. Both were built to provide a sheltered walk on the ground floor and a gallery above. The designs of both suggest French provenance and indeed the slightly thin quality of the Castle Ashby screen is not Italian.[1] On this account the Inigo Jones attribution seems unlikely. The entablature of the upper Ionic order is weak and some of the correct moulds are lacking: the elliptical arch in the centre of the lower Doric order is clumsy where it breaks through the entablature. Moreover, the strips across the engaged columns would not have been approved by Inigo Jones, who wrote: "columns with rings or garlands about them blamed"; and the pronounced scotia, or concave moulding, in their base is strangely unorthodox. Yet the Pantheon-like aedicules within the colonnade and the Palladian windows on the park and courtyard elevations reveal that the architect, whoever he may have been, was acquainted with ancient and Palladian motifs. Above all the quality of the masonry is good. On the whole, in spite of its merits and because of its demerits, it is wiser not to attribute the Castle Ashby screen to Inigo Jones.

In addition to the screen, other work within-doors was done in the same somewhat advanced style for the first and second Earls. The ceiling of the "King William III" dining-room dates from 1624. It is of a transitional type, coved and compartmented with deep ribs like the ceiling of the saloon at Forde Abbey, the flats filled with Flemish strapwork design. The ceiling of the chapel and the gallery also survive from this period. The west staircase balustrade and several landing overdoors

1 The lettered parapet on the screen may have replaced an original blank parapet. Bridges's notes of c. 1720 mention the lettered parapet over both fronts of the screen.

30 (above) Castle Ashby, Northamptonshire: part of connecting
screen, c. 1624–30
*Architect unknown*

31 Raynham Hall, Norfolk: East Centrepiece. Possibly by Inigo
Jones before 1637, or even by Sir R. Pratt after 1660

*"Country Life" photograph*

32 (*top left*) Becket Park, Berkshire: the Fishing Lodge, once a brewhouse, 1640

33 Charlton House, Greenwich: Garden House, 1630

34 Chesterton Windmill, Warwickshire, *c.* 1639

are carved in a semi-classical manner, and the panels of the pretty little bower room, painted green and gold with drops of flowers, recall the French interpretation under Louis XIII of Raphael arabesques.[1]

## 6 Forty Hall, Enfield, 1629–36

Forty Hall poses the same problem as Boston Manor. A square block in red brick with sloping roof, it appears at first sight a typical late Stuart country house of the middling sort. On closer inspection the octagonal chimney shafts show themselves to be Jacobean. On entry the hall screen, fireplaces and strapwork plaster ceilings display the same early style. So does the brick gateway, with its curved gable and ball finials in the back court. What therefore are we to assume? The house and appurtenances were in fact built for Sir Nicholas Raynton in Charles I's reign. When he died in 1646 he was buried in Enfield church under a monument which even at that date his widow or executors had designed in just such a Jacobean style as the gateway and screen at Forty Hall. At the very end of the century Forty Hall changed families. The next owners, Wolstenholme by name, would naturally wish to bring up to date the old-fashioned property they had bought. The simplest way, without pulling the house down and building anew, would surely be to give the windows classical surrounds, add to the walls stone strings and quoins, provide an eaves cornice and modernize the shape of the roof.

## 7 Chevening, Kent: before 1630

The original house at Chevening in Kent is supposed to have been built for the 13th Lord Dacre. This information is supplied by his descendant, the 17th Lord Dacre, and by Edward Hasted in his *History of Kent*.[2] Now since the 13th Lord Dacre died in 1630, that is the latest year in which Chevening could have been begun. Once again Colen Campbell, who gave a plate of it, believed that Inigo Jones was the architect of the house. Vertue and Hasted also stated the same thing. The triple attribution is not made any less credible by the fact that John Webb at a later date was working inside the house. Two designs of his for internal features survive. In a letter to his friend Sir Justinian Isham in 1655, Webb wrote: "I am now making ornaments of wainscot for a room in Kent for my lo. Dacres [the 14th baron] which is 31 fo: long, 22: broad and 24: fo. high w^ch. height if I forget not yours is to be . . . his room is very noble and he bestows much cost upon it." The room was probably the hall, which was much altered in 1720, for its dimensions almost exactly tally with those specified by Webb. Although Chevening was twice reconstituted in the eighteenth century, the centre block retains its original core and even window disposition(66). The saloon behind the hall is still an unspoilt seventeenth-century room. It is panelled in oak from floor to ceiling and between continuous pilasters are recessed arcades, framing plain planks butted together like the panels of the famous

---

[1] The panel landscapes of this enchanting little room are in the Dutch manner.
[2] Published 1778–9.

Haynes Grange room.[1] The enriched work is of pine and the pilaster capitals are of lead gilded. The room is a remarkable specimen of its date and was probably decorated by Webb at the same time as the hall.

Chevening can hardly have been built by Webb, for he only joined Inigo Jones's office in 1628 at the age of seventeen. Fortunately we know what the house looked like when built, from Campbell's plate and a still earlier drawing made on an estate map in 1679. It was a tall rectangular block of three storeys, an attic floor and basement. The material was evidently brick with stone dressings. The first floor was approached by steep steps. The roof, adorned with dormer windows, rose steeply and was crowned with a balustraded parapet. The style of the house was therefore something entirely different to those Inigo Jones buildings we have hitherto considered. Yet for that reason we need not hesitate to associate his name with it. There exists a drawing by Jones done in 1638 for a house in just such a style, entitled by him ''Upright for my lo Matravers his house at Loatsbury''. This was Lord Maltravers, the eldest son and heir of Lord Arundel. Whether the design was carried out is not known. The Chevening-Maltravers type of house omits the orders, and is not Palladian. It is basically modelled on the Genoese palace popularized by Rubens in his book *I Palazzi di Genova*. This book had immense influence on mid-seventeenth-century domestic architecture in England and will be considered at some length in a subsequent chapter.

### 8  *Charlton House, Greenwich, garden house, c. 1630*

In an early view of the grounds at Chevening, taken in the seventeenth century, appear a pair of small garden pavilions with very distinctive hipped roofs of French flavour. They have long ago disappeared, but in the grounds of Charlton House near Greenwich, on a raised mound overlooking the church and high road, is an identical pavilion, which tradition has always associated with Inigo Jones (33). It is of red brick and consists of three bays of door and two windows between Doric pilasters that carry an entablature. The pavilion bears no relation in style to the Jacobean house which was built in 1612 for Sir Adam Newton, then tutor to Henry Prince of Wales. Sir Adam died and was succeeded by his son, a young man, in 1630. The pavilion probably belongs to the improvements which the heir will have carried out at this time. (The two contemporary brick arches on the terrace are likewise classical in style.)

### 9  *Becket Park, Berkshire, Fishing lodge, c. 1630–40*

It is appropriate to refer here to the little fishing lodge, or China House as it once was called, built above the lake at Becket Park (32). Dr. Pococke, who saw it in 1757, called it a summer-house. It was formerly part of a brew-house. The fantastic overhanging eaves which give it a pagoda look are constructed upon fairly modern roof rafters, and were probably so designed when the adjacent Chinese

[1] Victoria and Albert Museum.

bridge was put up. The four sides of the building are identical. Each consists of a central panelled door between two windows. These preserve their mullions and transoms which are in stone, like the rest of the building, and have double arrises. The cramped disposition of door and windows is not altogether pleasing. Vertue's attribution of the fishing lodge to Inigo Jones is not apparently based on any documentary evidence.[1]

## 10   Stoke Bruerne Park, Northamptonshire, 1630–6

In 1619 James I established at Mortlake on the Thames the tapestry factory which acquired great fame throughout the seventeenth century. Sir Francis Crane was made the first director. He was a man of considerable artistic taste and business acumen. He became secretary to Prince Charles and eventually amassed a large fortune, not only out of the Mortlake factory but by using his influence with the Crown to create baronets and promote ambitious men to other high offices. Accordingly he was able to advance large sums of money to Charles after he became King and in return was granted valuable manors that had belonged to the Crown. One of these manors granted him in settlement of a debt of £10,000 was that of Stoke Bruerne in Northamptonshire.

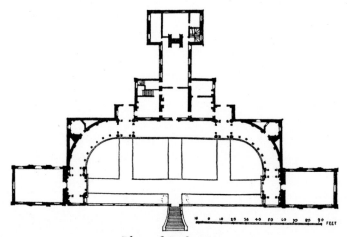

35.  Plan of Stoke Bruerne

In 1630 Sir Francis Crane started to transform an existing Tudor house set on slightly rising ground in a lank and insipid landscape. He partly rebuilt and entirely refaced the main block, to which he added curving colonnades with a pavilion at the end of each. Mr. Gotch claimed that Stoke Bruerne was the only country house that could with any assurance be attributed to Inigo Jones, but so far no documentary proof is forthcoming to establish this claim. Again we have the dubious word of

[1] Jones built other small lodges of this description, *vide* the pavilion at Theobalds for King James and the New Lodge in Hyde Park for King Charles (1634–5). The latter had a roof space of only 47 square feet.

Colen Campbell, who illustrated it, that it "was begun by Inigo Jones: the wings and the colonnades and all the foundations were made by him: but the front of the house was designed by another architect, the civil wars having also interrupted this work". There is some uncertainty what happened to Crane's central block and whether it ever was completed by him, for in Campbell's plate it is replaced by a structure which, although coinciding with the lines of the pavilions, is a little too baroque in feeling to belong to their date. Now Bridges, the Northamptonshire historian, was less dogmatic than Campbell. He said that Crane brought the model of his new house from Italy and in the execution of it "had the assistance of Inigo Jones". He also said that the house was finished before the wars and that Sir Francis Crane lived to entertain the King and Queen in it before his death in 1636.

Bridges was certainly correct in stating that the model for Stoke Bruerne came from Italy, for it is the earliest example in England of the Palladian country-house disposition of central block, curved colonnades and wings (p. 121). By the eighteenth century this disposition had become commonly accepted for a country house intended to make the grandest display and convey an impression of immensity. We see it at Kedleston, Hopetown, Castlecoole and in literally hundreds of houses throughout England, Scotland and Ireland. At Stoke Bruerne the centre block which Campbell illustrated was unfortunately burnt down in 1886, when a monstrous pseudo-Jacobean pile was tacked on to one of the pavilions so as to make complete nonsense of Sir Francis Crane's symmetrical arrangement. The pavilions, which still adhere to their original design, are, like so much noble architecture of our country today, tottering into irredeemable ruin (36).

Nevertheless, under a tangle of vegetation the remains of Crane's curved colonnades may be traced. The rear walls are divided into niched bays by Ionic pilasters which formerly balanced the disengaged columns in the front. The materials used for the colonnades and pavilions are the same. The pilasters, columns and dressings are of a tawny orange Duston sandstone, which stands out very prominently against a background of grey Lincolnshire limestone. Each quadrant arm runs into an open rectangular porch, which is an extension of the rectangular pavilion. In fact the whole plan of centre block, colonnade enclosure, porches and pavilions was made a geometrical interplay of rectangles. At the corners of both pavilions are large Ionic pilasters which, unlike the lesser columns of the colonnades and porches, are not diminished and so convey a faintly uneasy impression of staidness. They support a pulvinated frieze of plaster. The long front of each pavilion is broken by a central projection under a pediment. The projection now contains a Palladian window not shown in Campbell's drawing, where instead a plain central window was set under an elliptical tympanum. The pointed roofs of porch and pavilion are very effectively related to each other in spite of the porch front and return having lost their pediments. Altogether there is a pictorial quality about the composition of plan and elevations which is less Palladian than manneristic. It is what we might expect from a mind accustomed like Sir Francis Crane's to the architectural backgrounds of the

36 Stoke Bruerne Park, Northamptonshire: one of the Pavilion wings. Probably by Inigo Jones, 1630–6

37 Lindsey House, Lincoln's Inn Fields. Probably by Inigo Jones, c. 1640. Compare with Somerset House (fig. 21)

KIRBY HALL, NORTHAMPTONSHIRE

38 (*above*) Garden Portal, possibly to design of Inigo Jones

39 (*left*) Entrance to Great Hall

40 (*below*) Forecourt Gateway, almost certainly to designs of Nicholas Stone. All date from 1638–40

Mortlake tapestry designs. In the eighteenth century minor alterations were made to the outsides of the pavilions. The insides were entirely reconstructed.

The *Architectural Dictionary* suggests that Moses Glover was Sir Francis Crane's architect. Glover, an obscure painter and minor architect, is known for a large survey vellum he made of Syon House and Isleworth Hundred, and a design for rebuilding Petworth. On the other hand the claim made for Inigo Jones's association with Stoke Bruerne dates back to the early eighteenth century. Bridges, in the unpublished notes from which his *History of Northamptonshire* was compiled, stated that he obtained his information in answer to questions he put to the then owner of Stoke Bruerne, Mr. Arundel, who was the great-nephew of Sir Francis Crane.

11    *Chesterton Windmill, Warwickshire, 1632*

Some six miles north of Kineton, on the summit of a knoll which rises gently out of the Warwickshire plains, stands Chesterton windmill (34). This beautiful and unusual object is built upon six stout piers, which carry round-headed, splayed openings. Over them a cylindrical storey pierced with windows has a leaded dome made to revolve with the wind. Four vast sails are attached to the dome by a transverse beam. The material of the mill is a very finely chiselled ashlar. The mill formed part of the property of the Peyto family, whose house close to Chesterton church was demolished in 1802. All that remains of it is a classical garden portal of red brick on the boundary of the churchyard. Upon a lake at the foot of the knoll are the vestiges of a small mill house, evidently built at the same time as the windmill, with a pedimented front door and mullion windows with finely moulded architraves. In the church [1] are tabernacle monuments to the Peyto family sculptured by Nicholas Stone in 1639. The windmill and mill house are of a developed vernacular, rather than truly classical style. Both have the sort of tentative features associated with Stone's sculpture rather than Jones's architecture, to which the windmill has always been ascribed.

12    *Ham House, Surrey, alterations, 1637–9*

In 1633 a lease of Ham House was granted by Charles I to the friend of his childhood, William Murray. Murray began life as page and whipping-boy to Charles when a young Prince, and although he never rose to political eminence he remained all his life an influential figure in the background of the Court, and close to the King's ear.

When Murray acquired the manor of Ham he found there a house, already twenty years old and thoroughly Jacobean in character, which may have been built by John Smithson. He very soon began to bring the interior up to date, and the alterations he made were so novel, and contrasted so strikingly with the original Jacobean work, that until quite recently many of them were mistaken for work done in Charles II's

---

[1] Inside the church tower is the head of a chimneypiece in stone—a swan-necked pediment holding an escutcheon. The carving is superior. This relic doubtless came out of the Peyto mansion.

reign by Murray's daughter after she became Duchess of Lauderdale. Now since Ham is within easy riding distance of London and Hampton Court—the royal palace is but a few miles away—the King with his insatiable interest in the arts and architecture, must surely have visited the house he gave his friend and, probably, have advised him over its alterations. Inigo Jones was quartered in Hampton Court at the time the work at Ham House was under consideration, for there is a sketch he did of a wall and some trees, with a hill and windmill beyond, on which he inscribed: "Ham Court out of my garret window 1636." It is therefore not a wild conjecture that Inigo Jones supplied Murray with designs for some of those internal features carried out in a style which only he was capable of understanding. Furthermore the craftsmen engaged by Murray were all servants who worked at various times under the surveyor-general upon the royal palaces.

The name of the joiner who constructed "the great arch" between the hall and staircase, the doors and door-cases on the stair landings and the stair dado, was Thomas Carter, whose bills have survived. It does not follow that he was responsible for the stair panels as well, since beautiful and interesting as these are, they do not bear much relation to the style of his recorded work.[1] The doors and door-cases on the stair landings, in spite of individual treatment, are of a more developed classical style and the prototypes of doorways common twenty and more years later. Their shouldered heads and slightly top-heavy broken pediments are repeated in exaggerated patterns at Thorpe Hall near Stamford and the group of houses in that neighbourhood, which arose in the Commonwealth and post-Restoration decades. Such semi-classical door-cases as the Ham ones are not found elsewhere in England at this early date. Unfortunately, no other work by Thomas Carter outside Ham has been identified, and his chair for the Speaker in the House of Commons, steps leading to it and screen behind it no longer exist.[2] As well as the joiner's bill, that of the painter and gilder of Thomas Carter's woodwork is extant. He was Matthew Goodericke, the active assistant to the King's serjeant-painter and an official of high standing.

Thomas Carter was the maker of other wainscot at Ham, notably parts of the north drawing-room and the whole of the long gallery. In these two apartments his work is very distinctive. In the first his panels are built up in stages, the upper ones provided with pediments, shouldered heads and half pilasters, eccentric features reproduced later in the Thorpe group of houses. His door-cases in the north drawing-room resemble those on the stair landing. The gallery panelling, for which Carter's bill is itemized and dated 1639, is divided into bays by Ionic pilasters, and is of more straightforward classical design than the rest of the woodwork in the house.

Inigo Jones's other craftsmen employed by Murray were Joseph Kinsman and

[1] The stairs may be compared with those at Cromwell House, Highgate, built in 1637–8. The carving of the Ham stair panels is superior. They consist of military trophies of every description—shields, draped drums, battle axes, armour and even cannons.

[2] Public Record Office, Declared Accounts 2429/73.

Francis de Clein [1]. Joseph Kinsman was a plasterer and perhaps a brother of Edward, the stonemason and sculptor. He was paid in 1637 for stucco work at Somerset House and in 1638 for "a fret ceiling in the queen's bedchamber wrought with ovals and squares garnished with garlands and festoons and other enrichments" at Whitehall. His bills for work at Ham cover the ceiling over the great staircase and the soffits under the stairs; the ceilings and friezes of what is now the round gallery over the hall, and the north drawing-room. These ceilings are of a more advanced classical character than Carter's wainscot and a complete departure from traditional Jacobean patterns, for they consist of deep corniced ribs, their flats decorated with guilloche mould or wreaths of fruit and flower heads: the stair soffits are adorned with roundels of bay leaves in the manner of the Coleshill ceilings. Francis de Clein, a painter from Rostock and designer of tapestry at the Mortlake factory, had worked for the surveyor at Somerset House. At Ham he decorated that part of the north drawing-room left over by Carter and Kinsman. He did the four inset paintings over the doors and designed the strange twisted columns of the fireplace. They are rude adaptations from those in one of the Raphael cartoons, "The healing of the lame man at the temple gate", which de Clein copied for the Mortlake tapestry series.

## 13  *Kirby Hall, Northamptonshire,* 1638–40

Like a vast hulk stranded upon an ever-narrowing reef, the noble ruins of Kirby Hall still defy an ocean of surface-mining which threatens to engulf it. But inside the green garden purlieus the hideous disturbance outside is forgotten; the rooks caw among the elms, and an ancient serenity prevails.

The great house of the Hattons was begun in 1570 by Thomas Thorpe, senior, for a previous family, the Staffords. Their tenure of Kirby was short, for within five years it was sold to Queen Elizabeth's Lord Chancellor, Sir Christopher Hatton of Holdenby. It was his successor, a third Sir Christopher, scholar and antiquary, who in 1638–40 considerably altered the appearance of the Tudor building. Tradition has always maintained that Inigo Jones directed the improvements. Although documentary evidence is lacking, the Ministry of Works's official guidebook accepts the tradition. Three factors help to strengthen it: Hatton's subsequent appointment as Comptroller of the Household of Charles I, our knowledge that Nicholas Stone supplied certain chimneypieces and window-cases in 1638, and the fairly developed classical character of some of the additions.

The so-called Inigo Jones work at Kirby consisted in the refacing of the north wing of the great court both on the entrance and the inner fronts; the insertion of a central window on the porch of the south range of the court; the alteration of the great hall; the addition of the staircase hall; and the building of the two portals in the north walls of the forecourt and garden.

[1] De Clein as a young man studied at Venice, where he was known to Sir Henry Wotton. Other works by him were the gilt-panelled room at Holland House, now destroyed, and the painted dining-room at Bolsover Castle.

It is unlikely, but not of course impossible, that Nicholas Stone was the sole author of these changes. It is true that he was capable of architectural design as well as mere mason's work. But those surviving units supposed to be built to his own design—namely the wing at Cornbury Park and the Physic Garden gateways at Oxford—declare the Netherlandish training of his early years. His chimneypieces for Kirby cannot be identified, but there are other isolated features that bear the distinctive stamp of Stone's art. One is the garden doorway (38) on the south front leading to the staircase hall, with its rather clumsy trusses that remind us of his fireplace in the hall at Cornbury. Another is the entrance archway (38) into the forecourt with its double tiered niches (like those of the main Physic Garden gateway) and ball finials on Ionic scroll pedestals (like those on the wall piers of an east gate at Christ Church, Oxford).[1] But the majority of the 1638–40 features are of a purer classical design of which Stone was probably not capable. These are, notably, the whole north elevation, a marvel of balanced units[2]; the courtyard windows (dated 1638 and 1640), with their very correct architraves and pediments; the wooden doorways into the great hall (which for refined workmanship compare with those of Ashburnham House); and above all the garden portals, carved in rocaille work, with flanking niches resembling those in the Arch of Janus Quadrifons at Rome (40). These two garden ornaments are the loveliest compositions at Kirby, and the offspring of true scholarship and art.

## 14  *Ashburnham House, Westminster, c.* 1640

Ashburnham House, within the precincts of Westminster Abbey, now forms part of Westminster school buildings. It has never been satisfactorily dated nor has its authorship been established. The name by which the house is known derives from the year 1662, when it was leased by the Dean and Chapter of Westminster for £14 a year to William Ashburnham, member of a distinguished royalist family and friend of Samuel Pepys. Ashburnham then went to live in it. So we know that the present house was standing just after the Restoration: and there is no reason to assume that it had been built during the previous troubled twenty years. In 1629 one Sir Edward Powell rented a dwelling on its site, where he was definitely living in 1634. In 1640 his lease was transferred to fresh trustees for the benefit of Lady Powell. Therefore it seems that either Sir Edward rebuilt the house before 1634, or, more probably, his wife—presumably then a widow—did so in 1640.

Ashburnham House was greatly admired and repeatedly illustrated by Lord Burlington's group of architects, who treated it as a prototype of Jonesian architecture. Isaac Ware[3] attributed it to Inigo, and so did Batty Langley, who, for reasons he did not disclose, assumed that some features were added by Webb. The rather

---

[1] This is a conceit taken from Borromini and was possibly introduced to the Stone family by the younger Nicholas on his return from Rome in 1643.

[2] Observe the extremely successful end gables, pedimented and scrolled, not unlike those at Raynham.

[3] Ware illustrated the little Doric summer-house formerly adjacent to the cloister and attributed it to Inigo Jones. It was destroyed in 1883.

austere red-brick structure we see today is of course only a fragment of the seven-teenth-century building. A fire in 1731 caused much havoc, and when repairs were put in hand a top storey was added. Then in 1882 the greater part of what remained was demolished. Fortunately, however, what must always have been one of the spectacular parts, the staircase, was spared, as well as most of the drawing-room on the first floor.

The staircase is a notable architectural triumph over an awkward and restricted site—a circumstance which suggests that the plan of the pre-existing house had to some extent to be preserved. In this respect its architect showed the same ingenuity as Wren did in achieving monuments of classic beauty in several city churches whose irregular shapes were dictated by the congested areas presented. The Ashburnham House staircase may rank with Kent's at No. 44 Berkeley Square, in that both manage on a miniature scale to impose a sense of great magnificence. The site of the stairwell at Ashburnham House is an imperfect square, or to be exact, a rhomboid. But the irregularity has been very cunningly glossed over. To all appearances the seeming square has been subdivided into nine equi-sized lesser squares, of which four contain ranges of steps, as many others landings and one a filled space. Over six of the squares a coved ceiling with raised oval dome has been contrived (43). The ceiling is supported on the open side by diminishing Ionic columns, which form a screen to the remaining third of the area, and on the wall side by corresponding pilasters. The stair treads are wide and easy of ascent; they and the landings are inlaid in patterned oak. The oak balusters are vase shaped and moulded at the caps and bases; the wide handrail is a development of the Jacobean moulded rail at Ham House. Indeed the moulds of the balusters, rail, dado and wall panelling are remarkably correct, and finely carved for the period. Only at the intersections an occasional clumsiness betrays that the craftsmen were practising patterns of joinery with which they were not yet absolutely familiar. The oval dome, which is raised on groups of Ionic columns resting on plinths between balusters and lit from the sides, is beyond all praise. It is a masterpiece of aery elegance. The spandrels of the ceiling cove are filled with plaster scrolls of a baroque character which Inigo Jones thought per-missible for interiors. The whole stair unit forms a composition which is one of the glories of the seventeenth century. The walls have lately been furnished with imposing portraits of head masters and from the dome a suitable crystal chandelier has been hung.

One of a pair of noble doorways, their jambs enriched with scroll carving, leads to the ante-room and drawing-room on the first floor. This carving and that in the tympanum of the ante-room doorway have a post-Restoration look and so may have been added later by William Ashburnham. The drawing-room ceiling also had an oval dome which was removed when the upper storey was added to the house. These domes, or recessed cupolas, are rarely found in the seventeenth century. Two are shown in drawings by Inigo Jones for rooms, now destroyed, at Wilton. Jones likewise provided an octagonal one in the court-room of the Barber Surgeons' Hall, and William Samwell constructed two, which still survive, at the Grange, Alresford. The plaster ribs of the drawing-room ceiling at Ashburnham House have become much blunted by continuous whitewashing. The door has a kind of roll mould, or raised spine down the centre, as though it were composed of two wings. The same mould is repeated round the dado panels.

### 15   Lindsey House, Lincoln's Inn Fields, c. 1640

On 16th November 1618 a Royal Commission was set up which included among its members the Earls of Pembroke, Arundel and Northampton, and the surveyor-general. The commissioners were instructed to lay out the area of Lincoln's Inn Fields so that ''according to your wisdoms and discretions [it] may be framed and reduced both for sweetness, uniformity and comliness into such walks, partitions or other plots, and in such sort, manner and form, both for public health and pleasure, as by the said Inigo Jones is or shall be accordingly drawn by way of map . . .''. The directions seem to promise some evidence—of which we are so constantly in need—that Jones was personally responsible for the development of this quarter of London. But once again evidence eludes us. Professor E. S. de Beer has ascertained that, even if the area of Lincoln's Inn Fields was immediately plotted out by the commissioners, no buildings were erected upon it for at least twenty years, and then only on the west side of the present square. Of the houses forming a block on the west side, known as Arch Row, only Lindsey House (it was bought by an Earl of Lindsey in the early eighteenth century) is believed to have been built by Inigo Jones (37). But alas there exist no documents to prove this much! Vertue, however, ascribed the house to Jones (and even dated it 1640) and so did Colen Campbell, who illustrated it in *Vitruvius Britannicus*.

The ascription of Lindsey House to Jones is more than plausible, not only because he was instructed to lay out the Fields twenty years previously but because the style of the building suggests it. The façade has been a little altered since it was built. When in 1752 the house was divided into two residences the central door was duplicated. The *piano nobile* windows were at some time lowered. Originally they had aprons which coincided with the alignment of the pilaster plinths. Nevertheless enough of the façade remains—there is nothing of the inside left—to make it a very interesting relic. We notice at once that it closely resembles Jones's front for Somerset House, built a few years earlier, being an adaptation of the Palazzo Thiene courtyard theme. With its rusticated ground floor over a basement, and its giant order of Ionic pilasters supporting an entablature, Lindsey House stands the prototype of the English town house of which thousands were to appear in London and the provinces down to Regency times. It is a pleasing and very economical elevation. Ornament is sparse. The *piano nobile* windows have simple pediments of which the central one only is broken with a swag suspended between the points. The volutes of the pilaster columns are adorned in the same way with swags thrown between them. This is a typical Inigo Jones conceit which was copied by Wren in his early years at Trinity College, Cambridge, and by the Norfolk architect, Henry Bell, on his Customs House at King's Lynn.

All the houses of Arch Row have spacious forecourts enclosed by a low wall which somewhat impedes a view of the square from the lower windows. In front of Lindsey House are two rusticated brick piers, each bearing an urn-shaped stone finial. The piers and finials are shown in Campbell's plate, and if they were not built in 1640 will not date later than from Charles II's reign.

## 16   *Cranborne Manor, Dorset, 1647*

At his Jacobean manor-house in Cranborne village the 2nd Earl of Salisbury was obliged to carry out a good deal of repair of the damage caused by Parliamentary troops in the Civil War. The west end was so badly knocked about that a whole new front had to be built from the ground up. It consists of a small rectangular block of two storeys. Long and short dressed coigns clothe the angles. The most striking feature is a steep hipped roof sustained by stout cantilever brackets in wood. In fact here is one of the very first hipped roofs in England. It so happens that the name of the man who designed the block has been recorded. One Thomas Fort, a local builder, made a report in 1647 for Lord Salisbury on the repairs which had just been carried out. He was considerably impressed by what he saw. "As for the form of the roof", he wrote of the new block, "in that design which Captain Rider drew it is more agreeable to the form of the house than any other as yet demonstrated. . . . Howsoever it agrees to look on, I am sure its better for all that end of the house for the defence of the weather, for as fast as the weather cometh up, it flieth off every way. . . ." The following year Rider was paid by Lord Salisbury for his "plot" of the west wing and for making two special journeys to Cranborne from Wilton. Now about this time Inigo Jones and John Webb were preparing for Lord Pembroke plans for rebuilding Wilton after the fire. Rider was presumably working there in some capacity under the two architects.

In the Declared Accounts mention is made of a certain Richard Ryder, described as carpenter, having erected a temporary pavilion of deal boards 75 ft. long and 30 ft. high, within the paved court of Somerset House, for the performance of a masque. This was in 1632. The room must have been approved, if it was not actually designed, by the surveyor-general himself. A little later Richard Ryder built a new annex for the Queen's cook at Somerset House. Finally in 1646 Richard Ryder, carpenter, was paid for sundry work upon the roof of Lord Pembroke's lodgings, which this equivocal nobleman still retained at Whitehall. There can surely be little doubt that Richard Ryder, the erstwhile royal carpenter, was the same man as Captain Rider, who while working for Lord Pembroke at Wilton found time to add a wing to Cranborne Manor. In view of these associations Jones and Webb may have had a hand in the carpenter's "plot" for so influential a nobleman as Lord Salisbury. The Earl was an old friend of Jones, who, as long ago as James I's reign, was wont to dine "at the end of my Lord Salisbury's table". The Cranborne wing is not a monumental design, but in its overhanging eaves and heavy supporting brackets the influence of St. Paul's Church, Covent Garden, may be detected.

## 17 *Forde Abbey, Dorset, 1658*

Sir Edmund Prideaux, a strong supporter of Parliament against Charles I, was in 1647 made by Cromwell Solicitor-General, and the following year Attorney-General. He was one of the new Commonwealth men to acquire riches as well as prestige. He consequently had the means to make several large-scale improvements to the Cistercian Abbey at Forde which he had bought after the King's death. They amounted chiefly to a new upstairs saloon, dining-room, staircase and screen in the medieval chapel. The saloon is perhaps the most impressive of Prideaux's new apartments (41). It is almost a double cube, with a coved ceiling resting upon a Corinthian cornice. The walls are hung with Mortlake tapestries in delicate shades of blue and green which were given to a subsequent owner by Queen Anne. The dining-room is wainscoted with panels—of similar patterns to some in the lesser rooms at Wilton—between serried pilasters. The plaster ceilings of both saloon and dining-room are unusually elaborate (42). If we compare them with ceilings at the Queen's House or Coleshill—and the dining-room ceiling at Forde has the same disposition of ribs as the hall and saloon ceilings at Coleshill—we at once notice that they are of a transitional and fussy design. There is a total absence of plain ribs and unadorned panels. Both are crammed with foliage patterns and devices taken from the Jacobean emblem books. The effect is a little over-ornate and overpowering, for mastery of the stuccoist's craft in country districts was at this time still far from realized. The same shortcomings are observable in the joinery as in the plasterwork at Forde. The door-heads and overmantels are somewhat tentative in design and weak in execution. But these demerits do not detract from the liveliness of the carving, especially of the staircase, which is already of the pierced panel and broad handrail type. With their central cartouches the panels recall those earlier panels on the famous stairway at Aldermaston Court; but here in place of warriors on the newel posts are urns filled with fruits and flowers. The chapel screen is of charming Carolean design, with great pendants of fruit on the piers like the drops in the Wilton double cube.

On the plaster ceiling of the staircase appears the date 1658. It probably determines the year of the completion of Sir Edmund Prideaux's improvements. Yet Woolfe and Gandon,[1] who made measured drawings of the ceilings, and Hutchins, the Dorset historian, attributed them to Inigo Jones. In the first place, a man with Prideaux's record of active services for Parliament would never have approached, nor surely have been received, by Inigo Jones, whose association with his old patron Philip Lord Pembroke at Wilton is his nearest lapse from allegiance to his King. In the second place, the designs of the Commonwealth additions at Forde Abbey can by no means be reconciled to Inigo's uncompromising classical standards. And in the third place, Inigo Jones had already been dead six years before the works at Forde were completed.

[1] *Vitruvius Britannicus*, Vol. II, 1771.

41 (*above*) The Saloon

FORDE ABBEY, DORSET

42 (*left*) A Ceiling Panel, 1658, in the manner of, but not by, Inigo Jones

43    Ashburnham House, Westminster: the Staircase, 1640–62. Attributed without
evidence to John Webb, and worthy of him

# NICHOLAS STONE AND THE FLEMISH TRADITION

NICHOLAS STONE (1586–1647) was thirteen years younger than Inigo Jones, and although his span by seventeenth-century standards was a long one, he died five years before him. Of his life, because of the account and note-book[1] which he assiduously kept throughout the greater part of it, we know far more than of his great contemporary's. As a consequence of the publication of these records Stone has turned out to be a figure of considerable academic importance in the field of Carolean art. A study of his architecture reveals that he exercised, however unconsciously, a consistent counter-influence to that of Inigo Jones, in spite of his being closely associated with him for more than a generation. Their official positions as master mason and surveyor-general to the Crown necessarily brought them into constant touch. Stone, we have already seen, was obliged to work under Jones's direction in most of his larger official undertakings: the Banqueting House, Queen's House, Somerset House, St. Paul's Cathedral and elsewhere. He cannot have failed to recognize in his dynamic superior the genius of a style different from his own. Nevertheless, he probably saw in his own work just as faithful an interpretation of the classical antiquities and renaissance humanities as in the other's.

Nowhere is there a hint in word or action that the relationship of the two men was not mutually respectful and cordial. And yet underneath the master mason's correct façade did there lurk grains of jealousy and resentment? We know that he liked to convey the impression that he had designed some buildings of which he had in fact only been the builder. He showed a reluctance, even in his note-book, to let it be supposed that he worked to anyone else's dictation. Throughout Stone's note-book there are merely the briefest references to Inigo, notwithstanding the months and years on end when they worked together. These references are in all cases but one to Jones's official title—"the surveyor", he is called in the most impersonal manner. Whereas for Thomas Baldwin, Comptroller of H.M. Works,

---

[1] W. L. Spiers, *The Note-book and Account-book of Nicholas Stone*, Walpole Society, Vol. VII, 1919. Before this date they were generally known through extracts used by George Vertue and Horace Walpole.

Stone made a monument in Berkhamsted church at a loss to himself of several pounds and referred to him in the notes with touches of affection; and whereas to his "loving and kind friend" Henry Wickes, the Paymaster of H.M. Works, John Embree, the Sergeant-Plumber, Simon Basill and other colleagues he left money in his will to buy mourning rings, he yet took care, it seems almost studiedly, to refrain from any tokens of regard towards his old master.

In terms of architecture Nicholas Stone is important rather for what he represented than what he accomplished. In sculpture he is important for a great mass of documented work of originality and individuality. In architecture he was retrospective, in sculpture progressive; and in the ultimate assessment of Stone's career we must of course remember that he was a sculptor by profession and only an architect by accident or under compulsion. To begin with, Stone was nurtured by tradition and training in the Elizabethan concepts of masonry which derived from the text-books and pattern books of the Low Countries. If Jones's classicism had never been introduced to this country Stone's style, we feel sure, could not have been more manneristic. Hence he represents in the genealogy of English architecture that vernacular branch which was to continue, long after his own death, a descent parallel to the Mediterranean classicism so strangely grafted on to the family tree by the designer of the Banqueting House, and Queen's House.

In the early years of James I's reign the leading monumental sculptors and stone-masons at work in this island were still largely Flemings. Gerard and his son Nicolas Jansen, Cornelius Cuer and Maximilian Colt were the fashionable artists engaged by the high nobility and royalty to carve their effigies and design their proud canopied tombs. There is scarcely a cathedral choir or parish chancel in which we do not see, often towering above its indigenous neighbours, like the proverbial young cuckoo in a nest of thrushes, the splendid plumage of the gaily painted, impertinent foreigner. We have become so accustomed to these exotic monuments that we take them for granted and love them just as we do the alien cuckoos in the English landscape. Gradually, however, the native sculptors began to reassert themselves and absorb the Flemings. Provincial tomb-makers with English names arose, like William White (whose monument, dated 1614, to Sir John Newdigate, is found at Harefield, Middlesex), John Gildon at Hereford, and Samuel Baldwin at Stroud. They started by copying the London patterns of the fashionable Flemings, whose sons, still working here, had anglicized their father's surnames. Thus Jansen became Jonson and Schoermann Shurman. Nonetheless the Low Country training in sculpture, as in architecture, so carefully fostered by the Protestant Tudors, still persisted. When young Nicholas Stone from the west country came up to London to learn his craft he was instantly advised to go to Holland, there to affiliate himself to the only school of sculpture deemed suitable for a promising English student.[1] This he did, and was considered fortunate to be taken into apprenticeship by Hendrik de Keyser, master

[1] A generation later, however, Englishmen might return to the ultimate classical source, and so Stone's own son and namesake in 1638 went to Rome.

mason and leading sculptor in the city of Amsterdam. From 1606 until 1613 Stone was perfecting his art in Holland. According to Charles Stoakes, his great-nephew and ultimate heir, Stone built a gateway at the Zuider Kerk, the masterpiece upon which de Keyser was engaged during most of Stone's apprenticeship. At the end of his seven years the young Englishman was pronounced satisfactory by his master, and before he left Holland given consent to marry his daughter, Maria.

On his return to England Stone straightway received commissions, and in 1616 was first heard of working, already under Inigo Jones's directions, upon the King's chapel at Holyroodhouse, Edinburgh. In 1619 he was put in charge of the building of the Banqueting House for two years; thereafter he carried out for the surveyor-general minor work at several royal palaces. In 1626 Charles I made him "master mason and architect for all our buildings and reparations within our house and castle of Windsor"—an appointment for life at a salary of 1s. a day. By now his reputation was established and his career assured. But for a long time already Stone had been producing tombs and monuments, and it is essentially as a monumental sculptor that he attained distinction, and as an artist should be judged.

There can be no doubt that Stone was in every sense the only creator of the forty-five monuments recorded in his note-book. He discarded some of the conventional designs and attributes beloved by the Jacobean monumental sculptors, particularly the four-poster shaped tomb with towering obelisks and coarse strapwork ornaments. His larger monuments he usually provided with double arched canopies, supported by vast console brackets—very characteristic features of his work. Pediments within pediments were a conceit to which he was much addicted.[1] These, which were usually broken, he crowned with rectangular panels, sometimes cumbersome box-like objects, or with armorial escutcheons. Rich mantling he favoured, winged cherubs and the cardinal virtues made to recline upon the sides of his pediments, and given elongated necks so as to appear from below suitably foreshortened. As for the figures of the deceased, they were represented by recumbent, seated or standing effigies, and by detached busts. And in this particular work Stone excelled. He was the first, and greatest English renaissance sculptor of the human face and figure. Hitherto monumental figure sculpture in this country had been of a stylized character which could rarely be described as portraiture. Stone's heads and shoulders were either done from the life or posthumously from paintings, and were intended to be likenesses.

The monuments to the Hon. Francis Holles in Westminster Abbey (44) and Dr. John Donne in St. Paul's Cathedral (45) are important examples of Stone's natura-listic approach to sculpture of the human form. The first shows him for once working in the tradition set by Michelangelo. Upon a cylindrical plinth, which records in Shakesperian verse his heroic virtues, is the seated figure of the young soldier who died serving in Belgium at the age of eighteen. His pose is that of the pensive Medici, only with head looking upward instead of down. He wears a Roman helmet, lorica

1 This was about the only conceit he borrowed from Palladio.

and tunic (an early example of the classical martial dress in English sculpture). The effigy of Donne is one of the few relics to have escaped the fire which destroyed the old cathedral. The story, as told by Izaak Walton, of how the extraordinary pose was adopted is well known. When he felt death to be approaching, the Dean of St. Paul's stripped himself of all his clothes and, wrapping a winding sheet round himself, had it tied in a knot above his head. Then upon the wooden model of an urn he stood "with his lean, pale and death-like face", while his portrait was painted upon a panel. This has disappeared, but its translation by Nicholas Stone into marble remains one of the masterpieces of English portrait sculpture.

Nicholas Stone had three sons, all of whom died fairly young not long after their father. Henry (known rather absurdly as Old Stone) [1] was a painter of much talent who devoted most of it to copying Vandyke portraits. It seems that he could turn his hand to sculpture also, for he was in partnership for a time with the youngest of the brothers, John, an artist of promise. John applied at the Restoration for the post of Master Mason to the Crown, and was supported by Lord Hatton of Kirby, who affirmed that he was "a most honest cavalier . . . and a most skilful person in his profession of whom I have had much experience"—presumably in assisting the elder Stone at Kirby Hall. John Stone obtained the post, but was soon obliged to relinquish it on account of ill-health. Nicholas, who died of the plague in 1647 a few weeks after his father, was the son who co-operated most closely with him, managed his accounts for several years, and did a certain amount of monumental sculpture. He kept a diary of a tour he made in Italy and his records of visits to Bernini in Rome and the Grand Duke's gallery in Florence throw interesting light on a young artist's self-training in his student years.

The strong family bond of the labouring and professional classes in the Tudor and Stuart centuries was often strengthened by a common craft and consequently shared business interests. [2] Nicholas Stone's family was a case in point. We are constantly coming across the names of colleagues and pupils who were his relations. There was Gabriel Stacy, his cousin and clerk of the works, who laid the marble floor of the hall in the Queen's House, built a black marble cistern at Somerset House, and was left in charge of Stone's operations at Cornbury. There was Charles Stoakes, his nephew, the father of his great-nephew of the same name and ultimate heir, both probably small jobbing builders who assisted him. Stone himself had married the daughter of Holland's most distinguished sculptor and builder, and all his life kept up a correspondence with his wife's family. Her Keyser brothers and nephews were sculptors; so was his own sister's husband, Andreas Kearne, a German who worked for Stone in England. He carved the "shelion" on Stone's watergate at York House and helped to adorn country houses as far afield as Northamptonshire and York-

1 The portrait of Sir William Paston at Felbrigg attributed by its owner, Mr. Ketton-Cremer, to Henry Stone, is an extraordinarily competent work.

2 For example, six members of the Honey family were paviers working for the Crown and Commonwealth between 1630 and 1660.

44    (*above*) Monument of the Hon. Francis Holles,
Westminster Abbey, 1622

*Sculptor: Nicholas Stone*

45    (*left*) Standing Effigy of Dr. John Donne, St.
Paul's Cathedral, 1631

*Sculptor: Nicholas Stone*

46 Charles I's Equestrian Statue at Charing Cross, by Hubert le Sueur, 1630. The Post-Restoration pedestal by Joshua Marshall

shire. He was employed by Sir Justinian Isham for garden statuary at Lamport Hall, and Sir Arthur Ingram at Sheriff Hutton hunting lodge. Sir Henry Slingsby, writing in his diary about improvements he was making to his Yorkshire house, recorded: "The staircase that leads to the great chamber . . . there sits a blackamoor cast in lead by Andrew Carne a Dutchman, who also cut in stone the statue of the horse in the garden." Through the link of the Stone family, English sculpture, until the second half of the seventeenth century, still maintained a strong Flemish and German strain. Thomas Burman (1618–74), whose origin is unknown, became one of Stone's assistants and Bushnell's master. He carved the busts of Alice Lady Lucy in Charlecote church, and the pensive, melancholy Charles I at Honington Hall. John Schoermann, from Emden, was another assistant. He executed the tomb of Sir Thomas Lucy III in Charlecote church and part of that of Sir John Danvers, the regicide, in Chelsea Old Church. But such little work by these northern Europeans has been identified, that their individual characteristics are not easy to assess.

The sculptor who was Stone's most serious rival, working in England contemporaneously with him, was also a foreigner, but of an entirely different race and school. This was Hubert le Sueur (who died 1650), a Frenchman said to have received his early training under Giovanni da Bologna in Florence. In contrast with the reserved air of Stone's compositions, a Mediterranean spontaneity distinguishes the best of le Sueur's sculpture. In 1619 he was in England, brought over either by Lord Arundel or Inigo Jones, and to be found living in the Huguenot colony of the capital. Until the Civil War le Sueur remained in this country, only making occasional visits to Paris in search of statuary for Charles I, and possibly to Italy, since he was paid for obtaining certain "moulds and patterns" of antique figures from that peninsula. His most successful work, on account of which Henry Peacham rather rashly magnified him as "the most excellent statuary in all materials that ever this country enjoyed", is the equestrian statue of Charles I at Charing Cross (46). Balthazar Gerbier was instrumental in getting le Sueur the commission through Lord Weston, the Lord High Treasurer. There is nothing else of his sculpture in quite so baroque, poetical and free a manner. He made several busts of the King, all in bronze, except one in marble now in the Victoria and Albert Museum. The best is perhaps that at Stourhead, in which Charles wears a dragon helmet à la romaine. Although the pose of le Sueur's heads could, like that of his figures, be striking and bold, the features of his faces were too frequently glacial and expressionless.

The English pupil of Stone to achieve most distinction was Edward Marshall (1598–1675). Like his master he was possessed of the renaissance artist's versatility and is supposed to have designed and built houses [1] as well as sculptured monuments and effigies. In 1632 he was elected to the Livery of the Masons' Company of which he was master in 1649–50. He evidently associated himself with the parliamentary interest, for John Stone in his petition to Charles II for the post of master mason to the Crown, formerly held by his father, said: "There is a pretender, one

[1] Marshall built new premises for himself in Fetter Lane after the Fire of London.

Mr. Marshall, to this place who in no kind served your Majesty.'' Marshall's defection will not have commended him to the Stone family who were royalists to their finger-tips. Nevertheless it had not hindered his alliance with John Webb during the Commonwealth. He built Webb's portico at The Vyne in 1654, and the following year was recommended by Webb as carver to Sir Justinian Isham for the chimneypieces at Lamport. But he was not accepted, and a Frenchman was engaged to Webb's disappointment. A letter (now at Chatsworth) dated 1658 from Webb to Marshall asked him to make a clay model pedestal for Lord Northumberland and indicated that Marshall was at the time working for him at Gunnersbury House.

Characteristic features of his monuments are recessed columns, shouldered or lugged architraves (as on his tomb to John Palmer in St. Margaret's, Westminster), foliated volutes and realistically carved drapery. He was the father of Joshua Marshall, who built Temple Bar for Wren and made the plinth for le Sueur's equestrian statue of Charles I at Charing Cross.

*      *      *

Confusion over the precise authorship of certain buildings on which Stone is known to have been engaged has been caused not only by Stone's equivocal claims but also by Charles Stoakes's affirmations. In a supplement to his great-uncle's notebooks Stoakes made a list of buildings, some of which, in an access of family zeal, he attributed to Stone's designs when in fact they were built by him to the designs of Inigo Jones or others. But if Stoakes inclined to exaggerate Stone's creative powers, he was correct in several of his attributions. One of these was the York House watergate, still standing somewhat forlornly between the Strand and the Embankment.

### 1  York House, Watergate, 1624–6

In 1624 the Duke of Buckingham was presented with York House, a jumble of old buildings at the south-west end of the Strand, and began with feverish haste to reconstruct it. Although Inigo Jones had done occasional work for the Duke, it was Balthazar Gerbier who, having wormed his way into Buckingham's confidence, became his artistic adviser and personal architect. Gerbier hated Inigo Jones, of whose success he was transparently envious, and took great pains to see that he made no more architectural designs for his master than could be prevented.[1] From a letter he wrote to Buckingham on 2nd December 1624 it appears that he was responsible for the new buildings at York House. He excused his delay in meeting the Duke by referring to the many things he still had to do there. The great chamber was already being paved, ceilings were being whitewashed, the walls of one room even covered with velvet, and scaffolding was all over the place. In his letter he wrote, with what complacent satisfaction we may well imagine: ''Le Surveyor Enigo Jonsaesté à Jorck

[1] Gerbier was not entirely successful. There is a design in Jones's hand for a ceiling for Buckingham either at York House or New Hall in 1628.

hous pour veoir la mayson, et était comme confus et honteux . . . il en est fort jaloux.'' But, to judge from a mid-seventeenth-century drawing, Inigo had little reason to be put out, for Balthazar's new house, with its long battlemented front over an open colonnade and two projecting wings with pediments, was a very jejune composition.

If Jones was not responsible for York House there is little reason to suppose that he designed the watergate [1] (48). Exactly which year it was built is a mystery. Gerbier implies that it was built before work was begun on the house. This would be early in 1624. Colen Campbell, however, dates it from 1626 and there are reasons for believing this year the more probable. Had it been built in 1624 Gerbier would undoubtedly have designed it himself, when he was kept almost permanently at York House. But he makes no claim to have done so. Moreover Charles Stoakes makes a specific and rather convincingly worded claim that Nicholas Stone did. ''The water gate at York House'', writes Stoakes, ''he [Stone] designed and built, and the right-hand lion he did fronting the Thames. Mr. Kearne, a German, his brother by marrying his sister did the she lion.'' From which it may be deduced that Stone was solely responsible for this impressive entrance to a great nobleman's palace on the river, in the absence of Gerbier, who in the year 1626 was abroad on diplomatic service negotiating for a peace with Spain.

As originally built the gate led straight to the foreshore and the water when the tide was up. It now stands well below the level of the embankment; and the steps up to it have consequently disappeared. Therefore, as seen today from the risen land and without a podium, it is distressingly foreshortened. The Portland stone of which it was constructed is much weathered and decayed. Nevertheless the gate is a relic of nobility and charm. The two lions carved by Stone and Kearne still mount guard on the river front. Between them the arms of Villiers are displayed on an escutcheon surrounded by the garter and surmounted by a ducal coronet. The charge from Buckingham's shield, an escallop, is repeatedly in evidence on the entablature. A large one is made the crowning feature of the central pediment. On the land front the arms of Villiers impale those of his wife, Katharine Manners. An anchor for the Lord High Admiral's office is carved on a cartouche, and the motto *Fidei Coticula Crux*— the Cross is the touchstone of Faith—on the frieze. The style of the watergate is too manneristic for Inigo Jones. It indulges besides in a solecism of which Jones would not have been guilty. Columns and pilasters of different size are made to support one entablature. This solecism would not have troubled Nicholas Stone, whose approach to achitecture was that of the sculptor rather than the scholar.

## 2  The Physic Garden, Oxford, 1631–2

Henry Danvers, born the same year as Inigo Jones, was a typical Elizabethan in that he combined the rôles of man of fortune and man of culture. Before the great Queen's reign was over he had been page to Sir Philip Sidney in the Low Countries,

[1] Webb made a drawing of it in 1641 as he did of many other buildings not his own nor his master's.

143

fought under Count Maurice of Nassau, killed a man for insulting his brother, suffered exile in France and served as a major-general of the army in Ireland. Then, his picaresque career having become past history, he is found, as Earl of Danby, devoting his declining years to the improvement of the Botanic Garden which he had established at Oxford. Nicholas Stone tells us that in 1631 he was making three gateways in the garden to Danby's order.

The main north gate which faces Magdalen College is one of the first objects to impress the London visitor approaching the University from Magdalen Bridge (47). He cannot pass without being struck by the monumental quality of the arch with its emphatic pediments, vermiculated bands, and well-placed statuary. The treatment of its two end pediments within a greater is a variation of the Pantheon motif which Palladio delighted to reproduce upon his church façades. In plan the gateway is a rectangle with niches for statues [1] on the side as well as the front and back faces, thus following the precedent of the Arch of Janus Quadrifons. Its Roman derivations have raised the question whether Stone, who never visited Italy, could be the sole originator of the composition, as Charles Stoakes also affirmed. The answer probably is that the gateway was largely inspired by Serlio's indifferent woodcut of the Arch of Janus in his *Architectura*. There is a marginal note by Inigo Jones in his copy of *Vitruvius*, preserved at Chatsworth, which definitely proves that he at least disclaimed its authorship. Jones is commenting upon Vitruvius's axiom that a good architect must be endowed with the creative instinct as well as versed in the principal arts and sciences. He goes on to paraphrase Vitruvius's text thus: "that in all the arts and doctrines the architect should be able to do more (which is in matter of architecture) than they who [sic] any particular thing by their exercise and industry have brought to perfect clearness. Example of this", he then goes on to write, "of some mathematicians of Oxford that designed for a gate for the garden of Simples lamely". Who these mathematicians were to whom Inigo refers so scathingly, unless Danby was one of them, we do not know. As usual, Inigo's sentence is strangely involved and the meaning slightly ambiguous. But it is clear that he disapproved of the gateway for being in his judgment inartistic and lacking style—faults which we are not disposed to find in it. He certainly implied that a group of people had a hand in its design.

The pair of gates in the west and east walls of the garden are smaller and simpler, but again repeat Palladio's church façade theme of a pediment within a pediment. The jewel-like blocks round the opening of each are a Jacobean touch which we expect from Nicholas Stone. Possibly, therefore, the design of these lesser gateways was entirely his own, whereas that of the great gateway was the outcome of combined inspirations.

3   *Cornbury Park, Oxfordshire*, 1632–3

Stone says that the year in which he finished the Botanic Garden gateways—they

[1] Those of Charles I and Charles II are later insertions. The bust of Lord Danby in the tympanum may be contemporary and by Stone.

bear the date 1632—he agreed to design and build for Lord Danby a new wing at Cornbury, in Wychwood Forest, and to direct the workmen. He paid in all thirty-three visits to Cornbury, many of them no doubt from Oxford, a distance of some twelve miles, and received £1,000 for his pains. His contractor was Timothy Strong (d. 1636) from Barrington, near Burford. Timothy was the grandfather of that Thomas Strong who owned stone quarries at Burford and was a master mason of importance under Wren in the building of St. Paul's Cathedral. As previously stated, Gabriel Stacy remained at Cornbury as deputy-supervisor in the short intervals between his cousin's frequent visits.

The Danby wing, for which Stone was responsible, still stands between the Eliza-bethan wing, in which Robert Lord Leicester died, and the Charles II wing built for Lord Clarendon. When the latter wing was erected by Hugh May, Stone's front was a good deal altered in roof, parapet and fenestration. But there are elements remain-ing which give this only survival of Nicholas Stone's domestic architecture consider-able interest.[1]

Stone's two-storey front, facing south, consists of a first floor with seven windows, and a ground floor with six windows and a portico. Whereas May clearly added the architraves to the upper windows he left the surrounds and pronounced keys of the lower windows as Stone made them. The small *œil-de-bœuf* window and panel at the extreme south-west end and the semi-classical balustraded portico with niches are Stone's work. Behind the elevation Stone's rooms have been greatly altered, but the flagged floor of his hall, the close laying of which John Evelyn so much admired, is still there and a hooded fireplace on massive consoles. The fire-place is taken straight out of Serlio's fourth book of *Architectura*. Other relics of Stone are two bedroom ceilings in transitional patterns, midway between the Jacobean and Carolean.

## 4    The Goldsmiths' Hall, Foster Lane, 1634–40

In 1634 the Goldsmith's Company decided to rebuild their city hall in Foster Lane because of its inadequate accommodation. A minute of a meeting that same year recorded the following information: "It being made known to the Court that the foundations are in readiness for the new buildings it is debated whether before the works are commenced, the King's Surveyor shall be sent for to view the same; but it is agreed that the buildings shall go forward without sending for any to view the same . . .". Nevertheless this bold show of independence was not sustained for long. An ambitious undertaking of the sort could not safely be concealed from the vigilance of the Lords Commissioners for New Buildings. Before the court could meet again the King's surveyor had been consulted. On his advice several plans for the new hall were prepared and submitted to the commissioners. Inigo Jones was subsequently invited to hear a petition of the Company read to Lord Arundel and other commissioners for permission to build and select a suitable plan. After an

1 Tart Hall, St. James's, built by Stone for Lady Arundel, c. 1639, entirely disappeared in George I's reign.

inspection of the site by Jones and Arundel a plan by Nicholas Stone was warmly commended by the commissioners. Accordingly the master mason was appointed by the Company to be their surveyor at a quarterly salary of £10. His assistant was to be a Mr. Hook[1] ; his overseer John Parker; his plumber John Grove (either he or his son worked under Webb at the Queen's House as plasterer); his carpenter Mr. Jarman (presumably Edward, who was to build the Royal Exchange); his plasterer Mr. Kinsman (probably Joseph who was working at Ham House about this time); his carver Mr. Taylor (either John, or Zachary ?), who agreed to do a specific job "as well as any man" and received £50. Finally, in 1638 when the building was nearing completion, the name occurs of a new mason, Mills—perhaps William Mills, who between 1637 and 1640 worked for the Crown at the Tower of London.

There is an interesting sequel to the part the commissioners played before the new hall could be begun. A minute of 1635 records that the court solemnly voted that a gratuity might be given Inigo Jones "for his favour" throughout the delicate proceedings. It took the form of a Spanish gold chain. The last mention of the royal surveyor's name was in 1636, when the Company consulted him about the roof and some wainscoting, particularly a screen, for the new hall.

Nothing now remains of the building of which, Charles Stoakes proudly asserted, although the site provided not a single right angle, Stone contrived every room to be square. The hall suffered in the Fire of London and was finally swept away in 1829. Contemporary prints show Stone's main frontage along Foster Lane to have been a rectangular structure with a central break and an aedicule over the pedimented entrance door. Evidently the ground floor had high rooms, for there were small square windows over others of normal dimensions. The attic floor had small round windows. The projecting eaves were upheld by large wooden brackets.

## 5   St. Mary's Portico, Oxford, 1637

A casual study of this enchanting, disarming and muddled piece of architecture, almost surely designed by Nicholas Stone in his maturity (it is one of Stoakes's attributions), and quite certainly executed by John Jackson, is enough to show how far removed was the master mason's best work from the surveyor-general's scholarly creations (49). Its design is an improvement upon the rugged outlines of Stone's gate at the Zuider Kerk in Amsterdam, the contours of which it nevertheless repeats. In no sense can the design be termed classical. The crowded detail introduced is often quite Gothic, notably the socle, or bracket on which the figure of Our Lady stands, the grimacing masks, the gargoyles and the cauliflowers that adorn it, and the soffit of the arch. The twisted barley-sugar columns and swan-neck pediments, which give the composition its chief character, may have been inspired by the

---

[1] This man evidently shared the quarrelsome nature of his greater namesake. The Company's minutes record that Hooke abused one of the wardens and was ordered to apologize and shake hands. The words were spoken but the handshaking was deferred. Was he the father of Robert Hooke?

Rubens panel on the Banqueting House ceiling, in which James I, enthroned within a tabernacle of this description, points to the figures of Peace and Plenty.

\* \* \*

The sixteen-thirties, which saw Nicholas Stone at his most prolific, were the decade which marked the height of William Laud's Erastianism. Laud, as the Defender of the Faith's divinely appointed champion against the Commons, had raised the secular authority of the Anglican Church to a dangerous pinnacle, on which for a time he managed with the perilous skill of a tightrope walker to balance before crashing to the ground and nearly bringing the whole structure with him. Particularly at the two Universities was the Laudian High Church régime firmly entrenched. Its remarkable leader impressed his personality upon every interest with which the régime concerned itself. Building was one of the interests into which he projected his energies with customary impetuosity and impatience. Totally ignorant of the science of architecture, with which he was not the least bothered, he determined to make his buildings express a doctrinaire ideal. As a humanist he conveyed to them a certain renaissance touch, but as one who had no sympathies with the Continent or Rome, he did not impart to them true classical scholarship. Instead Laud, who intended the High Church movement to be a reversion to what he supposed was pre-Reformation spiritual independence of the Pope, gave to his architecture a Romanesque instead of Roman flavour, in round arches which often repudiated the essential adjuncts of abacus and capital. On the other hand symbolism of all kinds was the hall-mark of his new liturgy and it was this that particularly horrified the Puritans who identified it—erroneously as it happened—with papistry. Existing churches and university chapels were consequently transformed by Laud with richly coloured glass depicting the history of the saints and Our Lady and even oil-paintings of the birth, passion, resurrection and ascension of Our Lord. Turkey carpets, tapestries, gold and silver candlesticks, communion plate, altar tables and furnishings of sweet-smelling cedar and rare inlaid woods were introduced. Statuary and sculpture were essential adornments. Hence too the sculptural quality of Laud's new buildings and his employment of the subordinate stonemason to translate his ideas into material form with the least recalcitrance and demur, rather than the uncompliant architect, with his preconceived notions about abstract style and design.

### 6 St. Catherine Cree, Leadenhall Street, 1630

In 1630 the new church of St. Catherine Cree in the City of London was consecrated by Laud, then Bishop of London. The occasion drew upon the Bishop severe criticism on account of the High Church, self-glorifying ceremonial with which he conducted it. ("Open, open, ye everlasting doors", the congregation were made to chant at his approach, "that the King of Glory may enter in!") The architecture of the church was disliked for the same Laudian associations. Today, however, there is little symbolic ornamentation left upon the only elevation visible (that fronting Leadenhall Street) to offend the sternest member of the lowest denomination. The rather ugly, square, raised heads to the windows remain as they were constructed, but the pediments over them and the cresting of the aisle roof have gone. Of the little square tower, the cupola and doorhead have been modified. Originally the door had a curved broken pediment with projecting box panel of the Nicholas Stone type, the whole much enriched with carving.

The interior has not been greatly altered (51). It is spacious, light and not without beauty in spite of its extraordinary hybrid style. The aisles are separated from the nave by round-headed Romanesque arches borne on composite capitals. The soffit of each architrave, which rests on no abacus, is adorned with classical panels bearing rosettes. Pilasters between the clerestory windows support the thick ribs of the nave vault. Classical acanthus scrolls support the Gothic ribs of the aisle vaults. The detail is a shameless mixture of classical and Gothic, for triglyphs and bosses, swags and crockets jostle together in a happy abandon which even the builders of Henry VIII's reign would have deemed unsuitable. No such scruples disturbed the designer of St. Catherine Cree, whose style seems nothing more nor less than a doctrinal defiance of Puritanism and Romanism as identified with Gothic and classical respectively. We feel that the designer set out to jumble together the ingredients of the two styles with deliberate disrespect. Professor Geoffrey Webb has suggested that Thomas Baldwin may have been the architect of the church. At first it is hard to believe that the man who held the important post of Comptroller of H.M. Works and co-operated so long and closely with the surveyor-general could have been guilty of the positive solecisms here presented. If, however, Baldwin, who was the friend of Stone, really had a directing hand in the Lincoln's Inn chapel and the Oxford Convocation House,[1] then his partial responsibility for the appearance of St. Catherine Cree is rather more understandable.

### 7   St. Helen's, Bishopsgate, door, 1633

The neighbouring church of St. Helen, Bishopsgate, has a south door of a semi-classical type, which, like St. Catherine Cree, has often been ascribed to Inigo Jones's design (52). It belongs in fact to the Laudian school of architecture, and can only have been built by a very unsophisticated mason. It is a stalwart, uncouth feature, and the top-heavy head, with date carved on the keystone, is absurdly out of proportion to the rest of it. It is the earliest example of a doorway with a shouldered architrave over two flanking half-pilasters, that strange Carolean conceit which is next found upon Thomas Carter's wainscot at Ham House and later at Thorpe Hall and kindred houses in the Stamford district.

### 8   St. John's College, Oxford, 1631–6

The late Mr. Arthur Bolton oddly enough subscribed to the legend that Inigo Jones was responsible for the cloister quadrangle at St. John's College, Oxford. He also

---

[1] According to Anthony à Wood.

47  Physic Garden, Oxford: Great Gateway built, if not designed, by Nicholas Stone, 1632

48  York House Watergate, Buckingham Street, Strand. Designed and built by Nicholas Stone, 1623–6

49   St. Mary's, Oxford. Portico added 1637 by Nicholas Stone

professed to see in the arcades a relation to those of the Ospedale Maggiore at Milan, a *quattrocento* structure begun in a transitional style by Antonio Filarete.

The whole idea of the quadrangle was Laud's. At the time he conceived it he was Bishop of London and Chancellor of Oxford University. It was carried out under his direction and at his expense—it cost him £5,000—for the honour of the college at which, in the previous century, he had been an undergraduate and of which years later he had become President. His successor in that office was his friend and disciple, William Juxon, who supported the undertaking as enthusiastically as he supported Laud's High Church policy. The college building accounts survive in great detail. Nowhere do they make mention of Inigo Jones's name. To start with, the names of Richard Maude, Hugh Davies and Robert Smith, all three masons, appear in partnership. In 1633 these men were dismissed and a William Hill was employed. He seems to have been even more unsatisfactory and his misconduct caused the agent who kept the accounts much expense, which it took him a long time to clear. Hill too was dismissed and replaced by John Jackson, a mason from London. Jackson had probably been working for Laud already at Lambeth. Under his charge the new work at St. John's was to be completed. Grey marble, veined with blue, was found by Juxon while hunting near Woodstock and used for the columns; stone was fetched from Heddington and Burford quarries, and timber from Shotover and Stow woods.

The accounts do not divulge who drew the designs of the several features. The great central porticos facing each other are in the tradition of those earlier Jacobean frontispieces at Merton and Wadham colleges, only more classical (56). It is tempting to speculate whether Nicholas Stone designed the porticos and arcades, since the two principal stone carvers, who worked at St. John's, Goor and Ackers, were his assistants. Much of the detail, such as the consoles supporting the tabernacles for the King's and Queen's statues,[1] the arabesques on the dies of the columns of the porticos, the angels in the spandrels and the cartouches on the soffits of the arcades, have their counterparts in Nicholas Stone's portico of St. Mary's. The flavour of the carved work is thoroughly Flemish. Moreover, the busts in the spandrels of the arcades, and the books, keys, rulers, compasses and other symbolism[2] along the friezes, are carved with that customary vigour which Stone imparted to his sculptural efforts. The doorways and the strapwork panels below the bay windows on the garden front are likewise Flemish in character. Yet neither Stone's note-book, nor the college accounts make any mention of work done by him at St. John's.

Jackson experienced continuous vexation in trying to enlist suitable masons. Perhaps Laud and Juxon were reluctant to pay them proper wages. A marginal note in the accounts discloses that Valentine and Simeon Strong (Valentine was the son of Timothy, Stone's contractor at Cornbury) were engaged in 1634. "These men would not come but at extraordinary rates: Mr. Jackson yielded to give them"

[1] They were sculptured by le Sueur and possibly cast in metal by Francesco Fanelli (*fl.* 1610–65), native of Florence, who styled himself *Scultore del Re della Gran Bretagna,* and published a book of engravings in 1642.

[2] John Evelyn noticed the store of mathematical instruments given to the college by Laud.

what they demanded, "but concealed from the other" workmen what they were getting. William Stacy, another mason (was he a relation of Gabriel, Stone's cousin, who laid the hall floor at the Queen's House ?) was paid for help in paving the entry to the library: David Woodfeild, joiner, for a model and seats in the library: and Edward Bromfield,[1] carpenter, for work on the west range and the great double staircase, as well as for "mending a wheelbarrow and the back gate".

## 9  Lambeth Palace, 1633 and 1663

Soon after he began embellishing his old college at Oxford, Laud, who had been made Archbishop of Canterbury in 1633, was building at Lambeth Palace. It was natural that he should employ some of the same workmen at both places. John Jackson, whom Laud sent from London to replace the unsatisfactory William Hill about the year 1634, had probably been serving the Archbishop at Lambeth. He may have been responsible for Laud's Tower which is dated 1633 with the initials "W.L." carved upon it. Another employee, Adam Browne, joiner, almost certainly worked at both places. In the St. John's College accounts there is a payment to a Mr. Browne for a platt in February 1633. At Lambeth Palace a surviving bill records that Adam Browne the same year made the beautiful turned altar rails for the chapel, an altar table, the pulpit and a piece of wainscot "that parts the pew for the lords". He was likewise responsible, we can only suppose, for the west gallery, the screen with oval openings, the pews with cherub bench ends and the stalls [2] with Archbishop's canopy—all of which things were bombed to fragments in the last war.

Thirty years later the faithful William Juxon, having lived to see the execution of the Archbishop and then of the King, the long decade of Cromwell's rule and the happy return of the Stuart dynasty, was himself reigning at Lambeth. He too launched out into much needed building activity, for which unfortunately all the accounts are missing. The palace, which had been sold during the Commonwealth, suffered fearful neglect and the fifteenth-century great hall was completely demolished. Juxon piously set about rebuilding it. He was a man eighty years old and naturally conservative, so his hall deliberately followed the previous one in plan and disposition, which were medieval, and the Laudian patterns to which he was accustomed in detail. It is even possible that Juxon employed John Jackson. He was still alive, for about this time we hear of him petitioning the King for payment of £5,000 owed him by His late Majesty. Samuel Pepy's description of Juxon's great hall as "a new old-fashioned hall as much as possible" explains very aptly what contemporaries thought of its style. Inside, the fine hammer-beam roof, an extraordinarily late example, has pendants of acanthus leaves under an egg-and-tongue mould, and scroll carving in the spandrels of the braces.

---

[1] Bromfield, with Thomas Mayo, made the "seats of the Convocation House," adjoining the Bodleian Library.
[2] The standards may be compared with those in Lincoln's Inn chapel, 1618–23. Now there is a payment to "Adam Browne, joiner, for making of a great press of wainscot for to hold King James and Queen Anne statues" in Westminster Abbey, 1624–5. Thus he was one of the surveyor-general's men.

Laud's and Juxon's master mason, John Jackson, was certainly busy towards the end of the Commonwealth working at Oxford. The chapel at Brasenose of which he was overseer is a fair example of the astonishing muddles into which the most capable English masons fell when left to their own devices. Without the guiding influence of an architect or client versed in classical principles a mason's undirected interpretation of them could be lamentable indeed. The north façade of the chapel within the quadrangle is basically Gothic. Tall Decorated windows have been framed with classical trimmings. These are indiscriminately applied to the Gothic structure like an assortment of ribbons bought at a haberdashery to bedeck some ancient female. The east end of the chapel facing the street has an even more bewildering mutton-dressed-as-lamb aspect. The absurdity of the composition is only paralleled by Bishop Wren's façade of Peterhouse chapel at Cambridge. Over the head of a Gothic window a giant drip mould or entablature has been made to rise like a tidal wave and then collapse into a broken pediment with swan-neck scrolls. Whereupon the designer, uncertain whether to crown the edifice with a Gothic or classical superstructure, has compromised with a curved gable splashed with surf-like crockets which clamber up to a finial of indeterminable provenance. The strange medley is only redeemed by the pleasing dark-brown tone of the stonework and the excellence of its carving by the mason, Simon White (53).

11  *Burford Priory, Chapel, 1661–2*

The hybrid guise in which sacred buildings were being dressed during and immediately after the Commonwealth reflects the ambiguous state into which the Anglican worship had fallen after the failure of Laud's Erastianism. Puritanism had temporarily triumphed; episcopacy was at a discount. The return of the monarchy meant the re-establishment of the bishoprics, but the hierarchy had learnt a severe lesson not soon to be forgotten. Until affairs properly righted themselves the Church remained undecided in policy because uncertain how it stood with the people.

In 1661 Speaker William Lenthall, who had steered a moderate course with delicacy and some dignity throughout the difficult times, chose to build a private chapel to his house at Burford in Oxfordshire. It is distinguished for the compromising character of its style. The resemblance of several features to the Oxford university buildings of Nicholas Stone and his school opens up the possibility that John Jackson worked here also.

The windows of the chapel are still simplified Gothic, as at Brasenose. Classical trimmings have also been introduced, but the juxtaposition of the two is not so absurd and the result, especially inside, is very charming. Outside, a pilastered Ionic order on a high plinth supports a deep entablature and gabled parapet. The entablature is not allowed to interfere with convenience and in the most engaging manner is stepped up to give room for a door into a gallery. Little pediments also project above the parapet, as at Brasenose. Inside, a segmental ceiling with guilloche ribs has been carried out in plaster (50). The columns supporting the gallery are spirally fluted and their capitals are fashioned with birds' heads instead of volutes. The main entrance door is framed by two angels on pedestals upholding a stone panel carved to represent the burning bush. The bold swagged pedestals supporting the angels are similar to those supporting the barley-sugar columns of St. Mary's portico.

*      *      *

12   *Holy Trinity Church, Berwick-on-Tweed,* 1652

In the seventeenth century it was a long distance from the Thames to the Tweed. Holy Trinity in Berwick is one of the few parish churches of the Commonwealth. It was built between 1648 and 1652 at the instance of the Puritan Governor of the important border town, to the design, it is said, of Cromwell's surveyor-general. This would have been Inigo's erstwhile foreman at St. Paul's Cathedral in the sixteen-thirties, Edward Carter, who died and was buried in St. Paul's, Covent Garden, in 1653.

Holy Trinity is of extraordinary interest in the history of our indigenous building. The church is neither a hang-over of the medieval, like its contemporary, the chapel at Staunton Harold, in Leicestershire, which is integrally Perpendicular, nor a Gothic revival structure with applied classical ornament, like Brasenose College chapel. In a sense it has evolved from St. Catherine Cree (while omitting all Laudian attributes), to which it bears resemblances in the raised square-headed windows of the nave, the west door and the Romanesque arches separating nave from aisles. The windows of the aisles and west end are of a rudimentary Venetian type. The squat west cupolas hardly convey to the church a dignity forfeited by the omission of a tower (a peal of bells in the neighbouring town hall having been considered adequate). The church is a plain, unpretentious, deliberately unbeautiful structure designed to serve a straightforward Low Church purpose, and is wonderfully expressive of the spiritual economy of the Cromwellian interlude.

*      *      *

At Cambridge during Charles I's reign an analogous movement in building to the one at Oxford was taking its course. It could hardly yet be termed architecture, for as at Oxford the professional architect had not yet made an appearance. Meanwhile university building was still left to the discretion of the leading dons, who employed families of masons to carry out their requirements as in Elizabethan and Jacobean times. At Cambridge, also, the sixteen-thirties were marked by the ascendancy of High Church party rule, and so the faces of the new colleges breathed the spirit of Laud's Erastianism. In other words, at the dictation of autocratic churchmen bent upon extravagant forms of adornment and symbolism, façades assumed an assertive, tendentious aspect to which the master mason, ignorant of classical rules and proud of his individualism, applied his skill. Since the influence of Inigo Jones was less

154

50 Speaker Lenthall's Chapel, Burford
Priory, Oxfordshire

*Architect: possibly John Jackson, 1661*

*"Country Life" photograph*

51 St. Catherine Cree, Leadenhall Street, London: Interior,
1630. An example of the Laudian
school of sculptor-builders

52   St. Helen's, Bishopsgate: South
      Door, dated 1633

53   Brasenose College Chapel, Oxford.
A shameless mixture of Gothic and classical
motifs

*Master mason: John Jackson, 1656–9*

54   Clare College, Cambridge: East Range, 1638–41

*Master mason: Thomas Grumbold*

felt at Cambridge than at Oxford the indigenous manner of building flourished unchecked until Wren's classicism set it at nought. And by a paradox, Wren's early association with Cambridge was brought about because of the High Church dominance of the university. His uncle, Bishop Matthew Wren, was a prominent and uncompromising member of the Laudian clergy and, as Master of Peterhouse, happened to be responsible for the most flagrant piece of High Church building at Cambridge. This was the astonishing façade which the Bishop imposed upon his college chapel when he re-edified it about 1635. The mason who carried out the work was George Thompson, but no name of an architect is given. This is not surprising, for doubtless there was none and the Bishop dictated the design himself. Over blind, elliptical arcades he placed a large central Gothic window between niches with crocketed canopies, and a fanciful skyline of indentures and a crested gable. The whole façade is rusticated and the upper stage above the arcades contained within a pair of flimsy fluted pilasters.

The leading Cambridge mason in the sixteen-thirties and 'forties was Thomas Grumball, or Grumbold, who came of a family of masons from Raundes in Northamptonshire.[1] He appears to have been a simple working man who in the course of operations developed idiosyncracies which became distinctive. They were inherited by a nephew Robert and developed by him into an almost recognizable style. Robert in fact began life like his uncle, a mere mason, and as a very young man worked in this capacity under John Webb at Lamport Hall between 1654 and 1657. Then between 1676 and 1683 he worked under Wren at Trinity College and on the chapel of St. Catherine's College. As a result of this experience he blossomed into an architect. Before the century was over he was engaged by the local aristocracy upon country-house practice [2] and by the Bishop of Ely upon rebuilding the north transept of his cathedral.

## 13  *Clare College, Cambridge, 1638–42*

Thomas Grumbold's first undertaking (1638–40) was the beautiful three-span bridge over the Cam at Clare College. For its design he received the remarkably modest fee of 3s. A curious feature of the bridge, which was repeated by both the Grumbolds on other occasions, is the way in which the balusters with square faces are set diagonally. Thomas's next undertakings were the east range (1638–41) and the south range (1640–2) of the buildings at Clare. The work was put out to contract, and the masons, carpenters and plumbers were paid daily wages in instalments. Brick was the material used for the core; it was faced with creamy-white stone, brought from Ketton and Weldon. Slate was fetched from Colly Weston and lead from Derbyshire. The Civil War interrupted the work, and during the Commonwealth

[1] Arthur and John Grumball, masons, were paid in 1636–7 for work on the stone chimneys at Holdenby House, Northamptonshire, one of the royal manors.

[2] Robert Grumbold (1638/9–1720) was employed in 1688 by the Earl of Elgin at Great Park House, Ampthill; and in 1694 by the 10th Earl of Kent at Wrest Park.

Thomas Grumbold died (1657). The great gate, or frontispiece, in Thomas's east range is still thoroughly Jacobean in style, but the rest of the façade and the south range are treated with vertical breaks in the window strips, which are quite novel and remarkably effective (54). Above them sharply pointed and semi-circular pediments of the dormer windows peep over a parapet. Tall arcaded chimney-stacks punctuate the roof line. John Evelyn, who was a great connoisseur of classical architecture, pronounced the college, when he saw it in 1654, to be "of a new and noble design, but not finished".

There has been a good deal of speculation whether Robert Grumbold personally designed the great west wing fronting the river. It embodies several ingredients, notably the parapet, the dormers and chimney-stacks, which are characteristics of the older Grumbold's work on the east and south ranges. But the elevation, composed of two main stages—Tuscan below and Ionic above—is a distinct development upon the uncle's elevations. The college building accounts imply that a John Westley, who died the same year as Thomas Grumbold, was its original designer, and that Robert, then a young man of twenty-eight, merely took over from him and continued the wing on lines already begun. At all events the river front was not properly finished until 1705, but which time Robert Grumbold had become a provincial architect of some repute. By the time the north range (1683–7) was begun Robert Grumbold was solely in charge, and certainly the designer, for there are payments to him for "raising the foundation" and "drawing a design" for the hall, which both without and within already shows the influence of Wren.

### 14  Christ's College, Cambridge: Fellows Building, 1640–2

A little after the older Grumbold started work at Clare, the Fellows Building at Christ's College was put in hand. Messrs. Willis and Clark [1] assert that no building accounts or records of its origins are preserved among the College archives. There is therefore no direct evidence that Thomas Grumbold had anything to do with it. Yet it possesses so many features similar to those at Clare that the older Grumbold almost surely was employed upon it.

Like Thomas Grumbold's ranges at Clare the Fellows Building at Christ's is only semi-classical in style. Consequently it is surprising to read that Evelyn judged it "a very noble erection . . . of exact architecture", which it certainly is not. The square windows have a strong Tudor flavour which is little mitigated by the thin architraves, and splayed bases to the surrounds of those on the first floor, or the blocked voussoirs and jambs of those on the ground floor. The balusters of the parapet are set diagonally, as on Clare Bridge. Above them peer the same sharply pointed and highly rounded dormer heads which seem to be the invariable stamp of a Grumbold building.

[1] R. Willis and J. W. Clark, *The Architectural History of Cambridge University*, 3 vols., 1886.

# CHAPTER SIX

# JOHN WEBB AND THE PALLADIAN TRADITION

THE rank John Webb holds in the early hierarchy of British architects—of whom he, far more justifiably than Inigo Jones, can claim to be the first professional—has consistently been underestimated. This is largely because he was always content to lurk in the shadow of his great master, to whom the disciple in pure veneration and humility never failed to give honour when it was due and often credit when it was not. Had Webb flourished in any subsequent era he would have been acclaimed an architect of exact, if limited scholarship, much power, and even originality, qualities which his work after Jones's death amply displayed. Had he lived during George I's reign he would have been regarded by the Burling-tonian group as the greatest of them all. It was frequently Webb's work which in mistake for Jones's, these literal students set themselves to imitate, and it was Webb himself who indirectly brought the influence of Palladio to bear upon early Georgian architecture almost to the exclusion of the other influences, from which Jones derived his various inspirations.

Even less is known of John Webb's life than of Inigo Jones's. Whereas Jones's career by virtue of his position of surveyor-general was punctuated by a number of official references, often of the driest possible kind, Webb's long subserviency called for no such records. Although he was for years the right-hand of the surveyor-general, there was seldom an occasion to refer to his name. After Jones's death, and during the Commonwealth, there was less occasion still; and throughout the fourteen remaining years of his life the sun of royal patronage which brilliantly illuminated many men of less talent and less sorely-proved loyalty than "Inigo Jones's man"— this is Evelyn's single reference to Webb—shone but fitfully upon him. Lack of official position once again meant lack of official references.

He was born in 1611, that is to say thirty-eight years after Inigo Jones. If we re-flect that in Tudor and Stuart times it was quite normal for young men to be married at eighteen, we realize that Webb could easily have been Jones's grandson. The wide gap in years makes the relationship between the two interesting. It is not usual for a very young man to revere the work and person of his grandfather's contem-poraries. The fact that Webb did so, speaks well for the compelling genius of Inigo

Jones. Moreover, Webb was of better birth than the other. His paternal family probably belonged to the lesser gentry and he had been educated at Merchant Taylors' School.[1] How it came about that in 1628 the schoolboy of seventeen attracted the notice of the King's surveyor is not known. At any rate Webb remained his pupil, assistant and unofficial deputy for close on a quarter of a century without enjoying any recognized position. In 1638 he is first mentioned as clerk to His Majesty's Surveyor of Works, but nothing more.[2] Webb tells us that he was at the start taken to live with Jones's family. Jones was not married and probably one of his spinster sisters kept house for him and was glad to look after the young apprentice, who soon was treated as a member of the family. The adopted relationship was made more real when Webb married Anne Jones, who may have been a niece, or at very least a cousin of his employer (for in Inigo's father's will no mention is made of another son). It is even possible that Anne was a natural child of the surveyor, because in the Somerset Visitation of 1672, made while Webb was yet alive, she is described as "the daughter and heir of Inigo Jones". One may suppose that this information was imparted by Webb himself, who towards the close of his life seems to have retired to Somerset for good. Certainly in his writings Webb speaks rather equivocally of Jones as his uncle. Anne's place in Inigo's affections was evidently a close one. She was left more money than any of the other legatees of his will, and each of her five children by Webb was handsomely provided with £1,000. Webb himself was made Jones's principal executor.

The few scrappy particulars of Webb's early history are to be gleaned out of that extraordinary verbiage which comprises the two volumes of the Stonehenge argument. The first, entitled *The Most Notable Antiquity of Great Britain, vulgarly called Stoneheng . . . restored,* was published by Webb in 1655. The volume purported to be written by Inigo Jones. In reality it was "some few indigested notes", as Webb explained in the text, made by Jones as long ago as 1620, when he had been commanded by James I, then staying at Wilton, to investigate the origin of the ruins. After his master's death Webb piously put the notes together and edited them. The resulting treatise set out to prove that Stonehenge was a Roman temple dedicated to Caelus, because it was open to the sky (here Vitruvius was quoted in evidence), and of circular shape (here Alberti was quoted), and because the upright stones were cut in pyramidal form as though reflecting the flames of the eternal fires. Jones had spent a lot of time on the site and was immensely impressed by the "beautiful proportions" of Stonehenge, which he seriously concluded had been built in the Tuscan order. He may have been sincere in this fantastic inference for, in *Coelum Britannicum,* he entitled a scene drawing of a cluster of prehistoric stones obviously suggested by Stonehenge, "the ruins of some great city of the ancient Romans, or

---

[1] The 1672 Somerset Visitation records that Webb's father, James, had married an unnamed daughter of — Dutton of Cheshire, described as gentleman.

[2] "John Webb, clerk, for engrossing and making two copies of a great book of survey of His Majesty's stables barns and coachhouses allowed him in reward lxs." Declared Accounts E 351/3272.

civilized Britains". On the other hand, we have Webb's word that he was "so far from exulting of this [theory] as that his notes were not found much less Stoneheng Restored written, until long after his death". It is therefore more likely that Jones was far from satisfied by his conclusions, which might even have been dictated by the King, and that he managed successfully to avoid publication of them during James's lifetime. If this was so, then Webb did his memory no service by resurrecting them. Webb wrote that he was induced to publish the work at the instance of his eminent friends Dr. Harvey and John Selden, who surely ought to have known better. How they and Webb could have believed such nonsense is a mystery. The result was that Jones's theory was in 1662 stoutly repudiated by Charles II's physician-in-ordinary, Dr. Walter Charleton, who, backed by the authority of Olius Wormius, an illustrious antiquary of European repute, made the counter mistake of attributing Stonehenge to the Danes. The refutation of his late master's thesis infuriated Webb, who promptly retaliated with the publication (1665) of his *A Vindication of Stone Heng restored,* in which he demolished Dr. Charleton and reaffirmed Jones's views. Webb over-emphasized Jones's infallibility and allowed himself to say the most abusive things of "this Doctor". After all, Charleton had been relatively polite about Jones's Roman attribution, which was a degree sillier than his own. The whole affair, which shows Webb in his least attractive light, has merely proved valuable for the scraps of biographical material parenthetically vouchsafed about Jones and Webb. The Stonehenge tomes make one agree with Horace Walpole's summary: "It is remark-able that whoever has treated of this monument has bestowed on it whatever class of antiquity he was peculiarly fond of."

When at the outbreak of the Civil War Inigo Jones, already an old man, left London, Webb stayed behind at Scotland Yard to superintend the surveyor's duties, which must in the capital, always hostile to the King's cause, have dwindled practic-ally to nothing. Webb, however, found time to act as a spy on the King's behalf. At the risk of his life he managed to send to the cavalier headquarters at Oxford inform-ation on the parliamentary forces, the numbers of their guns and men, and the plans of the London fortifications. He even served the royalist leaders in London, by carrying letters to and from the King. On one occasion he managed safely to smuggle the royal jewelry in his waistcoat pocket through the enemy lines to Beverley in Yorkshire, where Charles was then stationed, in spite of being plundered of every-thing else and for a time imprisoned on the way.

With these loyal services to his credit it is not surprising that at the Restoration Webb believed he stood a fair chance of appointment to the surveyor-generalship, the reversion of which seems to have been suggested if not actually promised him by Charles I. In his suit to Charles II in 1660 he reminded the King that he had in 1643 been thrust out of office and employment for his loyalty, that he "was by the especial command of your Majesty's Royal Father of ever blessed memory, brought up by Inigo Jones Esq<sup>r</sup>,[1] Your Majesty's late Surveyor of the Work in the study of

1 In the Declared Accounts Jones is first accorded the title of Esquire in 1628-9.

architecture, for enabling him to do your Royal Father and Your Majesty service in the said office''. And again Webb wrote: ''that he was brought up by his uncle Mr. Inigo Jones upon his late Majesty's command in the study of architecture, as well that which relates to building as for masques, triumphs and the like . . . there being scarce any of the great nobility or eminent gentry of England but he hath done service for in the matter of building, ordering of medals, statues and the like''. These passages are enlightening. They contain the reference to Inigo Jones as his uncle, a relationship presumably acquired through his wife, and the remark that his upbringing and training had been at the express command of the King. By this Webb presumably meant, not that Charles I commanded his surveyor-general specifically to take into apprenticeship him, John Webb, then aged seventeen, but gave his consent to the surveyor-general engaging a boy with a view to his becoming assistant and possibly ultimate successor. The reference to Webb having worked for a great many of the landed gentry was by that time very true, for after Jones's death and during the Commonwealth he was at last free to undertake private commissions on his own. In spite of their deprivations and impoverishment many cavaliers (and Webb seems to have worked almost exclusively for cavaliers) retired discreetly to their estates and set about improving them.

Webb was not successful in his petition for office. The post was granted to Sir John Denham, author of *Cooper's Hill,* the first descriptive epic in the English language, and soldier, whose military exploits during the Civil War were, notwithstanding his lack of architectural experience, considered a higher recommendation than the other's. Denham may not have been much of a creative architect—he built the original Burlington House in 1665, and laid out Pall Mall and some streets round Clarendon House, Piccadilly. But as surveyor-general he was occupied with many and varied duties. He acted as censor of new plays—a task for which he was doubtless better qualified than for certain others—and spent much time and labour in repairing the royal residences after their prolonged neglect during the Commonwealth. Preparations for the coronation, too, kept him busy for the first year of his appointment. He was a kindly man, praised his workmen for their patience in enduring long arrears of pay, and took pity on poor people, even giving them shelter in his own house when he was obliged to evict them from condemned premises. His contemporaries, moreover, did not all depreciate his merits, and on his death Christopher Wase lamented him in a long obsequial poem which began:

> What means this silence, that may seem to doom
> Denham to have an undistinguished tomb?

Poor Webb's disappointment was made manifest at the unpredictable choice of a man who although he ''may, as most gentry, have some knowledge of the theory of architecture . . . can have none of the practice, but must employ another''. This complaint was only too truly borne out by Denham's employment of Webb himself who was made his assistant surveyor of the building at Greenwich Palace. Evidently the King's advisers appreciated the delicacy of the situation for Webb was granted the same salary as Denham, namely £200 per annum, plus £1 13s. 10d. a month for travelling expenses.[1] As a slight recompense Webb was promised the reversion of the surveyor-generalship on the death of Denham, who in the first place happened to be four years his junior. Yet Denham predeceased him. After being driven insane by his wife's infidelity with the Duke of York, when he assured the King that he was not His Majesty's surveyor but the Holy Ghost, he died in 1669. Now at last Webb supposed that his long withheld promotion was assured. Not a bit of it. In spite of the promised reversion, the young Christopher Wren, whose rise to fortune during the 'sixties had been spectacular, was granted the coveted office. Denham just before his death had appointed Wren his deputy, probably at the King's request, and positively asked that he should be his successor, and that if Hugh May or anyone else put forward claims they were made without his consent. In vain Webb pleaded that his rival professed his unsuitability because of inexperience; and, when Wren's appointment seemed certain, that if only he, Webb, were made joint surveyor he would loyally serve with Wren and instruct him in his heavy duties, but under him who was "by far his inferior" he could not serve. In vain, too, he pointed out that at the Restoration he had, by order of Parliament, personally prepared all the royal palaces for the King's home-coming; that he had carried out the Woolwich fortifications, and at the Whitehall Theatre had made discoveries in the scenical art; that he had spent £1,000 of his own money on work at Greenwich Palace and received up to date a paltry £200 in return. These remonstrances were to no avail. Webb undoubtedly received shabby treatment, and it is clear that Denham had from the first opposed his reversion of the surveyorship. After this undeserved setback he did little more building, but retired sadly to the small estate which he had bought, soon after Inigo Jones's death, at Butleigh, near Ilchester in Somerset. He once more turned his energies to writing—never his strong suit—and published a lengthy essay on a subject about which he can surely have known little, "The Endeavouring a probability that the Language of the Empire of China is the Primitive Language". As a pathetic reminder of his bruised existence he dedicated the extraordinary treatise to his ungrateful sovereign, whose virtues he compared, not ineptly, to the winds and his subjects to the corn upon whom they incontinently blew. At Butleigh Court he died in 1674, aged sixty-three, and was buried in the small church which since his day has fallen a victim to the zeal of Gothic restorers and retains neither a trace of his architectural style nor a memory of his name. The house which he had built, and where he was succeeded by three generations of his family, has completely disappeared.[2]

Webb left in his will his "library and books and all prints and cuts and drawings

[1] Even so, during Denham's severe illness in 1666 it was Hugh May, and not Webb, who was made acting Surveyor-General.

[2] When Webb's Butleigh Court was destroyed, c. 1850, Inigo Jones's pocket-book was found in the walls. Its whereabouts now is unknown. The Victorian Butleigh Court, partly designed by the Prince Consort, was in its turn demolished in 1951.

of architecture" to his son William, and "my will and charge is that he shall keep them entire together without selling or embezzling any of them", a direction which within less than ten years was flagrantly disregarded. The widow of William sold them before 1681 to Mr. John Oliver, surveyor to the City of London. John Aubrey, writing soon after this time, related: "Mr. Oliver, the city surveyor, hath all his [Inigo Jones's] papers and designs, not only of St. Paul's Cath, etc. and the Banqueting house, but his design of all Whitehall, suitable to the Banqueting house; a rare thing, which see". In addition to Jones's and Webb's masque and architectural drawings the papers included a number of Palladio's drawings which Jones had acquired in Italy, and had set Webb to copy and vary by way of exercise. The Palladio drawings and the greater part of the rest were bought, presumably from Oliver, by Lord Burlington and Dr. George Clarke the politician, virtuoso and benefactor of Oxford university. Burlington's collection, to which the Earl added further Palladio drawings bought by him in Italy, descended to the Dukes of Devonshire, and is kept at Chatsworth. Dr. Clarke bequeathed his share in 1736 to Worcester College, Oxford. A third and much the least share in bulk somehow fell to the possession of a Mr. William Emmet of Bromley (c. 1717), whose descendants bequeathed them in 1848 to the British Museum.[1]

Webb's earliest drawings known to have been carried out, were two plans and an elevation for the theatre of the Barber Surgeons' Hall, dated 1636. The building was, we have seen, designed and built by Inigo Jones, so Webb was merely acting as his master's draftsman, a subordinate rôle he fulfilled on many a future occasion. Two years later Webb did another drawing, which he inscribed "for Mr. Penruddock 1638 for a lodge in a park in Hampshire". The Penruddocks, an ancient family who were to suffer severely in the Civil War fighting for the King—Sir John Penruddock remained a close friend of Webb—came from Compton Chamberlayne, which is actually in the neighbouring county, Wiltshire. Whether the two-storey lodge was built we cannot be sure. This same year Webb drew the very ambitious upright extension to Somerset House, upon which he wrote the words "not taken". No drawings by him exist for the Queen's House, which was finished by 1635, nor was he in charge of Jones's alterations to St. Paul's Cathedral, although Sir William Dugdale affirmed that the later cathedral accounts and reports contained several marginal references to "Joh. Web. gen.". We therefore assume that Webb, who joined Jones's office in 1628, was not given any responsible or creative work to perform before 1636. This is not surprising, because in the seventeenth century a young man's apprenticeship in whatever trade or profession habitually lasted seven years. How then would John Webb have occupied his time during this period?

Miss Margaret Whinney,[2] from close studies of Webb's architectural sketches, has concluded that the young apprentice was kept by his master close to the drawing-

---

[1] He may have been the son, or grandson, of Maurice Emmett, bricklayer, who worked under Webb at Greenwich Palace in 1664–72, and was the builder of the College of Heralds.

[2] M. Whinney, *Some Church Designs by John Webb*, Warburg Institute Journal, Vol. VI, 1943.

55  Holy  Trinity,  Berwick - on - Tweed

*Architect: probably Edward Carter; possibly John Embree, 1652*

56  St. John's College, Oxford: Frontispiece of Quadrangle, 1631–6.
*Designer unknown*
Statue of Charles I by Francesco Fanelli

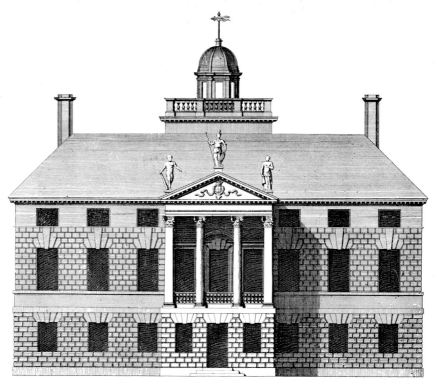

57 Amesbury Abbey, Wiltshire: original façade by John Webb, 1661, rebuilt 1834. (From C. Campbell's *Vitruvius Britannicus*, 1725)

58 Belvoir Castle, Rutland: façade designed by John Webb, 1654. (From W. Kent's *Designs of Inigo Jones*, 1727)

59 Oatlands Palace, Surrey: Garden Portal by Inigo Jones, 1617. (From John Vardy's *Some Designs of Inigo Jones*, 1744)

board doing exercises. She conjectures that Webb's many transcriptions of plates in Serlio's, Palladio's and Scamozzi's books as well as of Palladio's original drawings in Jones's possession, and essays at designs of his own based on these masters, were done during his early apprentice years. In particular she believes that Webb's several church designs belong to this period, including the one for a great cathedral with dome. The cathedral design is a patch-work composition, its features borrowed from the great Italian and even French masters. The treatment of its façade was derived from Maderna's Sta. Susanna in Rome, and of its dome from Bramante's dome for St. Peter's illustrated in Serlio; whereas its lantern and spire anticipate those of Mansard's Invalides. In that it is the first imaginative exercise upon a domed church in England it is of some academic interest. It is not beyond belief that Wren saw these drawings and even profited from them, just as he may have seen Webb's Greenwich Palace scheme and made use of it. There are, for example, units in Webb's cathedral design, such as the drum of the dome and the half section of the transept façade, which are repeated by Wren in his design for the new St. Paul's. So too is the spire reflected in the spire of St. Vedast Foster, and the elliptical pediment of Webb's campanile in the towers of Christ Church, Newgate, and St. Bride's.

Since Webb had certainly not travelled to Italy and probably not to France during Inigo Jones's lifetime, the ecclesiastical sketches done by him as a very young man can only have been suggested by his master, with the help of the architectural books and drawings in his library. In addition to the church designs, Webb likewise did innumerable sketches for small secular buildings, archways taken from Serlio and Scamozzi, and fountains and grottoes from Rossi's folio volume[1]: to these he appended notes of an earnest and naive kind such as students customarily compose. Among his student exercises are drawings of the Pitti Palace, the "Arch in Verona", the Louvre, and other Italian and French buildings which presumably he had never seen except in illustrations.

Webb's rigorous early training by Inigo Jones is what made him the first professional architect of the English Renaissance. He, in fact, enjoyed an advantage denied to his predecessors and even his own master. He was taught at an early age all the rudiments of the architectural science, moreover by a supreme artist, versed in the lores of ancient and renaissance Rome. By contrast, Inigo as a young man had no such training, and had never been apprenticed to an older architect. Consequently he remained throughout his life an amateur. The distinction is noticeable in the architectural drawings of the two men. Jones's were never very accomplished and rather pictorial sketches than finished elevations. He was far happier at figure drawing, his sketches of human heads, busts and caryatides being free and easy. Webb's sketches of such details were tight and uncomfortable in comparison, whereas the architectural drawings of his maturity were efficient and professional. Similarly, Jones's handwriting was large, sprawling and untidy: Webb's small, regular and neat.

Furthermore Webb's training covered a long period. In a sense it lasted until

[1] Rossi's *Nuova Racolta di Fontane di Roma*, 1618, seems to have inspired Webb.

Inigo Jones's death or so long as the old architect was capable of work at all. There is little doubt that until Commonwealth times Webb's individuality had not asserted itself and was entirely absorbed by his master's. He was merely Inigo Jones's instrument and could not be termed an architect in his own right. In other words he was the executant of Inigo Jones's ideas and conceptions, even his amanuensis. The many official reports made by the surveyor-general in his later years for the royal commissioners and Lord Treasurer were written out by the assistant. So too were several of Jones's architectural designs for private commissions completed by the other. For example, the elevation of a house for Sir Peter Killigrew in Blackfriars was in Webb's hand, but inscribed by him "Mr. Surveyor's Design". The building of Wilton for Lord Pembroke was carried out by Webb and certainly finished by him after Jones's death, but to Jones's dictation. Consequently we should not try and look for evidence of Webb's own inspirations much before 1652. Seldom can a great architect have been better served by a faithful, self-effacing and gifted ghost than Jones was served by Webb.

The story of the Whitehall Palace drawings probably explains the situation as well as any other. When first published in the early eighteenth century, at Lord Burlington's instigation by Colen Campbell[1] and William Kent,[2] they were all unhesitatingly ascribed to Inigo Jones. Webb's co-existence was at this time scarcely acknowledged. When architectural research started in earnest at the beginning of the twentieth century and scholars learnt to distinguish between the master's and disciple's handwritings, the drawings, since they are almost all in Webb's, were then attributed to Webb's inspiration. Today, however, the tendency is to re-attribute the early plans to Jones and the later ones to Webb. The total number of drawings is seventy and they have been grouped under four dates—1638, 1647–8, 17th October 1661 and 1661–5.[3]

Of these groups the first only dealt with a scheme which owed its inspiration solely to Jones. Webb had in 1638 only just emerged from his apprenticeship and for another ten years, at least, acted as Jones's subordinate. The drawings involved the demolition of the Banqueting House. No one but the builder of it would have dared countenance its disappearance. Webb in his schemes sought consistently to preserve it and Charles II pronounced it to be sacrosanct. The 1638 drawings are for smaller units of building than the later drawings. The façades are divided into storeys, like the Banqueting House, each with its separate order, and correspond in style with the

1 *Vitruvius Britannicus*, Vol. I, 1717. Campbell procured his illustrations from Mr. William Emmet's collection. He attributed them to the year 1639. He took liberties and altered some of the drawings.

2 *Designs of Inigo Jones*, 1727. Kent's illustrations were copies by Flitcroft of drawings in Lord Burlington's and Dr. Clarke's possession. Kent, or Flitcroft, embellished them in some particulars and altered the dimensions. Hulsbergh also reversed them in the engraving process. Kent's illustrations are all different to Campbell's. Thus by 1727 the public were already presented with two separate and conflicting schemes purporting to be by Inigo Jones.

3 For a technical and somewhat involved account of recent researches see Margaret Whinney's *John Webb's Drawings for Whitehall Palace*, Walpole Society, Vol. XXXI, 1942–3.

designs for Somerset House of that same year and the Covent Garden piazza of only a few years earlier. To this group William Sanderson indirectly referred in his *History of the Life and Reign of King Charles* (published in 1658), when he stated that an ample sum of money was contributed in the late sixteen-thirties by the citizens of London-derry ''by way of composition towards the erecting of a royal palace of his Majesty's Court in St. James's Park, according to a model drawn by Inigo Jones his excellent architector''.[1] For the second group of drawings there is Webb's word that he was at least mainly responsible. In his application for the post of surveyor at the Restora-tion, he reminded Charles II that, as Jones's deputy ''to execute the said place [Whitehall Palace] in his absence'' from London during the Civil War, he ''attended His Majesty [Charles I] in that capacity at Hampton Court and in the Isle of Wight, where he received His Majesty's command to design a palace for Whitehall, which he did until His Majesty's unfortunate calamity caused him to desist''. Since Charles I escaped on 15th November 1647 from Hampton Court Palace, where he had been in semi-captivity since June, and made for Carisbrooke Castle, where he remained until December 1648, we can calculate fairly accurately when it was that Webb began work on the second group of plans. That during this extremity of his affairs Charles could seriously give thought to rebuilding the palace shows how utterly out of touch he was with realities. Although Jones and Webb were no longer living under the same roof at this period, they must frequently have met over business as they did at Wilton. Consequently, the surveyor will almost certainly have seen and approved—possibly have inspired—such important drawings as the new Whitehall ones. Yet they are markedly different from those of the first group and already show affinities with Webb's post-Restoration façade for Greenwich Palace in simple, massive units and the use of the giant order. The two last groups, namely that dated 17th October 1661 and the other belonging to the years 1661–5, were of course entirely Webb's own.

So much has been written upon the merits and demerits of the abortive Whitehall Palace schemes that there is no need to reinvestigate them in detail (60). As long ago as the building of the Banqueting House, when Rubens wrote in 1621 about his projected ceiling canvases ''touchant la sale au nouveau palais'', a scheme for a com-plete new Whitehall Palace was first mooted. As late as 1698, after a disastrous fire had practically destroyed all that remained of the old jumble of buildings, Wren was still toying with the idea of adopting Webb's last scheme for a new palace for William III. Most writers on the subject have deplored the circumstances which prevented the fulfilment of Jones's and Webb's intention. But as we have explained, there were at least four different intentions, to the last of which, by Webb, the majority of the surviving drawings relate. It is difficult to be enthusiastic about most of the early elevations submitted to Charles I. The objection to nearly all of them is the same. They were dull. The façades were to be of immense lengths (1,280 ft. by 950 ft. were the overall dimensions), with a surfeit of small repetitive motives. They

[1] E. S. de Beer, *Whitehall Palace. Inigo Jones and Wren.* Notes and Queries, 30th December 1939.

were not to have any central crowning feature, but undersized cupolas at strategic points. The austere fronts were to be relieved at intervals by projecting bays crowded with statuary. Undoubtedly the finest unit would have been the great circular Persian court. It owed its derivation perhaps to the central court at Caprarola by Vignola; perhaps to the one—oval it is true—at Fontainebleau by Lescot; perhaps to the two, circular again, at the Tuileries Palace by Philibert de l'Orme, whose book was the only French architectural volume in Jones's library. In short the chief value of the Whitehall Palace drawings lies in their indication of the different prototypes Jones and Webb had in mind for the various units. We may trace the origin of these units to many sources, and if it is true that Webb was untravelled [1] we may see in them, as well as text-book influences, the fruits of Inigo Jones's extensive knowledge. For behind the monumental designs for Whitehall Palace were the shadows of the great palaces of the Continent which Jones had at one time or another visited and observed.

On the other hand no French influences are apparent in any of Webb's constructions which survive today or were ever carried out. Webb with the years has hardly been luckier with his buildings than was his master. It we exclude the work at Wilton to Jones's dictation, and the additions to the Queen's House, his only architectural units to survive are the centre block at Lamport Hall and the Charles II block at Greenwich. Mere scraps and fragments exist at other houses. Yet there exist a great quantity of measured elevations for country houses drawn by Webb in his independence, but never carried out. These drawings are far removed from the eclectic sketches deliberately done from architectural books in his student days. They all share one characteristic with the houses destroyed and the fragments of houses remaining which can be identified as his. They are exclusively and uncompromisingly Palladian. Because of this selective scholarship Webb's façades adhere far more tenaciously to the letter of architectural rules than Inigo Jones's. We sense behind their eminently correct, sparse and carefully measured planes the academic mind of the drawing-master rather than the untrammelled inspiration of the creative artist. They also amaze us by their anticipation of early Georgian country houses. And of course the explanation is that Webb's country-house drawings were purloined and adapted by Lord Burlington and his band of disciples, Kent, Campbell, Leoni, Flitcroft, Ripley and the rest of them. It was not Inigo Jones at all upon whom they modelled themselves, although, because of their ignorance to distinguish between a sprawling and a copy-book handwriting, they thought it was.

\*       \*       \*

1   *Lamport Hall, Northamptonshire, 1654–7*

In Lamport Hall, situated on the main road from Northampton to Market Harborough, Sir Justinian Isham, client, and John Webb, architect, composed the

1 In the list of warrants of the Lord Protector and Council there is mention of a pass to France having been issued in July 1656 to a John Webb. It is not known that the recipient availed himself of it. The Calendar of State Papers refers to another John Webb, formerly in the King's service.

60 Whitehall Palace. A picture by Thomas Sandby showing how Jones's and Webb's scheme for the Royal Palace might have appeared, if executed

61 Lees Court, Kent, 1652. Corner of the Hall, inspired by that of the Queen's House, Greenwich (cf. fig. 15)

62 Lamport Hall, Northants. Hall Fireplace designed by John Webb, 1655

63   (*above*) Portico built by Edward Marshall, 1654, and probably designed by John Webb

64   (*left*) Garden House, possibly designed by John Webb on a Greek-cross plan

best documented story of how a country house of this period came into being. The story is fully recorded in ten letters from Webb to Isham, which are preserved in the Lamport Hall library in the possession of Sir Justinian's direct descendant. Because of the harmonious relations that existed between client and architect, both of whom were persons of culture and excellent character, the correspondence is agreeable as well as informative.

Sir Justinian Isham, 2nd Baronet, came of a distinguished Northamptonshire family long settled at Lamport. He was born the year before and died the same year as John Webb. When the two men first became friends is not known, but since their interests and sympathies were identical, how and why they became friends is readily understandable. In his Stonehenge book Webb mentions Isham in terms of affection. Isham was a Cambridge man, educated at Christ's College, to which he was to contribute £20 towards the new Fellows Building in 1646. In his youth he travelled to Holland, France and possibly Italy. On the Continent his love of painting and architecture was born. He collected many architectural books for his library at Lamport and evidently read Italian. He certainly prided himself on his architectural knowledge, which Webb in the letters to his client had the tact and good sense not to question. Isham was constantly ventilating his architectural opinions, and in a letter to his friend Sir Ralph Verney in 1655 signed himself facetiously "Architrave, Frieze and Cornice". During the Civil War he championed the King's cause, in 1649 was imprisoned as a delinquent, and two years later, on succeeding to the baronetcy, forced to compound. Nevertheless his sufferings were not so severe that during the Commonwealth he could not afford to alter and improve his ancestral home.

At first Isham corresponded with the French-born architect and military engineer, David Papillon. He was an old man and a neighbour, who had bought property at Lubenham across the Leicestershire border and built himself a semi-fortified house which he called Papillon Hall.[1] In answer to Sir Justinian's proposals that he should add to the existing house at Lamport, Papillon wrote a letter, dated 12th May 1652, attempting to dissuade him, owing to the irregular structure of the old buildings, so repugnant, he expressed them, to the accepted rules of art. Instead, he submitted plans for an entirely new house which Isham seems to have rejected out of hand.

In 1654 Isham came to terms with John Webb and the next three years saw the addition to the old buildings, which were retained, of a west wing at Lamport. Webb's letters, dated between 1654 and 1657, were addressed to Isham from Scotland Yard. They were all written in Webb's meticulous handwriting and began "Sir" or "Honoured Sir", and ended "your assured friend to serve you, John Webb". They accompanied working drawings for parapets, balusters, window

[1] Papillon Hall has since the late war been totally demolished. This most interesting haunted house contained a "luck" in a pair of high-heeled brocaded shoes. The house was built in 1622–4 within a moat on the plan of an octagon. It originally had but one entrance and each room led into another. The pitched roof in the shape of a cross had leaded spaces whence views of the surrounding country were obtainable. It had pointed gables with ball finials. The windows had rounded brick heads. See plate in J. Nichols, *Leicestershire*, 1795. Lutyens enlarged it.

moulds, console scrolls and every possible detail, which were packed in a paste-board case and despatched to Northamptonshire by carrier. The letters provide an excellent account of how the architect set about his job. Webb was responsible for every original plan and design. He gave the most minute instructions for the masons, not to them direct, but through his client. Isham thereupon made precise notes how he would pass on these instructions. There was also a third person who played an important part in the operations, the contractor. His name was T. Sargenson of Coventry, and he provided the material. Thirteen letters of his to Sir Justinian are preserved. Although Sargenson sported a coat of arms his letters were phrased more deferentially than Webb's and ended "Your Worship, in all humble and dutiful service". They were concerned largely with Weldon stone and the necessity of laying in as large a stock as possible before the summer was over and while the roads remained dry and passable. We easily perceive how a difficult or opinionated client could by this distant and indirect means of communication make havoc of an architect's schemes. But although Isham at times differed from Webb, who was frequently obliged to defer to him, he never interfered with his architect's schemes once he himself had approved them. And it seems that he usually did at least tacitly approve them. Webb for his part was peculiarly discreet. He never directly vetoed Isham's counter-suggestions; at times he merely ignored them and reiterated his own. In addition to his rôle of architect Webb assumed that of adviser to Isham on artistic matters, helping him in the purchase of statuary and pictures for the house.

Webb's first letter, dated June 1654, to Sir Justinian accompanied what he called a "schitzo" of the front of the new block and recommended a portico—not carried out—which he said would not look "temple like" when he had done with it. The second letter was chiefly concerned with the basement or cellar windows, the need for the masons faithfully to observe the moulds of the architraves, of which full-scale profile drawings were to be sent, and the distance, once it was established, between the end windows and the angle dressings. Evidently Sir Justinian agreed what the distance ought to be, for Webb's third letter enclosed an amended design for the front which was ultimately carried out. This is the simple rusticated astylar elevation of five bays (67). Over the basement windows steps lead to a central doorway with broken pediment between four windows of alternate pointed and elliptical pediments. Above the *piano nobile* is a range of square windows under an entablature and balustrade. Webb's small raised pediment over the front (perhaps taken from Serlio) was removed by Francis Smith when in 1732 he added the side wings. The present rather cumbersome pediment was substituted by Henry Hakewill in 1821. What remains of Webb's modest façade is extremely accomplished and refined.

Webb's next four letters were written in 1655. He sent full-scale moulds for all stonework, subsequently executed, on the outside of the house, and designs for the "inside of your room and chimneypiece". He said he wanted the chimneypiece of the music hall to be wrought of Northamptonshire or Portland stone in London by Mr. Marshall (62). This was Edward Marshall, the monumental sculptor. But

Isham did not agree. In fact the lower stage of the chimneypiece was executed in Weldon stone and the upper in wood by the French Huguenot, Pierre Benier, who had in 1643 succeeded his brother Isaac as Sculptor in Ordinary to Charles I, a position confirmed in his favour by Charles II.[1] As to the chimneypiece, Webb did not favour cartouches of Flemish type. "My design is after the Italian manner"—he emphasized—with draped swags, now rather blunted by overpainting, and a pair of Isham swans. Benier also carved the stone escutcheon over the front door. Webb had advised against Benier to no avail and evidently disapproved of Isham's taste for foreign masons. "As for your French workmen", he wrote, "I desire always to employ our own countrymen" who are acquainted with local traditions, "for French fashions are, you know, fantastical". Nevertheless he submitted to Sir Justinian's choice, with a good grace, and sent down drawings of moulds for the chimneypiece. The other ornaments of the music hall he left to his client to select. Normandy glass, he said, cost as much as 45s. the case in London and would not go down in price until England was at peace with France again. He told Isham that a merchant in London had several paintings from Italy for sale, amongst them a copy after Titian which "quoad a copy is tolerable but I should suppose it is not so pleasing to your Lady because of the naked woman in it".[2] Presumably Lady Isham's scruples were overcome, for the picture, "Susanna and the Elders", is at Lamport today. The same year Sir Justinian did some more picture buying, for a small Vandyke of Christ and St. John the Baptist was acquired for £24 through Webb from a dealer, Maurice Wase, to whom he had introduced his client. This picture also is still in the house.

In June 1655 Sir Justinian, always an uncompromising royalist, was imprisoned until he consented to take the oath to respect the life of the Protector. After his release in October there were to be no more letters for two years. During the interval the house was being completed, for Webb's remaining three letters referred to designs for gate piers with the swan crest upon them, and instructions how the masons were to set them up. Sir Justinian was advised that "the gathering of some green" on them "is not amiss, it being a symptom of antiquity". No piers by Webb survive, and most of the piers now in the grounds date from later in the century and a few from Henry Hakewill's restorations in the early nineteenth century.

Webb's decoration has not fared so well within the house as without. The upper

---

[1] Pierre Benier was one of a large family of sculptors. He did the noble portrait bust of Sir Richard Shuckburgh (d. 1656) in Shuckburgh church, Warwicks. The prudery of Parliament obliged him as Sculptor in Ordinary in 1645 to cover "the naked place of divers statues and figures in the open gallery and in the garden" of St. James's Palace.

[2] Webb, like Inigo Jones, prided himself on his knowledge of pictures. At the Restoration of Charles II he asked to hang in Somerset House those royal pictures dispersed on Charles I's death which had now been recovered. There is other evidence that he dealt in pictures. At the Restoration one Henry Carter in a petition for compensation claimed back £20 he had paid at the sale of Charles I's pictures to John Webb for a naked Venus, a foot long.

part of the walls, the coves and ceiling of his great room or music hall were redecorated by Francis Smith, who did away with Webb's flat ceiling of one oval
wreath and scrolls in the spandrels. The large drops in the Wilton fashion which
Webb designed for his panels between the lower windows were dismantled. Fortunately Benier's chimneypiece to Webb's design and the wooden panelling, cornice
and door-cases of the lower half of the room were not touched. Nor were several
of the door-cases upstairs. But Webb's staircase has been cut about. Enough remains
to show that the balustrade was of the pierced-panel type with flowered sprays of
foliage issuing from an urn. This type of staircase with newel finials made of enlarged acorns and acanthus leaves is to be seen at Thorpe Hall, close to Peterborough,
a house being built at the same time as Lamport. Most probably the same joiner was
employed at both houses and it would be interesting to know at which he worked
first and to whose design. Sargenson, the contractor, paid a special visit to Thorpe in
order to get hints how to lay the roof at Lamport, for in a letter to Sir Justinian
dated 19th July 1655 he wrote, "Before we can appoint the floor for the platform
of lead on the top of the house we desire to know your mind how you will have it,
whether as my lord St. John's house is (which I went purposely to see) which is
level and plained on the top with small gutters under the lead to carry the water to
two great gutters on the sides." The information gleaned did not seem to bear much
relation to the way the roof at Lamport was carried out. Nevertheless the extract
from Sargenson's letter shows how craftsmen engaged on one house readily
travelled round the country in order to pick up useful hints from another, and how
quickly ideas were disseminated and shared by different members of the architectural
profession.

2  *Drayton House, Northamptonshire, 1653–5*

Webb's letters to Sir Justinian Isham contain additional interest in several
references to work the architect had in hand for other clients. Writing from Scotland
Yard in 1655 Webb tells Isham that he hopes soon to pay another visit to Lamport,
but is awaiting a summons from Lord Peterborough to go to Drayton nearby and will
come on from there. Henry Mordaunt, 2nd Earl of Peterborough, had served in the
parliamentary army, deserted to Charles I, and joined Lord Holland's rising when
the King was under duress at Hampton Court. During the Protectorate he was lying
low at Drayton hoping to escape notice. Peterborough had suffered severe fines for
his loyalty to the King and was now obliged to nurse his dwindled resources. Yet he
managed to do a little building and to anticipate the larger improvements to Drayton
which he was to carry out in the following reign.

There exist two drawings signed by Webb and dated 1653 for chimneypieces
at Drayton. One is entitled "for the bedchamber in the ground storey of Drayton".
The chimneypiece may be seen today in modified form in the magnificent state
bedroom. The overmantel is as Webb designed it, but the untidy fireplace is not

properly related to it and so cannot have been supervised by Webb. The overmantel, with its robust pediment and heavy swags of fruit and foliage, is typical of what we know of Webb's work. The second chimneypiece was intended for the "with-drawing-room to the bedchamber in the lower storey at Drayton", but was not put up. Since Webb was still working at Drayton, as he intimated to Isham, two years later he probably decorated the whole suite of rooms at the end of the north wing—where some door-cases with broken architraves survive—and possibly other parts of the house as well.[1]

## 3   Belvoir Castle, Rutland, 1654

In a letter to Isham written towards the end of 1654 Webb mentioned that he was just about to leave London for Belvoir where, it seems, he was bringing about alterations on a vast scale. Nothing of them remains today. Kent, in his *Designs*, gives a plan and the principal elevation (58), attributing them, as was usual with him, to Jones's inspiration and Webb's draftsmanship.[2] The rather odd plan of the castle is of H formation with a very long connecting stroke. A great transverse hall embracing two storeys was made to occupy the central axis. The principal elevation, not unlike Webb's Greenwich Palace block, had a central portico and end projections, on which were windows with splayed jambs like those on the corner towers of Wilton.

## 4   The Vyne, Hampshire, 1654

Chaloner Chute, Speaker of the House of Commons during Richard Cromwell's ephemeral Protectorate, had in 1653 bought The Vyne, near Basingstoke, from the Sandys family. To this most interesting old house, with its fifteenth-century chapel and Henry VIII long gallery, Chute immediately made alterations and additions. Horace Walpole stated that Chute employed John Webb for the purpose. Although there is no documentary proof,[3] all the evidence (including long family tradition) points to this. There are among the Jones-Webb papers (in the R.I.B.A. library) plans and elevations of some of the work done at The Vyne at this time, but they are inscribed by Lord Burlington's hand. This suggests, but does not prove, that Burlington, who had these drawings made, believed Webb (Inigo Jones being dead) the author of the alterations. Furthermore there are preserved at The Vyne dated

[1] Among the Webb letters at Lamport is a drawing dated 1667 by one Isaac Rowe, a servant to Lord Peterborough, for an octagonal panel under a pediment, surrounded by cupboards. There was some work, now destroyed, at Drayton by Rowe, who may have been trained by Webb.

[2] Inigo Jones probably visited Belvoir in 1621, 1634 and 1637, when preparations were being made for royal progresses to the castle.

[3] Perhaps the best evidence is the fact that Chute had married at Chevening four years previously the widow of the 13th Lord Dacre. Mrs. Chute's son by her former husband was the 14th Lord Dacre, for whom in 1655 John Webb wrote to Isham that he was decorating a room at Chevening.

accounts of the work done. They are in the handwriting of Edward Marshall, who charged for carving the stone capitals of the great portico and executing a number of chimneypieces. Now Marshall was during the Protectorate working for Webb at several places. Moreover, the character of many of the 1654 features at The Vyne resembles the character of much of Webb's known work.

First of all Chute had the base court removed and the doors and windows of the east front transformed. There are charges "for taking down the old windows and setting up the new, cut into square heads". Doorways with broken pediments containing the Chute arms were inserted. On the west front the great portico, said to be the first attached to an English country house, was set up (63). Sir Reginald Blomfield was over-severe in his strictures upon the clumsiness and lack of restraint shown in the portico. It is true that the openings behind the end pilasters *in antis* are unorthodox [1]; but they are not unpleasing. The pilasters and two columns which compose the tetrastyle are of brick covered with stucco, a treatment much favoured by Palladio. But the pediment, with its pronounced dentils, is of painted wood. The central cartouche of Chaloner Chute's arms was carved by Marshall. Inside the house several chimneypieces were inserted. The marble one in the gallery with broken pediment—containing a cartouche and swags—and shouldered architrave, is a very typical Webb design; so is another in the library, with half columns of palm trunks and palm branches on the entablature, a foreshadowing of the baroque treatment of his Greenwich Palace interiors. Another in the dining-room displays a mixture of styles that Webb would not have liked and has jambs in the Flemish fashion which he deprecated in a letter to Sir Justinian Isham. Possibly for this chimneypiece Marshall was solely responsible. The remainder, in bedrooms, are of far simpler character and anticipate those inserted by Wren at Hampton Court and elsewhere. There is a secondary staircase with waisted balusters which also must date from Webb's alterations.

Lastly, in the garden Chute set up two red-brick pavilions, of which one survives (64). This little building with domed roof is a rotunda in form and reminds us of those exercises which Webb in his apprentice years used to scribble out of his volume of Serlio. It has four pilastered and pedimented projections which give the building the plan of a Greek cross. It was originally plastered within and there are still to be seen traces of a simple modillioned cornice.

## 5  *Northumberland House, Charing Cross, 1657–8*

Webb was definitely making alterations for Lord Northumberland at his Jacobean palace at Charing Cross in 1657–8. There exists a very fanciful design by him of a chimneypiece which is reproduced in Vardy's *Some Designs of Inigo Jones* and dated 1657. The overmantel is distinguished by reversed scrolls of palm branches and draperies

[1] At least Webb would have claimed that Palladio did the same thing in the four porticos of the Villa Rotonda, at Vicenza.

which provide the decorative theme. In 1658 Webb wrote a letter addressed to "Mr. Marshall", asking him to make a clay model for a pedestal for Lord Northumberland.

## 6 Gunnersbury House, Middlesex, 1658

The same letter disclosed that Marshall was doing work for Webb at Gunnersbury House. This was a villa, on the outskirts of London close to Chiswick and Kew, built for John Maynard, then serjeant-at-law. Maynard was, like all Webb's clients, a royalist who had protested against Charles's deposition and then been imprisoned for hinting that Cromwell's government was a usurpation. Webb's design for Gunnersbury (65) came straight out of Palladio's book and was practically a copy of the Villa Cornaro at Piombino Dese only without its lower loggia. It consisted of ground floor approached by steps, *piano nobile* and attic. All but two bays of the piano nobile were taken up by a recessed hexastyle portico under a pediment, displaying in the tympanum a shield of Maynard's arms and long trails of mantling. Horace Walpole considered the portico far too large, but conceded that the staircase and saloon were very noble. The saloon was in fact a double cube, 25 ft. high, and led on to the portico. The rest of the rooms were in consequence too small, with the exception of the lower hall below the saloon, which had screens of columns at either end. Sir Roger Pratt found both portico and hall infringements of true architectural principles and criticized the planning of the house for being Italian in a northern climate. A pair of gate piers, each containing a niche under a pediment, resembled Webb's rather more elaborate gate piers at Amesbury and completed the Palladian character of Gunnersbury House. Nothing now remains of Webb's villa, which was pulled down soon after the death of Princess Amelia, one of George II's daughters, who had lived in it.

## 7 Amesbury Abbey, Wiltshire, 1661

Long before Catherine, eccentric Duchess of Queensbury, was to parade with the poet Gay along the terraced banks of the Avon at Amesbury, a Palladian villa had replaced the monastic buildings. This was in 1661. Amesbury Abbey was then the property of William Seymour, 2nd Duke of Somerset, in whose favour the titles of his great grandfather, the Lord Protector, had been revived. The authorities for stating that the new house was built and finished by Webb are George Vertue and Colen Campbell.[1] Amesbury was, like Gunnersbury, essentially a Palladian villa of cubical block type (57). "Here is a bold rustic basement", wrote Campbell in explanation of his plate of it in *Vitruvius Britannicus,* "which supports a regular loggio of the Composed order." This was a tetrastyle portico. The structure was crowned by a platformed projection from which rose above the balustrade a cupola to light

[1] The latter, however, ascribed its design to Jones. Kent ascribed Amesbury solely to Jones, as he did all Webb's buildings.

the stairwell. The feature was probably inspired not by Palladio but by the plates of Rubens's book the *Palazzi di Genova*. The main staircase contained a lesser stone circular stair within it. The house was greatly admired by James Fergusson who in his *History of Architecture* (1865-7) referred to it as the prototype of the English country house in the classical style. Webb's house was, however, long ago pulled down and in 1834 replaced by the present one built by Thomas Hopper on Webb's plan. The portico on a rusticated basement was repeated—only the tetrastyle became a hexa-style—and the cubical block, although inclining to heaviness, more or less follows the design of its Palladian predecessor. On the principal front the nine bays and the plain band between the rustication of first and ground floors have been retained. One simple chimneypiece in a ground-floor room and several doorways and dados by Webb were spared.

On the road Webb's twin gate piers still stand. They are essentially Palladian, essentially Webb-like. Doric half columns, supporting an entablature with pedi-ment, enclose a niche. The composition is a development of the Gunnersbury piers and a simplified version of those, also no doubt by Webb, with frost-work carving that used to stand in the east garden of Wilton. They in their turn find their English prototype in the piers at Holland House which, according to Vertue, were erected by Nicholas Stone as early as 1629.[1]

## 8    *Greenwich Palace, 1663–8*

Charles II was always ready to sponsor good ideas so long as they did not cost him any effort or expense. His taste and sound judgment were only surpassed by his genial Medicean cynicism, which counselled him to allow men less perspicacious and intelligent than himself to interfere with his affairs if they felt strongly impelled to do so. In other words he had strong views about few things and seldom positively discountenanced other peoples' even when they were wholly bad. It was doubtless this distressing passivity which enabled his advisers to make Sir John Denham his surveyor-general in place of Webb, whose claims and qualifications were far superior. Charles II certainly favoured a scheme to rebuild the royal palace of Greenwich. He must have known that Denham was quite unfitted to carry it out, and that Webb, whose scheme for Whitehall Palace he had approved, was just the right man for the purpose. Perhaps he asserted himself sufficiently to insist that Webb should in some measure be associated with the undertaking.

John Evelyn relates how, as early as 19th October 1661, he met Denham "to consult with him about the placing of his palace at Greenwich, which I would have had built between the river and the Queen's house [this was a silly proposal coming from so intelligent a virtuoso], so as a large square cut should have let in the Thames

---

1 Walpole said they were to the design of Inigo Jones. This is not improbable since Henry Rich, Earl of Holland, was an influential person at Court. Of Portland stone the piers have pediments and niches between Doric pilasters with vermiculated bands. They carry carved griffins supporting the arms of Rich impaling Cope.

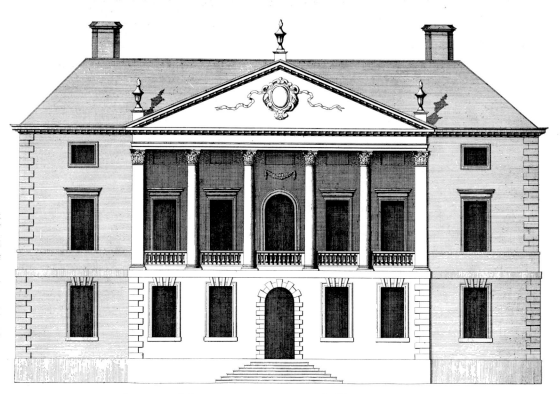

65    Gunnersbury, Middlesex. (From C. Campbell's *Vitruvius Britannicus, 1715*)
*Architect: John Webb, 1658*

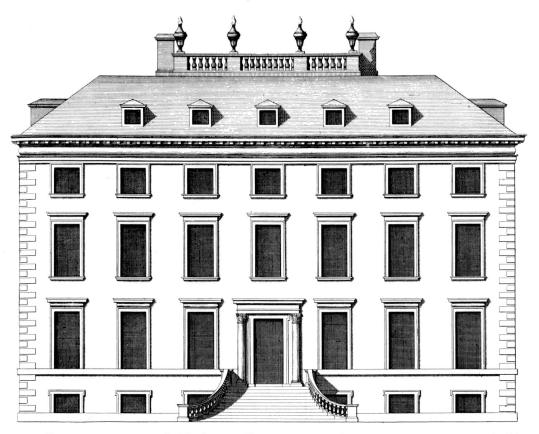

66    Chevening, Kent. Probably designed by Inigo Jones, about 1630. (From C. Campbell's
*Vitruvius Britannicus, 1717*)

67   Lamport Hall, Northamptonshire
*Architect: John Webb, 1654–70. Pediment altered by Henry Hakeville, 1821*

68   King Charles II's Block, Greenwich Palace
*Architect: John Webb, 1663–8*

like a bay, but Sir John was for setting it on piles at the very brink of the water, which I did not assent to; and so came away, knowing Sir John to be a better poet than architect, though he had Mr. Webb (Inigo Jones's man) to assist him''. In fact Webb was made assistant-surveyor to ensure that the new building at Greenwich should be planned and conducted properly. His appointment was phrased in a way that makes this quite clear, while at the same time protecting Denham's sensitive dignity. The royal decree ran as follows: ''Whereas we have thought fit to employ you [John Webb] for the erecting and building of our Palace at Greenwich, we do hereby require and authorise you to execute, act, and proceed there to your best skill and judgment in architecture, as our Surveyor-Assistant unto Sir John Denham, K$^{nt}$ of the Bath, Surveyor-General of our Works, Etc.''

The history of the various units which make Greenwich the most uniform, interesting and beautiful of all the royal palaces in the United Kingdom deserves a whole volume to itself. It is probably Webb who was responsible for the ultimate form the group of buildings took, although he designed and built but a fraction of them. Wiser than Denham, with his poetical and unpractical idea of making a kind of Venetian projection into the river, where the strong tides and currents would in no time have undermined the piles; wiser than Evelyn with his blind disregard of the commanding view of the river from the Queen's House on the hill above, Webb had the piety and artistic sense to make Inigo Jones's little building the focal point of his whole scheme. He had the imagination and vision to foresee the vast conglomeration of wings when he set his part of what is now called King Charles's block, not between the Queen's House and the Thames, but slightly to the west of a straight line drawn from one to the other (68). Furthermore he sited his long elevation to face not north or south, but east. Webb's plans and drawings, mostly signed, for his block date between 1663 and 1670, in which year he designed a chapel (never executed). In March 1664 Pepys recorded that the foundations of the block were laid.[1] By 1668 the building was completed. Thereupon a gap in the annals of Greenwich Palace appear. Money became short, the King's tepid enthusiasm evaporated.

In 1694 it was decided to make the palace into a hospital for seamen. There was actually talk of demolishing Webb's block, but Queen Mary refused her sanction because it had been built, as she supposed, to Inigo Jones's design. Instead she positively ordered it to be duplicated on the other side of the court. Already the master's name had become a legend, and Hawksmoor in some notes relating to his work at Greenwich about this time referred to the great opinion the world had of the buildings of Jones and Webb. Queen Mary constantly visited the site and cherished a desire to complete the palace, as had been intended by, in fact, Webb. The Queen then died, but her strongly expressed wishes were respected by King William, her widower, and Sir Christopher Wren, the surveyor-general. Sir

[1] Joshua Marshall was paid for laying the foundations, helping build the east and north fronts and for supplying a chimneypiece. One of his more prominent assistants was John Young, who carved shields and trophies on one of the pediments.

Christopher's son, in the *Parentalia,* relates how his father kept his ambitious project subservient to the two existing buildings of Jones and Webb. The famous architect "cheerfully engaged in the work, gratis, and contrived the new fabric, extensive, durable and magnificent, conformable to the graceful pavilion, which had been erected there by Charles II, and originally intended for his own palace . . .". The passage refers to the Queen Anne block which Wren quite simply made a repetition of the King Charles block, and placed symmetrically to the east of the straight line from the Queen's House to the Thames. Thus Wren had the magnanimity and genius to develop the principle of Webb's original scheme for Greenwich Palace. Henceforward a number of England's most prominent members of the architectural hierarchy—Vanbrugh, Hawksmoor, Campbell, Ripley, Athenian Stuart and Yenn—were to contribute towards the completion of the palace with which the illustrious names of Inigo Jones, John Webb and Christopher Wren were already associated.[1]

Webb's work of course only consisted of the east side of the King Charles block. Colen Campbell doubled it on the west side. Webb's east elevation, judged as an independent entity, is a little disappointing. We may admire the horizontal emphasis of the great length, broken by the central portico and two end pavilions. The treatment has its parallels in Webb's Whitehall Palace designs of this date and his abortive Durham House elevation of 1649. The end pavilions are adaptations of Palladio's Palazzo Valmarana façade at Vicenza in a giant order of pilasters supporting an attic storey. But Palladio made his giant order embrace the whole length of his façade, whereas here the limited treatment is too heavy for the narrowness of the pavilions. The heaviness is particularly accentuated by the depth of plinth on the attic storey of each pavilion. Also the lack of parapet to the centre block is a defect and the sudden rise of roof from the cornice ungainly. The composition as a whole is monotonous.

Webb left a number of drawings for the King's apartments, giving special attention to chimneypieces and directions as to how the marble for them should be fetched from Leghorn. Of these drawings the most delightful, dated 1665, is for the King's bedchamber; it shows within an alcove the bed under sprays of palm from the capitals of palm trunk columns. Another shows the detail of the alcove soffit in crowns against a pattern of honeysuckle.[2] Jones and Webb were particularly fond of palm-tree decoration. Jones had years before designed a floating island planted with palm trees, which he called a maritime chariot,—to be "drawn by sea monsters . . . with a sweet motion in the sea"—for Davenant's masque, *The Temple of Love.* Webb introduced the same theme in a chimneypiece for The Vyne. The Georgian architects held it in much affection. Vardy practically copied Webb's Greenwich Palace room

1 There exists at Wilton a plan of Greenwich Palace and its grounds in the hand of Wren. On the plan are shown, between the observatory and the Queen's House, a large hemicycle, against which is written "Grotto by Mr. Webb 1665", and between the grotto and the Queen's House, a garden layout by Lenôtre. Both these interesting features have entirely disappeared.

2 John Grove, who worked under Webb at the Queen's House, did the plaster ceilings.

in his drawing-room at Spencer House and Robert Adam adopted the palm theme in his tea-pavilion at Moor Park and state bedroom at Kedleston, where the posts of the gilt bed are palm trunks, the mirrors and torchères *en suite*.

Little of Webb's work is left inside King Charles's block, where Wren in transforming it into a hospital ward was obliged to make sweeping changes. But there remain several large stone doorways, noticeably influenced by Jones's doorways in the Queen's House, and at least one chimneypiece, of a massive but straightforward kind. The great staircase, with its Tijou-like balusters, is almost certainly a later contribution by Wren.[1]

*　　　*　　　*

To sum up the story of John Webb: he was unfairly treated in his life and has been unfairly treated since his death. His reverence for and devotion to his master accounted for the long subordination of his talents to the other's genius. Before Inigo Jones's death, therefore, Webb's architecture cannot be distinguished from Jones's. Until that event the names of Inigo Jones and John Webb are synonymous. There then ensued the decade of the Commonwealth when Webb, an ardent royalist, could hardly have expected official recognition. He certainly never received it. After the Restoration, when he was a middle-aged man in his fifties, there came the most grievous disappointments of his life, his supercession in the surveyorship, first by Denham and then nine years later by Wren. Of Webb's two most ambitious schemes, for Whitehall and Greenwich palaces, the first came to nothing whatever, the second amounted to a single unit. Of his country-house work we have seen what is left of it, fragmentary stuff indeed, here a chimneypiece, there a gate pier and the centre block of Lamport Hall the only elevation. There is not enough to enable the average person to appreciate the importance of the man who was the first professional architect of the English Renaissance. Yet the influence he had upon the development of our classical architecture was, if indirect, immense. He learnt from Inigo Jones the principles of antiquity, and applied them to his own architecture even more scrupulously than his master did to his. Whereas Jones in the Queen's House and the alterations to old St. Paul's adopted an assortment of classical influences, which were, notwithstanding, absolutely alien to this country, Webb in the Greenwich block and Lamport wing reduced them to a circumscribed style of balanced masses and chaste detail, to which he somehow imparted a spirit already English. And now we come to the final instance of Webb being the sport of posterity. The Burlingtonians, without knowing it, derived as much from Webb as they did from Jones. The country houses, which under the Whig ascendancy, adorned the English landscape, were practically copied from the designs which Webb originated after the death of Jones. Even so, it was Jones and not Webb who received the credit for them.

*　　　*　　　*

[1] Richard Cleare was a carver of the original staircase and Robert Streater painted most of the wainscot.

185

There are a number of houses attributed to Webb on no documentary evidence at all. Of them the claims of Ramsbury Manor, Ashdown House, Thorpe Hall and Thorney Abbey House have long remained unquestioned. But the first, although built for the son of Webb's old patron, Philip Earl of Pembroke, was not begun until after Webb's death. The second, for stylistic reasons to be discerned later, is not likely to have been of Webb's design. The third and fourth have recently found their true authors. There are still three others which for reasons of date, history and style fit in with the tradition attached to each and so may to some extent be associated with Webb.

## 9 Lees Court, Kent, 1652

This unusual house was built the year of Inigo Jones's death for Sir George Sondes, a royalist who had suffered grievously in the Civil War. He had compounded heavily for his estates, sequestrated by Parliament, but somehow managed to raise enough money to spend on building. Hasted, the historian of Kent, states that the front of Lees Court was designed by Inigo Jones soon after the death of Charles I (69). This is not altogether impossible, for the composition is essentially scholarly. Yet the interior (if it is fair to judge from photographs what was entirely gutted by fire in 1912), seems not quite up to Jones's impeccable standards.

The long, unbroken front was rebuilt exactly as it stood before the fire. It is of two storeys and consists of thirteen bays formed by a giant order of Ionic pilasters of stucco, their wreathed capitals of stone. They carry an entablature upon which are fitted in an ungainly manner huge console brackets to support an overhanging roof. This distinguishing feature recalls the treatment of St. Paul's Church, Covent Garden. Clumsy though it be it is, not without a peculiar appeal and even beauty, notably in the deep shadow cast by the eaves. Now the entablature has breaks over each pilaster and this alone suggests that at least an attic storey with possibly a balustrade, as at Lindsey House, was originally contemplated. At once the absurd squatness of the house, looking in its present state like a magnified orangery, is explained. Badeslade's drawing of the façade in the early eighteenth century provides a balustrade which apparently was never carried out, owing to Sir George's limited funds having become exhausted. Badeslade may therefore have made his drawing from the architect's original design, then possibly still in existence. Bearing this in mind it is easy enough to see that the architect of Lees Court took his design straight from Palladio's woodcut of a house for Count Giacomo Angarano, to which he merely added four bays. Even his windows without architraves and surrounds are the same, and he has only varied Palladio's design by raising the ground-floor window-heads of the four central bays in an attempt to give height to a front which he deliberately lengthened. Moreover, the material used is brick, stuccoed over, in the manner much favoured by Palladio.

If Jones designed the front—and after all he was not too decrepit in 1650 to

69  Lees Court, Kent. Architect possibly John Webb, 1652, who took his elevation straight from Palladio

70 Swakeleys, Middlesex: Gable, 1629–38

71 Hampstead Marshall, Berkshire: pair of Gatepiers designed by Sir Balthazar Gerbier and carved by Edward Pierce, jun., *c.* 1663

72 Swakeleys, Middlesex: Hall Screen, 1629–38

visit Coleshill and give advice to Roger Pratt—did Webb after his death decorate the interior ? It is an interesting speculation. The great hall occupied two storeys, and a gallery at first-floor level was carried right round on carved cantilever brackets like those in the hall of the Queen's House (15). The gallery balusters, too, were waisted in the Italian Renaissance shape Jones introduced at the Queen's House. The handrail moulds were identical. All the wainscoting seems to have been painted white and gold. The floor was marbled in black and white. The design of the plaster ceiling was the same as that in the west bridge room at Greenwich, a central oval with rectangular and square panels on the outsides. The flats of the ribs were decorated with those swags of fruit and bunched drapery pendants found on the double cube ceiling at Wilton. Although it is never wise to judge from photographs, it seems that the quality of the Lees Court ceiling was inferior to the others. Certainly the photographs show that the door-cases, especially their heads, were a little thin and weak in design compared with those at the Queen's House and Wilton. But after a careful analysis of the Palladian front and the rooms formerly behind it it is difficult to associate any other architects than Jones and Webb with Lees Court.

## 10   Cobham Hall, Kent, 1662

For long it was held that the centre block between the two Tudor wings of Cobham Hall was rebuilt by James 4th Duke of Lennox (and 1st of Richmond) to designs supplied by Inigo Jones, some time between 1633, when the Duke came of age and the outbreak of the Civil War; and that Charles, the 6th and last Duke, completed the work in 1662, the date appearing on the façade. The sources to which the tradition can be traced are once again Vertue and Campbell. It is true that a drawing made during Jones's lifetime, in 1648, by Webb exists, entitled "purfyle of the Duke's Palace at Cobham". But this design was never carried out. What probably happened was that drawings were prepared in Jones's office for the 4th Duke of Lennox, a nobleman of high rank and importance at Court, but shelved, and that Webb after the Restoration made a new design for the 6th Duke which was carried out. Correspondence between the last duchess, La Belle Stuart, and her husband, who was the 6th Duke of Lennox, reveals that building was still in progress as late as 1670–2. Horace Walpole, who accepted Vertue's attribution to Jones, recorded after a visit to Cobham that there was a portrait of the architect in the house (it is there today), as though its presence confirmed his connection with it. In this portrait Inigo is depicted as a man of sixty to sixty-five years old, which certainly coincides with his age between 1633 and 1638 when the 4th Duke may have contemplated alterations to Cobham.

Campbell's plate shows the block as a detached entity and so makes it appear more important than it actually is. He also made the attic windows smaller than they are and put sunk panels above them. The block, of small red bricks, is adorned with four Corinthian pilasters, cement rendered, supporting a stone entablature with modillioned cornice. Over the entablature is a heavy attic storey resembling that of Webb's Greenwich Palace block. Campbell calls the composition a "pilastrade", with attic "of the highest proportion". In the centre is a Tuscan doorway with curved broken pediment. Under the lintel of the door are two circular discs which have a distinctly unclassical look. It is small details such as these which make one hesitate before wholeheartedly ascribing the block to a Palladian purist such as Webb had become by the time of the Restoration.

## 11  *Farnham Castle, Surrey, 1662–72*

George Morley was a divine of strong royalist sympathies who left England on the death of Charles I and ministered to cavalier exiles wherever he went on the Continent. At the Restoration he was made Bishop of Worcester and in 1662 advanced to the see of Winchester. Farnham Castle was the episcopal country seat and during the ensuing ten years of the Bishop's tenure of the see he, according to Anthony à Wood, carried out improvements and made alterations there. Morley happened to be a cousin of Sir John Denham, who in 1642 had unsuccessfully defended the castle, of which he was then governor, against the parliamentary forces. Denham was now the surveyor-general and his active assistant was John Webb. This is how Webb's name is linked with Farnham Castle, where the alterations to some extent bear the stamp of his style.

Bishop Morley's work consisted, in the main, of the staircase, landing gallery and chapel. The stairs and gallery are rough-and-ready joiner's work, pleasant, but unrefined in design and execution. The chapel on the contrary is far superior. A beautiful and unusual door between two round-headed latticed windows is the entrance to it. The panels of the door are perforated and carved with winged cherub heads and old men in the sun. The wall panelling is treated architecturally, and between the deeply framed fields great Wilton drops are suspended from cherubim, their wings folded under their chins. Over the fields are crossed sprays of Webb's favourite palm. The chapel is the product of an architect of more than the amateur talents which Sir John Denham possessed.

# CHAPTER SEVEN

# GERBIER, MILLS, PRATT AND THE RUBENS SCHOOL

THE startling Italianism introduced to England by Inigo Jones was by no means on the wane at the conclusion of the old surveyor-general's career and on the collapse of Charles I's regime. On the contrary, John Webb, albeit discredited, unfairly we may think, as a political and artistic reactionary, doggedly and bravely adhered to the Inigo Jones tenets. His compositions, which spanned the awkward era between Jones's and Wren's working lives, were attempts at purging the traditional building style of those mannerist tendencies to which even Inigo's eclecticism was occasionally sympathetic. In these attempts Webb failed signally, for side by side with his strict classicism the indigenous mannerist style persisted in flourishing. The parallel movement was something of which we should perhaps be glad. In a sense it represented the popular, as opposed to esoteri, ccourt style. It resolutely declined in the second half of the seventeenth century to be dragooned into an academic strait-jacket. Instead it slowly blossomed into the style which of all others we are inclined to consider the most essentially English, the late Stuart or Queen Anne.

Carolean indigenous architecture had several ingredients. It had of course developed primarily out of the Jacobean style. And Jacobeanism was that unbroken Gothic tradition of building, leavened with certain Flemish influences. Ever since the dismissal of Italian artisans by Henry VIII stylistic tributaries from the Low Countries had continued to flow into our native stream. Their origin was the close religious and commercial affinities between England and the Low Countries established by the Reformation. We have seen the effects which visiting Flemish stone-masons and building surveyors, like Maximilian Colt and Giles de Whitt, had upon the form of Elizabethan church monuments and country houses. Throughout the reigns of James I and Charles I, even when Inigo Jones as royal surveyor was giving the official stamp of his approval to the Italian style, fresh Flemish influences continued to arrive and be absorbed. But England, a great maritime power, was moving into ever closer touch with Holland than Flanders. Since the inhabitants of Holland became in the seventeenth century the recognized exponents of the Protestant philosophy of life, as well as the leaders in the sciences and arts, we can easily perceive how Dutch influence over here was steadily mounting.

In 1619 Jones was busily engaged upon the new Banqueting House. That same year one of the Smithson family from Bolsover, probably John, was making uprights for "My Lady Cooke's house in Holborn" and a new building at St. James's Palace. Both of Smithson's uprights are traditional, that is to say integrally Jacobean. The distinguishing feature of each design is, however, something new, namely a large overall gable of scrolled curves crowned with a pediment. Neither of these Smithson uprights was perhaps executed, but there exists today a house—the earliest extant—with just this distinguishing feature which was being carried out the very same year. It is Raynham Hall in Norfolk, to which we have referred already at some length. The widely spread gable, with involuted scroll base, curved and diminishing contours, culminating in a triangular apex outlined against the sky, is a feature so compelling that it provides a distinctive category of Carolean house which has been rather arbitrarily designated as "Dutch". The "Dutch" epithet is furthermore accentuated by the material, brick (sometimes skilfully moulded like fine stonework), in which most houses of the group are constructed. Incidentally the traditional character of the group is maintained in the case of country houses (with the notable exception of Raynham) by the old-fashioned H plan.

1   *Swakeleys House, nr. Uxbridge, Middlesex, 1629–38*

A whole decade after Raynham was begun, a "Dutch" house was being built within a few miles of London, always the leading city in art and fashion. Lord Mayor Wright may not have been abreast with court notions about architecture, and his city connections may have pointed to Puritan sympathies, but most surely he desired an up-to-date design for his country residence in which to invest much trouble and money. He certainly attained in Swakeleys something novel and bizarre. In its regimented gables (70) and its pediments used as extensions to string courses over windows, Swakeleys presents an arresting surface, peaked and undulating like the disturbed motion of a wavy sea. Basically it is still a Jacobean mansion in its wings, porch (leading to screens passage), bay window projections, pitched roofs and clustered chimney-stacks. The material is a coarse brick, of which the bond is still English, but the window surrounds and dressings are covered with a plaster composition simulating stone. Samuel Pepys paid Swakeleys a visit in 1665 and the impression which the house, then some thirty years old, made upon him is not without significance. The new owner, Sir Robert Viner, also destined to become lord mayor, was a rich goldsmith who had just bought the property. He "took us up and down with great respect, and showed us all his house and grounds; and it is a place not very modern in the garden nor house, but the most uniform in all that ever I saw; and some things to excess. Pretty to see over the screen of the hall (put up by Sir J. Harrington, a Long-Parliament man) the King's head, and the Lord of Essex on one side, and Fairfax on the other; and upon the other side of the screen the parson of the parish, and the lord of the manor and his sisters. The windowcases, doorcases and chimneys of all the house are marble.'' Thereafter Pepys's attentions were distracted by the remains of a black boy, dead of a consumption, which, having been dried in an oven, were exposed to view in a box. The classical screen (72) which Pepys noticed with hardly less enthusiasm than the black boy, was probably added just before the Civil War, since the royal lions on the pediment and the bust of Charles I—the parliamentarian generals, the parson, squire and his sisters have all disappeared—were not likely ornaments in Long-Parliament days. The classical fireplace in the hall, and the bold ceiling of the upstairs saloon in fifteen deeply ribbed compartments, likewise belong to this date. But the structure of the house, with its curved and pedimented gables, dates from the late 'twenties and early 'thirties and accounts for Pepys's comment that Swakeleys was a house ''not very modern'' in its conception.

2    *Kew Palace,* 1631

With Kew Palace, actually built for a Dutch merchant, we advance a stage further (80). The spreading H plan of Stratfield Saye and West Horsley Place, two other ''Dutch'' houses built about 1630, has shrunk to a compact rectangle with no wings, but the merest projections, or rather window bays. Conversely, the low elevations have shot upwards into four storeys. The porch projection is a modified form of the old Oxford College frontispiece and is carried through the first three storeys in the three orders. A fourth, or attic, storey comes within the pedimented curved gables. A transition from the old internal disposition has taken place, for an axial passage cuts through the middle of the house, although the offices are still kept to one side of the passage and the withdrawing-rooms to the other. Kew Palace is an early example of Flemish bonding, and the gauged and rubbed brickwork of exceptionally refined quality is the first sign of a decorative art that became extremely popular as the century progressed.

3    *Broome Park, Kent,* 1635–8

''Ap. 1635 Sir Basil Dixwell laid the foundation of the house at Broome.'' Mr. Henry Oxinden, a near neighbour, took the keenest interest in every stage of the house's construction. He noted in his diary precisely how the work proceeded. First of all he took account of Sir Basil's preparation of the site, and the dyking and quicksetting of the great pasture fields around the house. By November the walls were practically complete. In the next year the stables were up. By September 1637 the joiners were well advanced with wainscoting the rooms. By Michaelmas 1638 they and the painters had finished their jobs. The total cost of the house amounted to £8,000. Oxinden was vastly impressed by what he witnessed going on. ''That superlative house", he called it, "now a building whose rare fabric and unparalleled beauty cannot choose but afford an infinite delight . . ."; and indeed of its sort, the "Dutch" group, Broome surpassed them all. Its sophisticated designer probably took some hints from Kew Palace, and was very probably a London man.

In Broome we have a mixture of English and Flemish bonds; and the absolute perfection of gauged and moulded brickwork (82). The rose-pink courses are beautifully laid and rise into gables more fanciful than any to be seen outside Holland. The skyline is contorted by broken pediments within pediments, and a multiplicity of scrolls. On one front a chimney crowns a double pediment, its shaft emerging as it were from a window in the gable below it. English mannerism of the Carolean age never became more extravagant than at Broome. Even at Rothamsted Park in Hertfordshire, where the alternate gables are given ogival pediments, the skyline contours are comparatively regular and orthodox. And yet in a structural sense Broome marks a further development upon its "Dutch" predecessors. If with one sweep of the hand we cut out the fantastic skyline we are left with a perfectly classical structure of two storeys within a giant order of pilasters resting on a pronounced plinth. The caps of the pilasters carry a continuous cornice with moulded projection, which throws a deep, sharp shadow, when the sun is shining, over the frieze.

Although Broome Park marks the peak of the "Dutch" group of buildings, later examples are worth studying. The old Grammar School (1636) in the High Street of Rye is in every sense a humbler affair (76). The ambitious remnants of Slyfield Manor, near Bookham (1640) likewise come within this group.

During the Commonwealth and after the Restoration the pedimented gable house is seldom found, and then only in remote country districts. It appears in Yorkshire at Moulton Hall near Richmond, and at Ledston Hall near Pontefract, where curvilinear gables, with involuted scrolls of a half-hearted sort, were added to a house already begun thirty years earlier by Lord Strafford, probably in the same style. Both these houses, beautiful in themselves,[1] are rather pale reflections in stone of an out-of-date style which, translated into glowing red brick, had in the south of England shed a warm lustre on the architecture of the previous reign.

*      *      *

The so-called "Dutch" style was only one manifestation of Low Country influence in England during Charles I's reign. Nicholas Stone's Flemish style we have already considered. There were yet others.

A slightly later and ultimately more sobering influence upon the vernacular architecture came from Flanders although indirectly. It came through an individual who left almost as deep a mark upon English art of the seventeenth century as Holbein had done upon English art of the sixteenth. He was no less a person than Peter Paul Rubens. Like Holbein, Rubens was of course primarily a painter. But he

---

[1] Moulton Hall is remarkable for its façade of projecting and recessed bands of ashlar, an original and effective form of decoration.

was a man of even greater versatility, rarer virtues, and more cosmopolitan accomplishments. His vastly inquiring mind assimilated the humanistic culture of the leading states of Europe, in all of which he was welcomed as an artist and scholar of international renown. In 1629 he was sent by Philip IV of Spain on an embassy to London to conclude peace with England. Here he was wooed for his favours almost like a crowned head and treated at the Court of Charles I with every possible honour. At the end of a year's stay he had been induced to paint for the King the huge canvas "War and Peace", now in the National Gallery, and to accept the commission to paint the Banqueting House ceiling. In return he was loaded with presents of jewelry and made a knight. In spite of a narrow escape from drowning, when his boat capsized on the way to Greenwich, Rubens formed a favourable opinion of this "island in which, instead of the barbarism to be expected in such a climate, at so great a distance from the culture of Italy . . .", he found a respectable standard of civilization. He was astonished by the treasures in English collections and the wealth and discrimination of their owners.

In 1622 Rubens had published the second volume of a book called *I Palazzi di Genova* which he dedicated to Don Carlo Grimaldo. It consisted of a record of baroque Genoese palaces drawn by himself and a short introductory text. In the text he pointed out that at the time of writing the Gothic manner of building was being abandoned and the Greek and Roman manners adopted universally. He implied that the baroque was the most suitable style for modern use and he mentioned as northern examples of it the Jesuit churches in Brussels and Antwerp. Rubens was preaching what he had practised, for between 1615 and 1618 he designed and decorated additions to an old house he had bought for himself in Antwerp (73). He built a studio, crowned with wide eaves and a hipped roof. He joined it to the old house by a triple arched portico so as to enclose a courtyard. The façade of the new studio he adorned with broken pediments, niches, caryatides, and all sorts of sculptural adjuncts meant to accentuate the lights and shadows of the surface. Into the studio and a domed gallery overhead he put his collection of sculpture and pictures, including nineteen Titians and seventeen Tintorettos. Surrounded by these treasures an army of pupils and assistants was kept busily at work on his own canvases, while passages from the great poets were read aloud. Rubens also built an Italian summer-house in the garden, which he made an integral part of the architectural composition. The portico and summer-house he several times introduced to the backgrounds of portraits of his two wives and himself. The Antwerp house was in fact a Flemish interpretation of a Genoese baroque palace. It became a shrine to which men of taste from the whole world resorted. Its importance as an architectural landmark cannot therefore be exaggerated.

It was after his stay in England that the effects of Rubens's publication became apparent. Someone within official circles, versed in the *Palazzi di Genova* and acquainted with Rubens's Antwerp house, was interpreting Rubens's architectural ideas into English practice. While in London Rubens had lodged in the house of his friend and compatriot, Balthazar Gerbier,[1] and this man has in consequence been credited with the rôle of interpreter. He was very resourceful and ready to turn his talents into any direction. Undoubtedly he was gifted. He was a fluent linguist, an accomplished miniaturist and draftsman, an ingenious inventor. He patented a "turning door" which admitted only one person at a time. He was always publishing tracts on some subject or another. Two of them were widely circulated among his contemporaries and are still remembered. They are *A brief Discourse concerning the three chief principles of Magnificent Buildings* and *Counsel and Advice to all Builders*, published in 1662 and 1664 successively.

Upon these two pamphlets Gerbier's precarious reputation stands. The first is the more readable because it deals with architecture generally. It is flavoured with humour and common sense. It is rather inconsequential and does not fail to convey Gerbier's notorious rancour in oblique depreciations of Inigo Jones, and conceit in visible puffs of his own prowess in architecture. Solidity, conveniency, and ornament he maintains to be the three architectural virtues which he keeps constantly within his purview. One requires no remarkable perspicacity to deduce from Gerbier's catalogue of precepts and prejudices that he favours the same baroque style for magnificent buildings as Rubens advocated forty years previously in the preface to his book on the Genoese palaces. All the same he refrains from committing himself openly to an opinion on style and tries to confine himself to practical matters. Houses, he says, should have even levels. Window transoms should be at least six foot above the floor; wooden casements should be double. Ornament, he implies, must be bold but carefully placed: surfaces otherwise spatial and plain, and, if of brick, then their mortar joints should be thin. He inveighs against pilasters and tall chimneys. What he prefers then are astylar façades, but with deep cornices and wide projecting eaves, and he instances his famous simile of the broad brim of a good hat to a traveller on a rainy day. Wide staircases he praises and is particular about the dimensions of the treads—4 in. high and 18 in. deep for choice. The stairwell, moreover, should have no side windows, but be lit from a central cupola. And so on. The second pamphlet is more specifically a manual for builders and gives advice upon what are fair charges by the different crafts. Too many buildings, he concludes, are being erected by apprentices and journeymen, rather than by trained architects.

With these sundry observations in mind we are left to identify buildings with Gerbier's authorship. But here we come against great difficulties, for where today are any of them to be found? Several drawings [2] by him exist in a fluent baroque manner for triumphal arches, erected by the Mayor and Corporation of London in celebration of Charles II's return from exile. He is known to have done work for Buckingham at New Hall,[3] Essex and to have begun Hampstead Marshall in Berkshire

[1] Gerbier may have seen himself as another Rubens. He was made Charles I's diplomatic and art agent in the Low Countries and was knighted. He died in 1667.

[2] In the R.I.B.A. Library. Some heraldic illuminations by Gerbier are preserved in the Pepysian Library, Cambridge. They formerly belonged to Samuel Pepys.

[3] In December 1624 Gerbier gave orders to a carpenter to prepare a model.

73 Rubens's House, Antwerp: part of Stone Screen and Garden Pavilion designed by the artist, 1610

74   (*above*) The Street Façade

75   (*right*) The Staircase

for Lord Craven, at least forty years later. All these works have long ago disappeared, and of the great house which William Winde completed nothing now stands but isolated pairs of urned gate piers, sad, magnificent witnesses of a garden layout, almost certainly designed by Gerbier.

### 4 Hampstead Marshall, Berkshire, 1662

Gerbier's plans and drawings for Hampstead Marshall survive; and they clearly reveal the influence of Rubens's book.[1] They show the house to have been of enormous size, planned as a rectangle round a court. Gerbier's descriptions of the various rooms indicate the palatial scale of the establishment. Three separate dining-rooms, for the lord, his gentleman and servants were provided. The state rooms were served with the usual corners and cupboards for dependents. "The porter may lodge under these stairs in a commodious room", he wrote; and, again, "Room for the Secretary's clerk to put trunks and boxes in". There were rooms for an apothecary, distiller, confectioner, butler and platekeeper, a "room to bathe" and next door to it, a "room for the repose after bathing". The east, or entrance front with projecting porch and four window bays, was the most English part of the whole composition. The other elevations, with pedimented windows under deep stone swags, and hipped roofs with dormers, were decidedly Rubens-ian. Of the surviving brick gate piers (71), Gerbier in 1663 designed those with shell-headed niches and stone urns, including the ones "near the church yard"— which Edward Pierce jnr. carved. William Winde in 1673 designed the "piers before the portico", still standing. Gerbier likewise left a design in colour for the principal entrance gates which, if they were ever constructed, must have been splendid indeed. Their robust, pictorial quality was obviously derived from the highly mannerist garden architecture in the background of Rubens's paintings.

No other houses definitely by Gerbier are known. But if he was really the medium, through whom Rubens's architectural ideas were first transmitted to England, then he must have built other houses long before he published his pamphlets and embarked upon Hampstead Marshall. And there are a number of houses dating from the sixteen-'thirties and 'forties with just the characteristics that apply to the English counter-part of the Rubens palace; that is to say the rectangular block plan, straight, fairly unbroken elevations often without orders, and projecting eaves. In these respects the palaces built by Galeazzo Alessi and his followers in Genoa are the prototypes. Other distinguishing characteristics are the hipped roof and dormer windows, tall chimney-stacks (which incidentally Gerbier disliked), and window surrounds of fanciful shapes —all of which derive, not from Genoese sources, but from Rubens's house at Antwerp.

### 5 Cromwell House, Highgate, 1637–8

In Cromwell House, Highgate, we have an early example of the Rubens style town house in a row (74). Its scale, compared to that of a Genoese palace in the Via

[1] Gough MSS., a.2. Bodleian Library, Oxford.

Aurea, is, on the other hand, infinitely humble. The street elevation is rectangular, of two storeys within seven bays, and an attic. The material is red brick. The central doorway is a massive Doric structure taken straight from Rubens's book. A cornice, the hat's broad brim, projects over the two storeys. Above the cornice is a blank parapet, the hat's crown, and a range of dormers peering from a sloping roof. This in turn is topped with a square platform (reconstructed) and cupola, as upon the Palazzo Grimaldo and Palazzo Loncellino. The windows have eared architraves and convex friezes in cut brick, and the central window over the entrance has strapwork surrounds of a sort much in evidence at this period. They bear little relation to Genoese palace windows but derive from Flemish pattern books, such as Bloom and Dietterlin produced, Rubens favoured and John Webb derided as old fashioned and impure.[1]

The wide staircase is given much prominence (75). In plan it is a rhomboid. The pierced balustrade of strapwork is interlaced with a variety of martial trophies, cannons, pikes and shields. On the voluted newel caps stand little warriors more finely carved than the rest of the woodwork. Professor Richardson claims that the accoutrement is so accurate it could only have been designed by a military expert, which Gerbier was known to be. In this case the contemporary stairs at Ham House may likewise be of Gerbier's design, for they combine similar accoutrement in the carving. An unusual feature is the flat of the handrail moulded in two channels. The door-cases upon the stair landing, with their broken pediments and eared architraves are, with the window surrounds, peculiarly Flemish, and Gerbier will have seen their like in the house of Rubens's intimate friend, the printer Balthazar Moretus, at Antwerp. Upstairs the drawing-room ceiling is of transitional pattern.

### 6  Balls Park, Hertford, c. 1640

Another house which belongs to the Rubens category, though whether built by Sir Balthazar Gerbier does not much matter, is Balls Park, Hertford (77). It can be dated about 1640, when its owner, Sir John Harrison, a farmer of the customs, was still a wealthy man and had not yet lost his money in the King's cause. Balls is a square block in red brick built round an open court, now covered in. The four façades are a little amateurish, but the encasing of the two orders of end pilasters in rustication makes a decorative effect. The most noteworthy feature is the broad cornice supported by carved wood console brackets set in pairs. These very Genoese consoles give a sense of movement to an otherwise static composition.

### 7  Tyttenhanger Park, Hertfordshire, c. 1640–54

In the same county is Tyttenhanger Park, likewise built in the same rather coarse brick, coloured plum, and the rubbed portions a vivid scarlet. This house has been dated 1654, but appears to be earlier, for it has none of the refinements of the later

[1] There is no better example of Flemish pattern book influence than the extravagant arcaded panelling (c. 1635-40) of the hall at Aldenham House, Herts.

Rubens houses. To begin with, the plan of Tyttenhanger is transitional from the Jacobean H to the later rectangle, the arms particularly on the north front being truncated. Although more satisfying (because less altered) than Balls Park, it is even more amateurish, the alignment of the windows on the north and west fronts being all over the place. Nevertheless the regularity of the main south front, with its recessed centre, steeply pitched roof and confident little dormers, is enchanting. More than any other Carolean house Tyttenhanger foreshadows the later Stuart houses built under the influence of Wren. It is in its details that we find affinities to Cromwell House. The window over the entrance, and another asymmetrically set on the west front, are identical in their Flemish text-book surrounds to the window over the entrance of Cromwell House. The door-cases on the first-floor landing are even more broken, angular and eccentric than those at the other.

In Moyles Court (1650–60) near Ringwood, far away from the capital, we have a slightly less sophisticated version of Tyttenhanger. A Cromwellian contemporary of Moyles is Highnam Court (1658) near Gloucester, rebuilt, according to Ralph Bigland the Gloucester historian, by one of Inigo Jones's scholars, Carter. Edward Carter was already dead and no other of that name alive at the time can be suggested. Highnam is grouped stylistically with Tyttenhanger and Moyles. It has a deep cornice with carved brackets. A distinguishing feature is the shell-headed niche over the entrance which once held a figure of Hercules.

*       *       *

If Gerbier, the friend of Rubens, was the first person to adapt the Genoese palace style to English indigenous architecture, there were native surveyors and builders who consciously and unconsciously followed his lead.

8   *Great Queen Street houses, Lincoln's Inn Fields, c. 1640*

A slightly varying example of the Rubens house was a rectangular block of brick houses (now destroyed) on the south side of Great Queen Street, Lincoln's Inn Fields. In this block was to be found an early instance of town houses in a row, but not the first. Inigo Jones had introduced the planned terrace group of dwellings at Covent Garden as early as the sixteen-thirties. But the Great Queen Street houses were something less than this. They were not meant to form a whole terrace but an independent block, comprising two architectural units of four houses in all. A deep unbroken cornice united them. An unusual departure was the treatment of the façade. Each unit was divided into five bays by Corinthian pilasters from street level to cornice, the ground floor occupying the podium, or pedestal. Gerbier, who disliked the use of the orders on façades, severely criticized these particular pilasters, "through whose bodies", he growled, "lions are represented to creep", a touch which he pretended to consider the last straw of unorthodox decoration. His criticism of the giant order in use here may have been inspired by his disapproval of any novelty which infringed the Rubens convention. And it must be admitted that the effect was not wholly satisfactory. The great depth of the podium comprising the ground floor was out of all proportion to the height of the pilasters. Together the podium and pilasters were too overpowering.

The houses were for long ascribed to John Webb in spite of Vertue's note, now practically confirmed by Mr. Howard Colvin's researches, that their architect was Peter Mills.[1] Mills (c. 1600–1670), by profession a bricklayer, rose to be Surveyor to the City of London and ultimately one of the four important surveyors appointed by Charles II to draw up plans for rebuilding the City after the Great Fire. From the number of buildings now attributable to him it is clear that he did not embrace Inigo Jones's Italianism but attached himself through circumstance to the Low Church, Low Country interests identifiable with the sympathies of his employers, the corporation fathers. They of course were traditionally opposed to all influences emanating from the established Church and the Court. The old Furnival's Inn, Holborn, built about 1636 and long ago demolished, may have been to Mills's design and certainly comes within the same category as the Great Queen Street block. It too was an independent street block with a deep Genoese cornice on pilasters carried through two floors. Between the first and second-floor windows were scrolled panels or aprons, which featured on the Great Queen Street houses and conveyed a strong manneristic flavour to both compositions. Another comparable street block was Thanet House, Aldersgate, demolished in 1882. A giant order of Ionic pilasters, their capitals adorned with swags, enclosed a *piano nobile* and attic, of which the window surrounds were emphatically mitred.

9   *Thorpe Hall, Northamptonshire, 1654–6*

After these divagations around the London streets we may follow Peter Mills into the open country. Mr. Colvin has now proved beyond doubt that Mills was responsible for the design and execution of what is structurally the most Genoese [2] of all English palaces of the seventeenth century, even if its decorative detail still largely derives from the old Flemish pattern books. Thorpe Hall, outside Peterborough, stands as a work of art second only to Coleshill in country houses of the interregnum between Inigo Jones and Christopher Wren (78).

On 30th August 1654 John Evelyn noted in his diary how he and his wife on their way from the north to London passed by "a stately palace of St. John's (one deep in the blood of our good King) built out of the ruins of the bishop's palace and cloister". Oliver St. John had been, with Pym, Hampden, Bedford and Saye and Sele, one of the chief members of the parliamentary party at the beginning of the civil troubles in England. He was now Chief Justice of the Court of Common Pleas and Commissioner of the Treasury. He therefore belonged to the Commonwealth band of men in power

1 H. Colvin: "The Architect of Thorpe Hall", *Country Life*, 6 June 1952.
2 For a comparison see the Palazzo del Banco di Napoli, formerly, Cambiaso, in the Via Garibaldi, Genoa.

76  Old Grammar School, Rye, Sussex, 1636

77  Balls Park, Hertford: 1638–40

*"Country Life" photograph*

78 Thorpe Hall, Northamptonshire. The outcome of the Rubens
influence

*Architect: Peter Mills, 1654–6*

*"Country Life" photograph*

79    Thorney Abbey House, Cambridgeshire

*Mason: John Lovin of Peterborough, 1660*

80    Kew Palace, Surrey.
The Dutch type of house,
1631

who had acquired the means to aggrandize themselves. In order to build the stately palace in which to found himself a dynasty he would naturally not turn to a professional architect left over from the old monarchical regime, like John Webb. On the other hand Peter Mills, Surveyor to the City of London, was from the political point of view unexceptionable. So in the previous February he had come to terms with Mills. The house arose in the shape of an unbroken parallelogram, 88 ft. by 74 ft. Instead of brick Mills chose for his material a silvery freestone out of which the Ketton masons worked an ashlar extremely clean cut and finished. The north and south elevations are identical (except for the porches). Each consists of three floors of seven bays, under a wide eave supported by console brackets. The hipped roof contains three pedimented dormers on all four fronts. From a broad roof platform spring four tall rusticated chimney-stacks. Unfortunately a central cupola and balustered parapet were long ago removed: a drawing in 1721 shows them missing. The absence of these features adversely affects the proportions of the house when viewed from a distance, by accentuating the undue height of the chimneys.

The plan of Thorpe Hall is transitional from Jacobean to Palladian. It is axial, yet the hall to the east of the main entrance is approached through a screen. The party walls on either side the axis are symmetrically ranged, but the rooms are not. They provide a wonderful assortment of chimneypieces, ceilings, door-cases, panelling and staircases, which must be compared with their counterparts at Coleshill for a demonstration of the difference between Flemish and classical patterns in use during the same decade. The chimneypieces are wrought in costly marbles and stone and, like the garden architecture, show very manneristic treatment in heavy pediments, panels in the entablature and banded surrounds. The ceiling of the dining-room is of identical design to one found among Webb's drawings. The coincidence was one of the reasons which led Mr. Avray Tipping to suppose that Webb must have been the architect of Thorpe. But such repetitions of pattern are frequently seen in seventeenth-century decoration. Architects were shameless in cribbing designs from each other. Moreover they often left the choice of decorative patterns to the craftsmen they employed. Stuccoists and joiners kept stock patterns which they used over and over again. One need only refer to Edward Pierce, junior, who in a long life worked for Gerbier, Winde, Pratt, William Wilson and even Wren, to understand how the designs of a leading craftsman might be reproduced in several buildings.

Peter Mills devised his house within a six-acre rectangle which he enclosed with a wall. He laid out the garden with raised terrace walks, balustrades, gate piers, niches, portals and pavilions, all carefully related to the house in a component fashion which Rubens would have approved. There is no other Commonwealth garden for layout and architecture comparable to it. The architecture, like much of the decoration within the house, is curiously unorthodox. The stone piers and portals are, like the marble chimneypieces, not always correct in their proportions. The caps of the piers and the pedimented architraves of the portals are as top-heavy as such features worked by Nicholas Stone a generation earlier. But their carving is throughout impeccable. It is not impossible that Mills employed as sculptor young John Stone, who in 1656 made the eccentric monument to Sir Edward Spencer in Great Brington church in the same county. The marble urn, from which Sir Edward is struggling to emerge on the Resurrection day corresponds with the curious urns, with Ionic volutes, within the niches of the forecourt gate piers at Thorpe. Another mannerist conceit is the motif of lions' heads and half bodies, made to scramble from the stonework. This was the motif which Gerbier objected to on the pilasters of the Great Queen Street houses. If it was a hall-mark of Peter Mill's architecture, then Mr. Colvin's suggestion that Mills also built Balls Park, where lions' heads peer from collars on the pilasters of the entrance doorway, is thus far corroborated.

### 10   Wisbech Castle, Cambridgeshire, 1658

No wonder that Lord Clarendon at the Restoration asked St. John for particulars of his Northamptonshire seat, "which from the manner and style of its architecture", he averred, was "little used in England before". Lord Clarendon did not, rather naturally, make use of Peter Mills's services. He chose a more acceptable architect in the royalist, Roger Pratt, to build his great mansion in London. But Oliver St. John's confidential servant, John Thurloe, almost certainly patronized Mills. Thurloe, who was Secretary to the Council of Estate and one of the Protector's intimate friends, with whom he was wont "to lay aside his greatness", rebuilt the old castle at Wisbech in 1658. A contemporary oil-painting of Thurloe's new house (altered out of all recognition in 1815) shows very clearly its affinities with Thorpe Hall (85). Wisbech Castle was a two-storeyed house with semi-basement and attic storey. It had a pronounced cornice, hipped roof with dormers, and four chimney-stacks outside a balustraded platform. Instead of porch it had a Genoese stone balcony over the front door, like the one at Ashdown. The upper window heads cut into the frieze above them and were provided with aprons, as at Thorpe. Inside, remnants of doorways may still be seen with the heavy heads, ears, half-pilasters and uncouth scrolls characteristic of the Rubens-type house. Two overmantels from the castle have found their way into the coffee-room of the Rose and Crown Inn nearby. Remains of a Commonwealth garden layout may be traced; and three of four pairs of stone gate piers, leading to an oval enclosure, stand on their original sites.

### 11   Thorney Abbey House, Cambridgeshire, 1660

At the Restoration and well within the reign of Charles II other houses in the district, with Stamford as its centre, arose, of which Thorpe Hall may be considered their prototype. William, 5th Earl of Bedford, during the Civil War ran with the hare and hunted with the hounds, but really sympathized with the parliamentary party. When the end of Richard Cromwell's protectorate was in sight he retired discreetly to his 20,000-acre fen property at Thorney, in Cambridgeshire. Here he added to an existing Elizabethan dwelling a small square block to serve as a temporary retreat of dignity and ease (79). A few months before the King was recalled, Bedford had engaged a mason contractor from Peterborough, John Lovin,[1] to do the work for him. In its very modest way, Thorney Abbey House belongs unmistakably to the Rubens category of house. Each of its three elevations has mullioned windows grouped round a central door. The stone roofs are hipped and flared. There is no platform, but one central chimney-stack in which all the flues of the block meet. The stack is rusticated, panelled and has a proper entablature like the stacks at Thorpe. The staircase is almost identical to the subsidiary one at Thorpe and has acorn and acanthus leaf finials. The wainscot in the dining-room is a simplified version of the wainscot in the same room at Thorpe, with the same features in returned and mitred architraves. Again at Thorney a complete garden layout has survived, within a five-sided walled area—a balustraded terrace; gate piers with pilaster strips and scrolls; a portal with splayed sides; a raised mount and a canal in the shape of a parallelogram. Whether Lord Bedford, who was a friend of Chief Justice St. John, or even Peter Mills, supplied John Lovin with the designs for the house and gardens is not known. At the neighbouring village of Whittlesey are a pair of gate piers (replicas of a pair at Thorney) that belonged to a house in Market Street now demolished. They, and the delightful little market hall with hipped roof resting on a cluster of piers and columns, may also be the work of John Lovin.

## 12   South Luffenham Hall, Rutland

South Luffenham Hall, just within Rutland, is a simplified version of Thorney Abbey House. It too is small, square in plan, with a roof of steep pitch and two chimney-stacks. On each of its three fronts is a central door. The wainscoting inside is not, however, as elaborate as it is at Thorney. The garden has a raised terrace by the road wall and stone gate piers.

## 13   Lyndon Hall, Rutland, 1668

Lyndon Hall, Rutland is a slightly more ambitious residence than the two previous houses. It is a square block (a wing was added in 1860) of seven bays to each face, two storeys and an attic. The central door to each face has a swan-necked pediment and above it an eared window with inverted scrolls at the sides. In the garden a series of Thorpe-style gate piers with pilaster panels and a portal with swan-necked pediment still stand. A mass of notes made by the builder of the house, Sir Abel Barker, 1st Baronet, and M.P. for Rutland, are preserved by the present owner, his descendant. Barker was a rich farmer who bought the Lyndon estate in 1661. "10

1 John Lovin was perhaps the builder of Peterborough Town Hall, 1671. It is more primitive than Thorney House and the rest of the Stamford-Peterborough group of houses, but has similar features.

Martii 6⅞ ", his notes begin in a neat hand, "A house may be built in this manner, on all sides alike . . .". Thereupon he gives particulars and exact measurements of windows, roof, chimneys and moulds of all sorts as they are to be executed for him by a certain John Sturges. This man first of all supplied a model, which Sir Abel altered in some respects. John Sutton of Stamford was engaged as rough mason. From the notes we learn that the house originally had a platform "with rails and balusters". An interesting fact recorded is that Sir Abel closely followed Gerbier's directions how to build a country house. He also took hints out of Palladio. Then he made a list of some articles which he "bought at London in May 70 for furnishing the house". About the same time Barker built a lesser house half a mile away called Top Hall,[1] which in scale and appearance resembles Thorney Abbey House and South Luffenham Hall. Top Hall is raised on a terrace and was designed to be entered through a gate forecourt with gate piers on each of its three sides. Two pairs of piers still remain.

## 14   Walcot Hall, Northamptonshire, 1674

That the Rubens type of house persisted well within the age of Wren there is proof in Walcot Hall, close to Stamford. Bridges informs us that Sir Hugh Cholmley built the house in 1674 soon after purchasing the property. Cholmley was an intimate friend and gossip of Pepys. "Sir H. Cholmley tells me great news", is the preface to frequent snippets of political confidences which were grist to the pages of Samuel's insatiable diary. "He is a man that I love mightily", he wrote. Walcot is a rectangular block of the same scale and style as Thorpe, but not so finished. The material used is dressed stone. The windows of the *piano nobile*, which is approached by steps, are pedimented and have pulvinated friezes. The south and principal front has a pediment. The roof platform at Walcot was removed soon after the house was built. No doubt the wooden balusters soon perished and, as they served no structural purpose, were not replaced. Beneath an overgrown Victorian pinetum an extensive and complete garden layout of the period may still be traced.

As yet little is known about the provincial surveyors and master masons responsible for the group of houses in the area between Stamford and Peterborough. But it was surely from Peter Mills's Thorpe Hall that local builders acquired a style whose origin can be traced through Balthazar Gerbier, Peter Paul Rubens, back to Galeazzo Alessi. In the course of travel and years the style originating in Genoa necessarily became very much blurred before it reached Stamford. There with a little vision it can nonetheless be recognized. In St. George's Square and St. Mary's Street of this Northamptonshire city are several extremely modest houses, in whose rectangular elevations, regularly spaced windows with mitred heads, projecting

[1] At Harringworth, Northamptonshire, is a house next to the church, almost a duplicate of Top Hall, Lyndon. It has a central stack of six chimneys set in a valley between two ridges of roof.

cornices, pitched roofs and rusticated chimney-stacks, the distant influence of the palaces of the Grimaldi and Pallavicini princes rather incongruously asserts itself.

*     *     *

If Nicholas Stone was primarily a sculptor, Balthazar Gerbier a miniaturist, and Peter Mills a bricklayer—all of whom eventually turned to designing houses—Roger Pratt, who belonged to a generation younger than theirs, having been born in 1620 when the reign of James I was practically over, was somewhat different. If the older men were versatile, they were only amateurs of architecture. Pratt, on the contrary, although a gentleman and heir to property and means, became a professional architect. This is a distinction which before the age of Wren he alone shares with Webb, with whom he may be ranked. His voluminous note-books,[1] which provide a quantity of material from which to assess his architectural learning, have been preserved. They and what survive of his buildings prove that Pratt succeeded in resolving out of several conflicting influences an eclectic style of domestic architecture, which is one of the high achievements of English art at all times.

Pratt's father was the younger son of a squirearchal family in Norfolk. Roger matriculated at Magdalen College, Oxford, in 1637. There he will have noticed the gateways in the Physic Garden and the portico at St. Mary's Church, which Stone had only recently completed. Two years later he entered the Inner Temple. In 1640 his father died and Roger succeeded to his fortune. By now the clouds of war were gathering and he soon found it convenient as well as prudent to leave England for the Continent. So he travelled extensively in France, Italy, Flanders and Holland. For a whole year from November 1644–5 John Evelyn was his "cohabitant and contemporary at Rome". Evelyn retained a high opinion of his friend's abilities, even though he was not always in agreement with his views. After the King's death, when for better or worse the future constitution of England seemed determined, Pratt returned from the Continent and settled at the Inner Temple. As a result of his travels it soon became apparent that the young man's overriding interests had shifted from the law to architecture.

Pratt's note-books do more than reiterate the familiar use of the five orders and advise the best site and materials for a new building. These unavoidable particulars are admittedly included in a practical form remarkably free from pedantry. But the note-books contain other matter not hitherto expounded in English architectural writings. They give most valuable hints to the layman how to appreciate architecture, how to judge the merits of buildings. He is exhorted to study dimension and proportion and the relation of parts of a building to the whole. He is told wherein the beauties of a building lie: the ordering of surfaces, the balance of ornaments, the effect of lines and shadows. "And in these considerations", Pratt writes, "we ought not only to heed that things are so, but we must also Examine why they are so,

---

[1] *The Architecture of Sir Roger Pratt*, R. T. Gunther, 1928.

for in the best work, we shall at last perceive that most things are placed there as well for strength as beauty. . . .'' Beauty, he is never tired of implying, is the ultimate purpose of all art, architecture included.

Pratt incidentally gives a synopsis of the manner in which great houses in the second half of the seventeenth century often came to be built. If you as an owner requiring a house are yourself incapable of designing one, then he advises ''get some ingenious gentleman who has seen much of that kind abroad and been somewhat versed in the best authors of architecture, viz: Palladio, Scamozzi, Serlio, etc. to do it for you, and to give you a design for it in paper, though but roughly drawn''. This practice is better than employing a ''home-bred architect'', by whom we imagine he means a person like Lovin of Peterborough, Jackson of Lambeth or the Grumbolds of Cambridge, untravelled masons and surveyors. Show the design to other experienced men, he commends, for their criticism. When they and you have modified it to your satisfaction, get the carpenter to have a scale model made. This will serve to protect your reputation in the eyes of posterity, as well as to guide the foreman and his workmen during the operations. Finally, when once you have laid a stone, never alter your design.

In the library of his old home at Ryston there still reposes a collection of architectural books and treatises which Pratt acquired on the Continent. They include the familiar works of Vitruvius, Alberti, Serlio, Cataneo, Le Muet and du Cerceau. There must have been other authors now missing. No man, Pratt asserts, can so much as claim the title of architect who has not studied the architecture of ancient Rome, modern Italy and France, for England has no architecture that deserves the name—with only two exceptions, namely, the Banqueting House and the portico of St. Paul's Cathedral. He pays high tribute to the palaces of Genoa, which he has visited, and constantly refers to Rubens's book on them. But it is his concentration on French building which makes Pratt's notes and architecture so interesting. He is repeatedly quoting French authorities like Fréart and citing buildings like the Louvre and Luxembourg palaces. Pratt becomes the first English architect consciously to derive much from French influences. Moreover, he wishes us to recognize this fact. He writes that the ''houses of France in the extent and cheerfulness of their courts; multiplicity and curiosity of their ornaments and carvings; neatness and variety of their roofs; and delicacy of their whole composure, outdo the Italian ones''. He qualifies this enthusiasm to some extent by continuing: ''but these [the Italian houses] in the greatness of their breadth; loftiness of their height; distinctness, regularity and judgment in all their ornaments and proportions; manliness of their strength, and majesty of their aspect, do by far surpass'' the French. For the fundamental architectural canons he of course looks to the original source of all renaissance building. He does not go as far as Henry Peacham, who considers the French the best architects in the world. Even so he prefers the layout of French to Italian gardens. After the Restoration and the return of Charles II's court, French influences were to become manifest throughout England, but when Pratt began building during the

Commonwealth this was not yet the case. Nowhere does he advocate a grounding in Flemish or Dutch styles as a prerequisite for the budding English architect.

It is the notable abandonment of all Flemish detail in his own work which marks the development of Pratt's architecture. The Genoese palace motif is still of course sensed in the structure of Pratt's houses, but not as transmitted through the Flemish mannerist medium of Rubens. In fact he severely criticized the redundancy of ornament on the façades of the palaces Rubens illustrated. A chaste classicism is the keynote of his structural and decorative designs. It is what allies Pratt to Webb and Jones and distinguishes him from Gerbier and Mills. A careful contrast of his Coleshill with Mills's Thorpe at once bears this out, in spite of several more than superficial resemblances between the two buildings. There are certain invariable characteristics of Pratt's houses. Their fronts are long and low; and composed of half basement, two floors, and attic storey with roof dormers. A balustered parapet—Pratt regarded it as a kind of diadem to the whole house—with cupola and tall, panelled chimneys complete the skyline. The façades are astylar. In this respect Pratt is strangely prejudiced, for he only admires Roman palaces like the Farnese where the orders are not introduced, and describes the Palazzo Cancelleria as ill-built and unworthy of notice on account of the pilasters. The *piano nobile* is given much emphasis and is approached by outside steps. The interior planning is Palladian axial, and strictly symmetrical, with the two principal apartments in the centre conjoined and of equal length.

15  *Coleshill House, Berkshire, 1650–62*

The year after his return to England Pratt began his first and probably best building. This was Coleshill House, for his cousin Sir George Pratt, 2nd Baronet (83). "Sir G. Pratt", wrote his great-grandson and eventual successor, Sir Mark Pleydell, "began a seat in the pres$^t$ Cucumber garden and raised it one storey, when Pratt and Jones arriving caus$^d$ it to be pulled down and rebuilt where it now stands. Pratt and Jones were frequently here and Jones was also consulted ab$^t$ the ceiling." Now Sir Mark, writing in the following century, procured this remarkably interesting story from a seventy-eight-year-old joiner on the estate, called John Buffin, who died in 1711. Buffin, speaking of the two architects, claimed that he "often saw them both" at Coleshill. There is no reason why he should not, for in 1650 he would have been a youth of nineteen or twenty years of age. Since Pratt had just come back from Italy, and considered Inigo Jones the only architect England had produced, it is extremely likely that he hastened to pay homage to the ageing surveyor. The young disciple would therefore almost surely have consulted him about the first commission he was just about to undertake. Moreover, the presence in Inigo Jones's sketchbook (at Chatsworth) of three designs entitled by Webb "S$^r$ George Pratt at Coleshill near Faringdon in Berkshire", and (at the R.I.B.A.) of a design for a chimneypiece (since somewhat altered) entitled "Sir George Pratt his great chamber", gives substance to the story. The fact, too, that the designs are in Webb's hand does nothing to discredit Jones being the author of them, for in the old architect's last years the other was often his amanuensis. Since Inigo was to die two years later he can only have been Pratt's inspirer and adviser during the initial stages of the building of Coleshill, which was not completed until 1662. The direct connection of the great man with Coleshill helps to explain why the style of the building was so essentially classical when other country houses, like Thorpe and Wisbech, begun at a later date, were yet to show Flemish influences.

At all events the summary change of site, from the cucumber garden to its present one on a decided eminence, accords with Pratt's recommendation that a country house should be placed on a slope in park or at least pasture land, one furlong from the highroad. Jones's or Pratts's plan for Coleshill was an unbroken parallelogram 124 ft. by 62 ft. (81). The house was to be four levels high, with platform and cupola, such as Jones had already designed for Lord Maltravers, Mills was to design at Thorpe, and Stanton years later at Belton. The tall and very prominent chimneys sprang from the sloping roof outside the platform. This was in accordance with Pratt's principle which, although followed at Kingston Lacy, was not observed by him either at Horseheath or Clarendon House, where the chimneys were set within the platform. "Chimneys should be ornamental as at Mr. Secretary Thurloe's house at Wisbech",

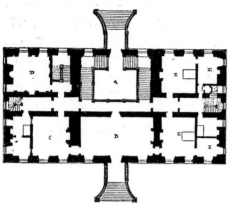

81. Plan of Coleshill

Pratt was to write in after years. Indeed his own at Coleshill are remarkably slender and decorative, and a glance at Le Muet's *Manière de bien bastir,* published in 1647, will divulge the origin of their beautifully carved sunk panels and entablatures. These stacks play a decisive part in the composition of Coleshill. With the central cupola they give the only vertical movement. And we notice how skilfully the architect contrived that, although the end chimneys should be made taller in order to enhance the dignity of the narrow north and south elevations, the tops of all of them remained level. Thus the horizontal harmony of Coleshill is nowhere disturbed, except by the crowning cupola where the punctuation is needed. From ground level to skyline a series of parallel lines in podium ledge, string-course, cornice, balustrade and chimney caps, emphasizes the astonishing geometrical perfection of the building. Seldom has such economy of line resulted in such majesty of form.

Because Pratt provided no orders, no pediment and no vertical wall breaks to relieve his two long fronts, the spacing of the windows necessarily had a determining part to play in the composition. He consequently gave relief to the severity of the

82    Broome Park, Kent, 1635–8. The most elaborate of the Dutch Skylines

83    Coleshill House, Berkshire: the perfection of English seventeenth-century classicism

*Architect: Sir Roger Pratt, 1650–62*

84    Coleshill House, Berkshire: Staircase Hall, 1660–2

*Architect: Sir Roger Pratt; Carver: Richard Cleare*

façades by putting wider spaces between the three centre windows than between the three at either end, an arrangement to which the dormers had to be adjusted. This manner of grouping is exactly opposed to the Venetian palace arrangement whereby the central windows are brought together. The Venetian arrangement, however, is what Pratt followed upon the side elevations, where he played as it were a contrapuntal melody within his architectural theme by setting each end window very close indeed to the angle. The heads and surrounds of the windows, as of the doors, are as purely classical in design as those at the Queen's House and the Banqueting House and show no inclination whatever towards the eccentricities of outline remarkable in the Stamford group of houses.

In his notes Pratt recommends what he calls ''a double building'' on an ''oblong square plan'' as most commodious, for the rather far-fetched reason that the occupants may move from one side of the house to the other as the weather dictates. All doors should be in line with one another and ''a clear vista through the very midde of the building where the principal entrances ought always to be placed''. He carried out these precepts at Coleshill, where the plan consists of two juxtaposed squares, on a central axis, the rooms on either side being symmetrically balanced. A house, Pratt goes on to say, must be ascended by steps for aesthetic as well as practical reasons, only a nobleman's house deserving a raised terrace. Since Sir George, his cousin, was merely a baronet, this noble appendage was omitted.

The hall into which the front door leads occupies two storeys and is dominated by the great double-flight staircase (84). Hitherto so much space had not been given to any staircase in an English house. The Coleshill one has not in the whole country got its fellow for magnificent simplicity. It was greatly admired and imitated by the Burlingtonian group of architects during the Inigo Jones revival. The crispness of the carving far surpasses that of the hall gallery at the Queen's House, and is rare before the coming of Grinling Gibbons. Pratt gives us the name of the joiner responsible for it. Richard Cleare [1] was at work upon the wainscot as late as 1662, when he presented his final account. He was an established London carver who later worked for Pratt at Clarendon House and for Wren at St. Olave's Church, Jewry. He carved the detail, like the festoons upon the stair strings, in London, sending them down by a man with a large basket. The classical door-cases in the hall and elsewhere were likewise carved by Cleare.

In his notes Pratt gives much practical advice upon plaster ceilings. If we are to believe Sir Mark Pleydell—and Buffin—Pratt was guided by Inigo Jones in his choice of pattern for one of those at Coleshill. And of course they all patently show the influence of those ceilings by Inigo at the Queen's House and the Banqueting House. By the time Pratt came to put them in place, however, Inigo Jones was dead. Other influences in the meantime came his way, such as Jean le Pautre's book of decorative designs, which were published in the year of Inigo's death. Le Pautre's ceilings

---

[1] He may have been a relation of William Cleer, the joiner of the panelling and screen behind the altar at Marlborough House chapel in Charles II's reign.

were notable for the extreme heaviness of their designs. Now the Coleshill ceilings, as is usual with English features under continental influence, are far less exaggerated than their prototypes, and the compartments between the ribs are comparatively free of ornament. Nevertheless the ribs themselves are deeper than those at Greenwich and Whitehall, and in the saloon have been given the same depth as the cornice whose dentils and moulds they exactly continue. Because of the lowness of the saloon the ceiling with cove, enriched with great swags suspended from cartouches, can be criticized as too heavy. On the other hand the ceiling of the hall, which is two storeys in height, is perfectly in scale.

"Exact and very uniform", was the verdict of Celia Fiennes upon Coleshill when she visited the house in the lifetime of its builder. Her words convey the secret of its composition. Coleshill is like a sonnet by Milton, wherein are compressed infinite subtleties of meaning. The pre-ordained framework may be circumscribed, and the traditional order exacting of strict obedience in the structure. Yet Roger Pratt in recognizing parallel obligations nevertheless introduced rich beauties and varieties of effect into the task he set himself at Coleshill and accomplished in its architecture one of England's greatest masterpieces.[1]

### 16   Kingston Lacy, Dorset, 1663–5

It is doubtful whether after Coleshill, Pratt ever excelled himself. At least it is impossible to judge from what remain of his other houses. Pratt was in every sense a perfectionist; he was able to devote his leisure to architecture without being dependent upon it for an income. Accordingly he took his time, built little, and that with the utmost thoroughness. Coleshill was finished in 1662, and in 1663 he began upon Kingston Lacy for Sir Ralph Bankes and finished it within two years. During the eighteenth century much of Pratt's work here was altered and in the nineteenth Sir Charles Barry, while reinstating what he believed to be many original features, obscured the rest with drastic innovations. Fortunately an original drawing, as well as Pratt's notes, show what the house looked like when first built (86).

Originally Kingston Lacy was of brick, with Portland and Chilmark stone dressings. It was the only one of Pratt's houses not faced with ashlar. As at Coleshill, the main fronts were nine windows in length, in groups of three, of which the middle was broken forward under a pediment containing a cartouche. The same horizontal effect was achieved by string-courses separating the *piano nobile* (likewise approached by steps) from the basement and first floor, a dentilled cornice and balustered platform, with cupola. Yet there was a difference to Coleshill in the proportions of Kingston Lacy. The latter house formed a block more nearly square than rectangular and the main elevation had less length, if the same height. With its break and pediment it was perhaps not so severe a composition as the other. But it was more conventional. It lacked the genius which the unusual window spacing, and the magic which the balanced chimneys convey to the design of Coleshill.

[1] Since these words were written Coleshill has been burnt and the shell disastrously levelled to the ground. This act of vandalism can never be too strongly censured.

17  *Horseheath, Cambridgeshire, 1663–5*

Over the same period Pratt was engaged upon a house for Lord Allington as far away as Cambridgeshire. Horseheath was demolished in 1777, but Colen Campbell gave a plate of it in *Vitruvius Britannicus*. So little did the name of Pratt convey half a century after his death that Campbell attributed the design to John Webb. But we have the authority of Evelyn, who wrote in his diary after a visit to Lord Allington: "His architect was Mr. Pratt." The house, he said, "is seated in a park, with a sweet prospect and stately avenue; but water still defective; the house has also its infirmities". Unfortunately Evelyn failed to specify what these were.

Campbell's plate reveals that Horseheath was rectangular in plan like Coleshill, but otherwise resembled Kingston Lacy in elevations. It was however larger, in that it had four windows on either side a central break under a pediment. The disposition of its four, instead of two, squat chimneys to each front was also the same, that is to say grouped within a platform around a cupola. The scale and cost of the house— Evelyn put it down as £20,000—were doubtless commensurate with Pratt's notions of what befitted a nobleman's estate and purse.

18  *Clarendon House, Piccadilly, London, 1664–6*

After the Restoration Pratt, as was to be expected of an architect with his experience and royalist sympathies, was kept busily engaged. The house he began in 1664 looking down St. James's Street, for the great Lord Clarendon was, like its owner, to enjoy an ephemeral splendour. It was deemed by connoisseurs one of the masterpieces of the time. Count Magalotti considered it one of the few buildings in London worth seeing, because it "was regularly disposed according to the rules of architecture", and this was more than could be said of most London houses built before the Great Fire in timber and plaster, with rickety gables and perilous overhangs. Its scale was altogether more grandiose than that of Coleshill, which after all was meant to be the home of a not very well-to-do baronet. Clarendon House was designed as a palace for the leading statesman of England, upon whom at the time the favour of a grateful sovereign and people shone uninterruptedly. Because Clarendon House stood a bare twenty years before it was pulled down, and the only visual records of it are indifferent prints, it is difficult for us to assess its architectural merits. Yet in judging it from these prints we find it hard to see in the pretentious and conventional front the nice serenity of Coleshill's astringent façade. On the other hand Pratt's detailed notes record the vast amount of thought and craftsmanship that went into its composition, and Evelyn's extravagant praises a certain surety of outstanding merits.

Clarendon House was, wrote Evelyn, "without hyperbolies, the best contriv'd, the most useful, graceful and magnificent house in England". Nothing, he went on, that he had seen abroad pleased him more. Nothing at home even approached it in excellence. He praised the judicious way "the walls were erected, the arches cut and turned, the timber braced, their scantlings and contignations disposed". And he confessed at first that he went to see it with prejudice and in a critical spirit. Years later Evelyn related in his diary how he drove past the house, which was being demolished, in the company of Clarendon's son, the second Earl, and how he turned away his head from the coach window lest he might have occasion to speak of it, "which must needs have grieved him". These delicate feelings did not prevent him from walking a few days later to view the ruins of his old friend's palace, "where I have often been so cheerful with him and sometimes so sad".

It was built not on a rectangular but an H plan and with the same number of storeys as at Coleshill. It had the same raised *piano nobile* over a basement. A balustered platform was brought forward over the projecting wings.

*      *      *

Pratt's architectural career was concentrated but short. He was in 1666 appointed, with Wren and May, a royal commissioner to supervise the rebuilding of the City after the Great Fire. Evelyn gives an interesting account of a meeting just before the Fire at which Wren and Pratt, amongst others, were present to discuss what was to be done with St. Paul's Cathedral, which had lain in a ruinous condition ever since the Civil War. He and Wren were in total disagreement with Pratt who, according to Evelyn, was for saving the body and steeple of the cathedral by patching them up. He implies that Pratt's conservatism opposed a rebuilding of the cathedral "with a noble cupola, a form of church building not as yet known in England, but of wonderful grace". However, "after much contest", Wren's and Evelyn's project "was at last assented to". It is somehow hard to suppose that Pratt was merely hostile to a new cathedral because it was to be in the classical style. He probably believed that Inigo Jones's re-edified cathedral and the portico which he greatly admired were not then in such hopeless plight that their total demolition was justified. Pratt's essay, "The New Way of Architecture for the outside of Churches", written several years later, shows, after all, a scientific interest in church building along classical lines, and a very thorough appreciation of modern churches in Rome and Paris, particularly the domes of St. Peter's, St. Andrea della Valle and the Sorbonne.

### 19  *Ryston Hall, Norfolk,* 1669

In 1668 Pratt was knighted for his architectural services, and married. The previous year he had inherited from a Pratt cousin the Ryston estate near Downham Market in Norfolk. The house he almost entirely rebuilt for himself. If ever a man had a proper sense of other people's and his own social standing it was Pratt. He made the new Ryston smaller in scale than Coleshill, but somewhat on the lines of Kingston Lacy, that is to say a block with a central break. He adopted his invariable scheme of a basement and *piano nobile* approached by outside steps. But he only

218

*"Country Life" photograph*

85    Wisbech    Castle,    Cambridgeshire.    (From    a    contemporary
painting in Wisbech Museum)

*"Country Life" photograph*

86    Kingston Lacy, Dorset. (From an original drawing in the house)
*Architect: Sir Roger Pratt, 1663–5*

87 Lodge Park, Sherborne, Gloucestershire, *c. 1650*.
(From a drawing inscribed in Lord Burlington's handwriting, R.I.B.A. library)

88 Aldermaston Court, Berkshire, 1636. Early regional classical
work. (From J. P. Neale's *Views of Seats,* 1828)

carried the first floor into the break, which he crowned with a semi-circular tympanum of a kind used by Le Muet, with a clock turret over it. On either side of his first-floor projection were attic floors. He took infinite trouble over details, and even the joiners and locksmiths he employed were London men. Today, little of Pratt's original house remains beyond the walls and one chimneypiece of white marble. But his own portrait by Lely showing him seated with a hand upon the bust of, perhaps, his wife, and his collection of architectural books are cherished by the Pratt descendant, who bears his christian name. He never built again, and until his death in 1684 devoted his life to agriculture and the welfare of his estate.

# CHAPTER EIGHT

# CAROLEAN CONCLUSION

IN assessing a whole age in terms of buildings we have to remember that great architecture is not necessarily representative of it. The changes of style which we have been tracing were by no means always consciously in the minds of the men who brought them about. On the contrary, only the outstanding artists, among them, truly knew what they were striving to achieve. The majority, the provincial surveyors or builders, merely followed what they believed to be the fashions of the moment. Not all clients, like Sir Justinian Isham or Lord Clarendon, intent upon raising themselves palaces, worried over the rules of the orders as laid down by the ancients; not all architects, like John Webb or Roger Pratt, bothered what Alberti or Serlio would have thought of the plats they devised for windows and door-cases. The majority of noblemen and squires, no matter how exalted their social status in the county, cared little for the arts and architecture. They cared a bit about their comfort and a good deal more about their dignity and prestige. So they engaged the best thought of builders in their district, and the builders in their turn, usually to the dictation of the clients, produced the most up-to-date plats with the help of whatever manuals and pattern-books were at hand. Fortunately, they could not easily go very wrong. The materials available, whether timber, brick or stone, were indigenous to the districts in which they moved. The tools and gear they used to fashion the materials were so unscientific that only skilled craftsmen could manipulate them. Consequently men's houses grew slowly out of the earth, like plants, and were variously pleasant. They never disfigured but always beautified a landscape. And the landscape of Stuart England was changing from the medieval wilderness of forest and moor into an ordered, cultivated garden. The enclosure system, which was the result of economic trends, determined the contours of England's face, which today we are deliberately and systematically disfiguring. The seventeenth century saw the rise of the small squire at the expense of the Crown. The vast tracts of crown property, formerly monastic property, were breaking up, and settling into lesser estates, which the gentry administered. Thenceforth each parish was to have its own squire. From north to south and west to east the well-to-do traveller to London, preceded by footmen axing a passage through the overgrown roads, would advance past cultivated farmlands and wooded parks abounding in red and fallow deer and fenced with wooden paling. He would see in the middle of every park the symbol of territorial government, in the country house, with the apostrophe as it were of manorial lordship close beside it, in the square or circular dovecote.

Large and small, the grey-roofed, pigeon-ridden country houses dominated the land. Ever since the Reformation the gentry had been creating new seats or improving old ones. Well into the reign of Charles I their notions of architecture remained for the most part traditional. That is to say they still practised what we call the Elizabethan or Jacobean style and only now and again a newer style, the Carolean, the development of which we have illustrated stage by stage in houses specially chosen because of the influences they distinctly reflect. But the majority of country houses in their simplicity combine so many influences—and few consciously—that we see them only as the ultimate expression of the age over which the distant figure of Inigo Jones was breathing a faint flavour of the new classicism.

Each region of England necessarily impressed its own stamp upon these modest squire's homes. In Berkshire, for example, West Woodhay Manor (1653) (90) and Aldermaston Court (1636) (88), before the first was altered and the second burnt during the nineteenth century, conformed to a regional type of Carolean squire's house. Both were of brick with stone dressings and had projecting wings, sloping roofs and massive chimney-stacks. Both were carefully symmetrical, yet, apart from a central Ionic porch in the one and two barley-sugar porches in the other, owed nothing to the five orders, Palladio or Rubens. Nevertheless both have recurrently been attributed to Inigo Jones on no grounds whatsoever.

In the west country is a group of houses which share certain semi-classical characteristics, thus suggesting that they emanated from the same builder or family of builders. The characteristics common to them all are a long unbroken front in stone, with no orders, two storeys of architraved windows and a balustered roof parapet. Of these buildings the first supposedly in date—for 1627 is a guess—is the south wing of Hinton St. George in Somerset. It was added about the time John Poulett was created a peer by Charles I as a suitable enhancement of his new dignity. It is of two storeys in Ham stone, nine windows long. Since the entrance is not in the middle of the elevation, probably two more bays were meant to extend westwards. Allan Cunningham, in his *Life of Inigo Jones,* attributed Hinton St. George to him without hesitation.

Ashton Court, outside Bristol, is now an enormous house of two long wings on either side of a Tudor gatehouse. The western wing was added in 1633 by Thomas Smyth, M.P. for Bridgewater. Smyth, an active royalist, was in this year one of those persons in the western counties appointed by the King to raise money for the repair of St. Paul's Cathedral. His wife was Florence, daughter of the 1st Lord Poulett of Hinton, and this relationship suggests the employment by Smyth of his father-in-law's builder. Although the great wing—it contains three rooms one of which, the gallery, is 93 ft. long—has since been stuccoed on the outside, the grouped windows remain unaltered. The lower windows have pediments alternately segmental and pointed, the upper entablatures without pediments. Between the first floor and the roof parapet are small port-hole windows to an attic floor. Collinson, the Somerset historian, assumed that the Ashton Court wing was designed by Jones.

In some estate settlements for Sherborne Park, in Gloucestershire, references are made under the years 1651 and 1652, to a "new park, lodge and paddock". They are taken to mean that what is now called Lodge Park on the Sherborne property had just been built for John Dutton, M.P. for Gloucester county. The A.P.S. dictionary suggests that Edward or Francis Carter was its architect. Francis Carter was dead by 1650, but Edward had three more years to run. Since he was then Cromwell's surveyor, it is unlikely, to say the least, that he would have found time or been willing to build a house for a Gloucestershire squire who had strained every nerve to repulse his master's troops from Oxford city. Amongst the Inigo Jones drawings is one of Lodge Park inscribed "The Lodge at Sherbourne", but the handwriting is Lord Burlington's (87). This enchanting little building has affinity to Ashton and Hinton in an unbroken façade of two storeys, the lower partly obscured by a projecting portico of three bays. Lastly, in the south wing of Brympton d'Evercy, near Yeovil (89), we have a fourth building, although reputedly dating as late as the sixteen-seventies, belonging to the Hinton group. And indeed the owner of Brympton in the sixteen-seventies, Sir John Sydenham, was like Smyth of Ashton, married to a Poulett wife. The comparatively late date of Brympton is in some measure confirmed by the improved quality of the stone carving to that of the other three houses. Here are two storeys again, but each ten bays wide. The windows are pedimented, segmentally and pointedly. Again the orders are missing on this long front. No name of an architect has yet been suggested for Brympton, and Cunningham's Inigo Jones guess is of course as ill-founded here as at Hinton.

Somewhere, therefore, in the west country lived a dynastic family of builders, busily producing houses, or new wings of houses, for royalist gentry to the formula we have been describing. In the course of fifty years or so there was little develop- ment of the formula, as we have seen in glancing firstly at the wing of Hinton and lastly at the wing of Brympton d'Evercy. In other words style changed imperceptibly in country districts far from London, and the very nature of hereditary builders, like all sure craftsmen, was conservative. The sort of building family we have in mind— and no claim is made for their connection with the Hinton group of houses—were the Somerset Arnolds established near Ilminster, only a few miles from Hinton. They first appeared working for Mrs. Wadham, upon her new Jacobean college at Oxford, between 1610 and 1613, in the persons of John and William Arnold. John, it seems, acted as her steward in control of the business and William, a master mason, as designer of plats and uprights. He was also paid £1 a week for superintending the builders, as well as additional monies by way of piece-work, for carving. From the accounts at Wadham we learn that two of three other men working under William were also Arnolds, Edmond and Thomas, but their relationship to the steward and master mason is not explained. The accounts furthermore disclose that no working

1 Another dynastic family was the Strongs, *vide* pp. 145 and 151.

drawings were used. The designer roughed out a plat and upright for which he was paid little. On their approval by the client the designer explained to the workmen on the spot by word of mouth more or less what he wanted done. Is it therefore surprising that style was an instinctive rather than deliberate impulse among country builders, like the Arnolds? Yet William Arnold was a professional man of some standing, and presumably education, who could command high fees. He was described in Mrs. Wadham's will as "gentleman", and, when engaged by George Luttrell in 1617 to remodel the centre front of Dunster Castle, as of "great experience in architecture". By now he had acquired a small estate for himself at Charlton Musgrove on the eastern confines of Somerset. A later member of the family was engaged first by Inigo Jones and then by Wren as carver at St. Paul's Cathedral. The Arnolds were probably typical of provincial families engaged in the building crafts. Some of them rose to more than local eminence, but did not fail to return from time to time to their homes and families, to whom they discreetly imparted second-hand architectural notions gleaned in Oxford, Cambridge or London.

Up and down the provinces the lesser Carolean houses retained traditional decencies under a thin guise of classical bravado. At Stanway, in Gloucestershire, we are confronted with perhaps the most beautiful example of an English country house, in which traditional forms are merged in the classical. No photographs can do justice to the group of church, gatehouse and hall, peering ruefully over a high wall with *œil-de-bœuf* openings most tantalizingly set above eye level, because the harmonizing factor is the golden Cotswold limestone, of which all the seemingly unrelated units are composed (92). This group of buildings of different dates and divergent styles appears to have grown together out of the hill, at the foot of which for hundreds of years they have nestled unaltered, undisturbed. Stanway is the very meaning of tradition, which makes styles of building into mere pedantic symbols of speech and exalts the picturesque to the supreme quality in architecture. The master mason who contrived the shell-crested gatehouse may not have been a student of the antique, like Inigo Jones (to whom of course it has been accredited), or Pratt, since he knew next to nothing of pure forms. But in his masterly reconciliation of a Gothic arch, Jacobean curvilinear gable and semi-classical porch he was a craftsman, whose innate sense of line and curve saved him from follies and enabled him to produce a poem of movement and rhythm.

\*       \*       \*

How were these country houses furnished in the times of James I, Charles I and Cromwell? Unfortunately the conversation-piece painting, which graphically discloses the interiors of gentlemen's houses a hundred years later, was not yet fashionable. As usual it is easier to form a picture of the rooms of a great than a small house because more contents and more inventories have been handed down in rich families than in poor. Indeed, an untouched specimen of the yeoman's or even merchant's house, complete with contents, of early Stuart times is a great rarity, almost a thing unknown.[1] On the other hand the inventories taken at Standon Lordship, for the Sadleir family in 1623, and at Tart Hall for Lady Arundel in 1641, give full and detailed accounts of the contents of two houses of the grand sort in Jacobean and Carolean times.

In the first place furnishings were, according to our standards, exceedingly sparse. Much emphasis however was laid upon stuffs and hangings of all sorts and their quality was often exactly described. They were valued as much for warmth, particularly for covering large draughty windows in winter evenings, as for decoration of bare walls. Not every room would be wainscoted or hung with arras, Mortlake or common verdure tapestries. In Lord William Howard's accounts at Naworth Castle allowance is made "for one suit of landscape hangings, containing 148 ells, at 6s. an ell". Since an ell was about forty-five inches, Lord William had ordered a large consignment of printed cloth to cover the walls of several rooms. Sir Henry Slingsby in 1640 describes the leather hangings he has just provided for the lodging chamber of his Yorkshire house: "calf skins silver'd, and wrought upon with a large flower in blue worsted; they came short of the ground, having the breadth of a panel of wainscot below them and a frieze and cornice above them. The chimneypiece" he adds, "is painted answerable in blue and silver". Worsted was a fine wool textile woven in Norfolk. Window curtains for the principal rooms would be of taffeta or silk, and for lesser rooms of woollen damask from Tournai.

Floor carpets were comparatively rare. The hall was usually paved in the familiar pattern of large square flagstones and, set diagonally at their corners, smaller squares of touch.[2] The floors of other rooms were boarded. Only rarely was a Persian carpet allowed to be walked upon and mention is made of "a foot carpet" for such a purpose. Rush mats were the usual substitute, and Gerbier, who was furnishing New Hall and York House for the Duke of Buckingham, in 1625, wrote to him as follows: "Madame has not given orders about the furniture of Persian cloth of gold nor for matting the other apartments; that should be done in time, for new mats for a month or two have an ill smell. Half of our Dutch mats have come." [3]

Great attention was naturally paid by the rich to beds. The days were not remarkable for comfort even in great houses, so there was all the more reason for the nights to be made as luxurious as possible. The Standon Lordship inventory gives particulars of every sort of bed. There are double beds with testers, livery bedsteads, half-tester beds, field beds, boarded beds, trundle beds. The tester beds, still of oak, were draped with curtains and valances of velvets, silks or satins in blue, yellow, green or crimson, or simply of crewel work. Sometimes they were made of cloth

[1] Townend, Troutbeck, Westmorland, c. 1626, was built and lived in by the Browne family until 1944. It is a near approach to a continuous yeoman home with contents—all of dark oak.

[2] "paved with diamond pavier made of freestone, as the halls of some of our great gentlemen in England are (amongst the rest that of my honourable and thrice worthy Maecenas Sir Edward Phelips, in his magnificent house of Montacute, in the county of Somerset, within a mile of Odcombe, my sweet native soil", T. Coryat, Crudities, 1611.

[3] The master mat-layer was an important officer under the royal surveyor.

of gold and silver, like those famous hangings at Knole, or satin "sprigged" with leaf, flower and insect. One tester was even made of bear skin, with finials of plumes, a decoration we associate with beds later in the century. The bedding was usually ordinary straw or plaited rush; sometimes a mattress was provided, filled with feathers. There would be a bolster and pillows. The Tart Hall inventory gives a description of Lady Arundel's younger son's bedroom which was probably typical of any noble youth's at the end of Charles I's reign. There was the bedstead standing on a yellow leather mat, on which to put bare feet on a frosty morning. The bed had a feather mattress, bolster, great pillow and little pillow: a pair of coarse blankets and a pair of fine woollen blankets. There is no mention of sheets. Over the blankets was laid a crimson quilt of Indian silk lined with yellow sarcenet. There were curtains hanging from the tester, and a double valance. The head of the bed was covered with yellow taffeta to match the pillows. Under the bed was kept a little wooden trundle bed with a flock quilt, presumably for the young man's page, who would sleep on it either outside the door or, if he was a favourite, in his master's bedroom. There was little additional furniture. In the room were one Indian armchair and three single chairs of oak, an oval table with a drawer, some religious paintings, and a pewter chamber-pot. The indispensable tongs and shovel were kept in the fireplace. Next door was a little closet in which stood an oak press of three shelves, covered with a Turkey carpet, and an oak livery cupboard for clothes.

The next most important items of furniture for comfort were the stool and chair. The stool was still the more common of the two. In the early half of Charles I's reign it was usually bare. The joint stool—often erroneously called today the coffin stool—was of oak, occasionally relieved with a squab or cushion. At a dinner party at Wilton given after the Restoration in honour of the future Grand Duke Cosimo III of Tuscany, only one armchair was provided for the distinguished guest. The prince was somewhat shocked by the paucity of the furniture after the customary luxury of Florence and felt constrained to offer it to the sister of his host, Lord Pembroke. She accepted it with alacrity and another had to be fetched for the prince. But at a farewell dinner party given him by Charles II at Whitehall, Cosimo offered the only armchair to the King, who declined it and sat like the rest of the company on a stool. Chairs with arms were therefore seldom used for meals, and probably a house of decent size would not for any purpose have more than two or three; these with straight carved backs and wooden seats would be reserved for the lord and lady, their aged relations or infirm guests. In the Standon Lordship inventory only two chairs were upholstered, and they belonged to the "King's Chamber". In Cromwellian times the chair with leather back and seat, held to the frame with stout brass nails, made its appearance.

Tables with turned or bulbous legs, and stretchers to rest the human feet off the cold and draughty floor had developed little in shape or refinement since Elizabeth's reign, and are rarely found of superior material and craftsmanship. Over them the Persian or Turkey carpet was habitually draped. Sometimes calf-skin cloths were used instead, and at Tart Hall most of the tables in the house seemed to have "a cover of red leather bordered with blue gilt leather". Woods like fruit and yew were chosen for tables of smaller size, with hinged tops and gates. At Hatfield there is a small square table on bulbous legs of King James's time, which is wholly covered in scale work of mother-of-pearl, but it is an unusual specimen. Court cupboards, buffets and chests of this period are only too familiar, and their designs were the legacy of a century. Their traditional shapes were almost invariable and the richer kind had rather more inlay of mahogany, ebony, mother-of-pearl or bone in the panels. Bone became a much favoured inlay and at Tart Hall two little birdcages— "and therein two canary birds"—were adorned with bone. But what we call marquetry furniture was scarcely known in England before the Restoration and only became fashionable with the Dutch influence of Daniel Marot at the end of the century. At Snowshill Manor, near Broadway, there is a large writing-table of oak inlaid with sycamore and other woods stained so as to look almost like seaweed marquetry. In a central oval is inlaid a crucifixion scene with the words "Remember Thy End". The piece is dated 1622.

We may well ask whether Inigo Jones, who certainly saw and observed the more refined furniture of Italy and France, was satisfied with the cumbersome pieces manufactured in the reigns of the first James and Charles, and whether he designed pieces better suited to the renaissance architecture he introduced to England. "Where within the [dwellings?] used by the ancients the varied and composed ornaments both of the house itself and the movables within it are most commendable." This phrase, like most of Jones's notes, is expressed oddly but means that he recognized the necessity for furniture, like decoration, to conform to the architecture of a room. That he did upon occasion design furniture is implicit in his responsibility as King's Surveyor for furnishing the royal palaces. John Chamberlain, in a letter to Dudley Carleton in 1616, practically says as much. He refers to an impending progress by James I to Edinburgh from London: "from hence many things are sent, but specially a pair of organs that cost above £400 besides all manner of furniture for a chapel (which Inigo Jones tells me he hath the charge of) with pictures of the apostles . . .". Moreover, one undated design by Inigo for a piece of furniture has survived [1] (91). It is a cabinet, in unspecified material, architecturally treated. It has a broken pediment in which a sunk cartouche contains a bust. There are cartouches on the panels below and niches and masks. The design is rather fussy and unattractive. Surprisingly enough it reveals not so much Italian as Flemish influence. But since no other drawing of his for furniture exists we can hardly judge him by this single specimen.

At the beginning of the century the nobility affected much silver plate. They habitually ate off silver dishes and drank out of silver goblets, whereas the lesser gentry and merchantmen used pewter. By 1642 vast quantities of the cavalier silver

[1] In the Gibbs Collection, Radcliffe Camera, Oxford. See W. Grant Keith, *Burlington Magazine*, Vol. XXII, 1912.

89  Brympton D'Evercy, Somerset: provincial classical façade, 1670–80

90 West Woodhay House, Berkshire, 1635: provincial classical doorway. (Within recent years it has been brought forward to form a portico)

91 Design by Inigo Jones for a Cabinet

92 Stanway House, Gloucestershire: the Gatehouse, an example of Cotswold compromise between Gothic and classical

loyally disappeared into the melting furnaces for the King's benefit; whereupon Venetian glass was imported in some quantity, at least for drinking purposes. The silver of the first Stuart reign largely followed realistic and architectural formulas that came from Germany and the Low Countries. Wine cups were made in the form of sliced pineapples, sweetmeat dishes were pierced with strapwork, and standing cups and salts built up in tiers of scrollwork crowned with a "pyramid" or steeple. Gradually these patterns gave place to simpler shapes and decoration; and gilding was left off. Until the Civil War sent them back to the Continent, the leading silversmiths in England were still foreigners. The result of their disappearance was an improved skill on the part of native silversmiths. English work, plain and austere under the Commonwealth on account of the economic and moral stringencies, again developed into vigorous floral patterns in the post-Restoration era, when wealth and gaiety returned to the nation.

In the average country household books played a surprisingly small part, and a well-stocked library was as unusual as a collection of gramophone disks is today. In other words a library was not a general necessity so much as a specialist's indulgence. At Standon Lordship the only books were the Bible and four old chronicle books, kept in the dining-room. Henry Peacham actually gave a list of the English books which he considered the minimum a gentleman need keep. It was confined to Thomas More's *Life of Richard III*, Philip Sidney's *Arcadia*, Francis Bacon's *Essays*, Richard Hooker's *Politie* and John Hayward's *Life of Henry IV*. Peacham's curious choice was not meant to be exclusive, but he implied that a gentleman's reading in his native tongue could perfectly well stop short there. The classics were of course another matter, and Sir Symonds D'Ewes tells us in his autobiography that for a youth of eighteen Macrobius's *Saturnals* and Gellius's *Attic Nights* made stimulating reading. An astonishing thing about the educated classes of these times is their apparent incapacity for being bored. Unless a national crisis intervened, an English country gentleman's preoccupations, other than sport, were the recurrent deaths of his own and his relations' children at or soon after birth, the genealogies of his own and his wife's families, law-suits with his neighbours, the plagues in London and a hearty dread (assuming that he was a Protestant) of the Catholic religion. Around these interests his domestic and social life revolved.

As for the arts, country gentlemen paid them little if any attention. Painters were creatures exotic and classless whose art men of birth would rarely condescend to practise. Usually they were foreigners and papists and so politically and socially suspect. Country gentlemen recognized that the King and nobility consorted with these fellows, but when the King's surveyor was ordered to construct a new pair of stairs outside Vandyke's lodgings at Blackfriars, specially to enable Charles and Henrietta to land there from their barge, they were shocked. Nevertheless courtiers, because of their secure rank, could afford, if they had the talent, to dabble in painting and music. They were merely following the whim of their royal master, who took drawing lessons from Rubens and Vandyke, and music lessons from John Cooper.

Peacham went so far as to allow that it was fitter for a gentleman to be an executant in music than in painting, if he had to be serious about either. He compared the status of an artist to that of an inn-keeper. Yet Peacham, being a man of culture—he had once been a schoolmaster—was proud when his countrymen (gentlemen excepted of course) excelled in these pursuits. There was that embarrassing example (because he came of a distinguished East Anglian family), in Sir Nathaniel Bacon, whose proficiency at portraiture was undeniable. Peacham deemed him equal to the greatest masters of painting. William Dobson (fortunately of humbler origin), was another native painter of a younger generation. Among musicians there were William Byrd, "Our phoenix", Peacham described him in those ineffably poetic phrases of the age, "preferred above all not so much for light madrigals as motets and music of piety and devotion"; Peter Philips, organist at Brussels to the Archduke Albert, and composer likewise of madrigals and motets; and John Dowland, immortal lutanist whose *Lachrymae* were dedicated to Queen Anne.

There are exceptions to be taken to every generalization. A Norfolk baronet, Sir William Paston, was intensely interested in the arts.[1] Sir William, although a prominent figure in his county, did not move in court circles. He preferred to consider himself a countryman. At Oxnead, his home near Aylsham, he assembled works of art of various kinds: porcelain, silver plate, crystal, agate and semi-precious stones. Sculpture, antique and contemporary, and landscape paintings he collected in large quantity. He was a patron of Nicholas Stone, whom he commissioned to decorate his house with chimneypieces and his garden with fountains, statues and terminal figures.[2] Raphael's *Holy Family*—eventually bought by the Empress Catherine of Russia at the famous Houghton Hall sale—was originally in his possession.

Probably few other country squires living before the Restoration collected on the same scale as Sir William Paston. Yet he was a lesser collector compared with the Duke of Buckingham and Lord Arundel. They in their turn were tyros in the field when we recall the achievements of Charles I. His collections of paintings, statuary, tapestries, cameos, coins and objects of nearly every branch of virtù have never since been excelled in quantity or quality by a single individual. They had an immense influence upon contemporary artists and visiting foreigners. For the King's judgment of works of art was as discriminating as his taste. His ambassadors and agents acquired for him masterpieces all over Europe. Kenelm Digby brought him sculptural fragments from Apollo's temple at Delos. Daniel Nys purchased for him for £18,000 the whole of the Duke of Mantua's collection, including Titians, Corregios, Raphaels

[1] See a privately printed essay on Sir William Paston, by R. W. Ketton-Cremer, 1951.
[2] Stone did one of his best busts in Lady Katherine Paston, 1636, in Oxnead church, and perhaps composed the touching lines in almost Shakespearean verse, which begin, punningly:

> Needs she another monument of Stone
> Who had so many better than this one
> All which were noble hearts whom her decease
> Transmuted into marble Niobes . . .

and Andrea del Sartos. Mantegna's *Triumphs* were included. Through Rubens he bought the Raphael cartoons. The Spanish King preferred to give him two Titians, when he was in Madrid, to his own daughter, whom he vowed he would sooner throw into a well headlong. The French King exchanged with him a Leonardo for a Holbein. The Pope tried to bribe him with the pictures he most coveted.

Charles furthermore patronized the greatest living artists. He was sculptured by Bernini [1] and Fanelli and le Sueur. He was painted by Rubens and Dobson and Vandyke. The last was accounted by his English contemporaries one of the greatest masters of all times and by Charles I a second Titian. The poet, Robert Herrick, in verse addressed to his artist nephew, exhorted him:

> On, as thou hast begun, brave youth, and get
> The palm from Urbin, Titian, Tintoret;

and then, after bidding him outdo Brueghel, Holbein and Rubens, apostrophized him thus:

> So draw, and paint, as none may do the like,
> No, not the glory of the world, Vandyke.

Through the medium of the "glory of the world" Charles I raised the cavalier ideal to such heights that posterity has never succeeded in taking a clear view of it through the clouds of romance in which it is still shrouded.

---

[1] There is at Arundel Castle a bust of Charles I by François Dusart, signed and dated 1636. Vertue believed it to be a copy of the lost Bernini—or to be done from Vandyke's triple portrait—for Lord Arundel.

# INDEX

The numbers in **Heavy Type** denote the *Figure Numbers* of the illustrations

Ackers, Harry, stone carver, 151
Adam, Robert, architect, 70 (note), 185
Alberti, L. B., architect and scholar, 160, 210, 222
Albury Park, Surrey, 36
Aldenham House, Hertfordshire, 200 (note)
Aldermaston Court, Berkshire, 132, 223; **88**
Aldersgate, City of London, 202
Alessi, Galeazzo, Genoese architect, 199, 208
Alresford, 130
Amelia, Princess, 179
Amesbury Abbey, Wiltshire: account of, 179–80; **57**
Ammanati, Bartolomeo, architect, 69
Ampthill, 106 (and note), 109, 157 (note)
Amsterdam, 112, 137, 146
Anet, Château d', 59
Angarano, Count Giacomo, House for, 186
Annandale, Earl of (*see* Murray, John)
Anne, Piazza d', Leghorn, 84 (note)
Anne of Denmark, Queen Consort of England, 22, 25, 26, 29, 42, 65, 66, 69, 232; her hearse, 73
*Antichità di Roma, L'*, 33 (note)
Antoninus and Faustina, Temple of, Rome, 54
Antwerp, 71, 79 (note), 195, 199, 200
*Arcadia*, Philip Sidney's, 103
Arch Row, Lincoln's Inn Fields, 130, 131
*Arches of Triumph . . . for James I*, 43
*Architectura*, by Serlio, 65, 90, 106, 144
*Architectural History of Cambridge*, 158 (and note)
*Architecture of Sir Roger Pratt*, 114 (note), 209
Arnold, Edmond, builder, 224
Arnold, John, steward, 224
Arnold, Thomas, builder, 224
Arnold, William, master mason, 224–5
Arundel Castle, Sussex, 233 (note)
Arundel, Earl of (*see* Howard, Thomas)
Arundel, Earl of, house for, at Greenwich, 64
Arundel House, Strand, 64, 75
Arundel, Mr. Francis, 125
Ashburnham House, Westminster, 95; account of, 128–30; **43**
Ashburnham, William, royalist, 128, 129

Ashdown House, Berkshire, 186, 206
Ashton Court, Somerset, 223–4
*Athenae Oxonienses*, 43 (note)
Aubrey, John, antiquary, 83, 99, 101, 109, 164
Audley End, Essex, 60
Augustus, Caesar, 34, 54, 55, 114
Avon, River, Wiltshire, 179
Aylsham, 232
Aytoun, William, master mason, 25

Bacon, Francis, 1st Viscount St. Albans, 30, 231
Bacon, Sir Nathaniel, painter, 232
Badeslade, T., architectural draughtsman, 186
Baker, John, blacksmith, 111
Baker, Richard, 19
Baldwin, Samuel, monumental sculptor, 136
Baldwin, Thomas, Comptroller of Works, 30–1, 74, 110, 135, 148
Balls Park, Hertford, 206; **77**; account of, 200
Banco di Napoli, Palazzo del, Genoa, 202 (note)
Bandinelli, Baccio, painter, 39
Bankes, Sir Ralph, 216
Banqueting House, Whitehall, 32, 49, 69 (note), 70, 72, 99 (and note), 101, 104, 109, 112, 135, 136, 137, 147, 164, 168, 169, 192, 195, 210, 215, 216; **1**; account of, 73–9
Barbarano, Palazzo, Vincenza, 74
Barber Surgeons' Company 94
Barber Surgeons' Hall, 94–5, 129, 164
Barberini, Cardinal, 36
Barberini, Matteo, Pope Urban VIII, 33 (note)
Barker, Sir Abel, 1st Baronet, 207–8
Barrington, 145
Barry, Sir Charles, architect, 76, 216
Basilica of Constantine, Rome, 33
Basilicana, Vicenza, 82 (note)
Basill, Edward, clerk of works, 65
Basill, Simon, jun., 136
Basill, Simon, sen., surveyor-general, 32, 35, 63
Basing House, Hampshire, 51, 96
Basingstoke, 177
Beaufort House, Chelsea, 79, 80
Becket Park, Berkshire, 120–1; **32**
Bedford, Francis, 4th Earl of, 85
Bedford, William, 5th Earl and 1st Duke of, 202, 206–7

Beds and bedrooms, 226–7
Bell, C .F. (with Percy Simpson), *Designs by Inigo Jones for Masques*, 26 (note), 39
Bell, Henry, architect, 131
Belton House, Linconshire, 212
Belvoir Castle, Rutland, 21 (and note), 22; **58**; account of, 177 (and note)
Bemerton, 20
Benci, Ginevra, 36
Benier, Isaac, sculptor, 175
Benier, Pierre, sculptor, 175 (and note), 176
Berkeley Square, London, staircase at No. 44: 129
Berkhamsted Church, 136
Bernini, G. L., architect, 42 (note), 53, 138, 233 (and note)
Berwick-on-Tweed, 154; **55**
Beverley, Yorkshire, 95, 161
Bigland, Ralph, Gloucestershire historian, 201
Bishopsgate, City of London, 148
Black Books of Lincoln's Inn, 109–10
Blackfriars, London, 84, 168, 231
Blenheim Palace, Oxfordshire, 31 (note)
Blickling Hall, Norfolk, 106, 111, 113
Blomfield, Sir Reginald, architectural historian, 178
Bloom (*or* Blum) Hans—*Description of the Five Orders*, 200
Bodleian Library, Oxford, 152 (note), 199 (note)
Bologna, Giovanni da, sculptor, 20, 84 (note), 141
Bolsover Castle, Derbyshire, 56, 127 (note), 192
Bolton, Arthur, architectural historian, 148
Bolton, Edmund, scholar, 28 (and note)
Bookham, 194
Books and libraries, 231
Borghese, Camillo, Pope Paul V, 27
Borromini, Francesco, architect, 53, 128 (note)
Børsen, The, Copenhagen, 22 (and note), 25
Boston Manor, Brentford, 119; account of, 115
Botanic Garden, Oxford, 144
Bramante, D. L., architect, 33, 83, 167
Brasenose College, Oxford, 154; **53**; account of, 153

Brenta, River, 35, 54
Brentford, 115
Brice, Ralph, King's master carpenter, 74 (note)
Bridges, John, county historian, 115, 116 (and note), 122, 125, 208
*Brief Discourse concerning . . . Magnificent Buildings,* 196
*Britannia Triumphans,* masque, 40
British Museum, 44 (note), 110 (note), 164
Broadway, Worcestershire, 228
Brooke, Christopher, poet and lawyer, 109–11
Broome Park, Kent, **82**; account of, 193–4
Broomfield, Edward, carpenter, 152 (and note)
Browne, Adam, joiner, 110 (and note), 152 (and note)
Browne family of Townend, 226 (note)
Browne, Henry, squire, 104
Browne, John, joiner, 110 (note)
Bruce family, 106
Brunelleschi, F., architect, 61
Brympton d'Evercy, Somerset, 224; **89**
Buckingham, Duke of (*see* Villiers, George)
Buffin, John, joiner, 211, 215
Bunyan, John, 105
Buonarotti, M.A., opera composer, 29
Burbage, James, actor, 41
Burford, 145, 151, 153; **50**
Burford Priory chapel, **50**; account of, 153–4
Burlington House, Piccadilly, 162
Burlington, Richard Boyle, 3rd Earl of, 39, 50, 80, 85, 94, 105, 116, 128, 164, 168 (and note), 170, 177, 224
Burman, Thomas, sculptor, 141
Bushell, Thomas, engineer, 100
Bushnell, John, sculptor, 141
Butleigh Church, 163
Butleigh Court, Somerset, 163 (and note)
Byrd, William, composer, 232

Cabinet, Jones's design for, 228; **91**
Caelus, sun god, 61, 160
Callot, Jacques, artist, 40, 60
Cambiaso, Palazzo di, Genoa, 202 (note)
Cambridge (University), 31, 131, 153, 154–8, 210, 225
Campbell, Colen, architect and historian, 85, 89 (and note), 100 (and note), 102, 115, 116, 119, 120, 122, 130, 131, 143, 168 (and note), 170, 179 (and note), 184, 189, 190, 217
Campion, Thomas, dramatist, 32; **3**
Cancelleria, Palazzo, Rome, 211
Caprarola, Palace of, 170
Caravaggio, painter, 39
Carfax, Oxford, 110
Carisbrooke Castle, Isle of Wight, 169
Carleton, Sir Dudley, 1st Viscount Dorchester, diplomatist, 32, 35, 66, 72, 80, 83, 228

Carlisle, Henry, 4th Earl of, 115 (note)
Carnarvon, Anna Sophia, Countess of, 101
Carpets, 226
Carr (*or* Ker), Robert, 1st Earl of Somerset, 27
Carter, Edward, surveyor-general, 31, 91 (and note), 94, 96, 154, 224
Carter, Francis, carpenter, 30–1, 74, 224
Carter, Henry, 175 (note)
Carter, Thomas, joiner, 126–7, 148
Cary, George, gilder and painter, 70 (and note)
Castle Ashby, Northamptonshire, 115–19; **30**
Castlecoole, N. Ireland, 122
Cataneo, Pietro—*L'Architettura di,* 210
Cecil family, 95
Cecil, Robert, 1st Earl of Salisbury, 29 (note), 99
Cecil, William, 2nd Earl of Salisbury, 131
Cento, 39
Cesari, Giuseppe, painter, 103
Chairs and stools, 227
Chaloner, Sir Thomas, the younger, Prince Henry's Governor, 29 (note)
Chamberlain, John, letter-writer, 66, 69, 72, 73, 80, 83, 90, 93, 228
Chambers, Sir William, architect, 89
Chambord, Château de, 34
Chancery Lane, City of London, 109
Chapman, George, poet, 32, 89–90, 109; monument to, 89–90
Charing Cross, London, 141, 142, 178
Charlecote Church, Warwickshire, 141
Charles I, Prince of Wales and King, 29, 31, 35 (and note) 36, 46, 52, 59, 60, 65, 66, 75, 76 (note), 79, 81, 83, 84, 86, 93, 95, 96, 99, 121, 125, 141, 142, 144 (note), 161–2, 169, 175, 186, 223, 231, 232, 233 (and note)
Charles II block, Greenwich, 170, 177, 183–5, 190, **46**
Charles II, King, 75, 96, 113, 141, 144 (note), 161 168, 169, 175, 180, 227
Charleton Musgrove, 225
Charleton, Walter, physician, 61, 161
Charlton House, Greenwich, 120; **33**
Chatsworth House library, Derbyshire, 26, 33, 36, 50, 54 (note), 74, 111, 142, 144, 164, 211; garden at, 100
Chelsea, 79, 80; Church, 141
Chesterton Windmill, church and mill house, Warwickshire, 125; **34**
Chevening, Kent, 119–20, 177 (note); **66**
Chiswick House, 50 (and note), 179; gateway, 79–80; **17**
Cholmley, Sir Hugh, 208
Christ Church Hall, Oxford, masque in, 27, 43; east gate at, 128

Christ Church, Newgate, 167
Christianus IV, King of Denmark, 21, 22, 25
Christmas, John, monumental sculptor, 71
Christmas, Mathias, monumental sculptor, 71
Christ's College, Cambridge, Fellows Building, 173; account of, 158
Chute, Chaloner, Speaker, 177–8
Cimandio, Roman, 35
*Cinque Ordini d'Architettura,* 55 (note)
City of London, 74, 84, 94, 147, 164, 218
City of Sleep, the, 41; **4**
Clare College, Cambridge, **54**; account of, 157–8; bridge at, 157
Clarendon, Earls of (*see* Hyde)
Clarendon House, Piccadilly, 162, 212, 215; account of, 217–8
Clarke, Dr. George, virtuoso, 164, 168 (note)
Clarke, John, freemason, 110
Clarke, J. W. (and R. Willis)—*Architectural History of Cambridge,* 158 (and note)
Cleare, Richard, joiner and carver, 185 (note), 215 (and note)
Cleer, William, joiner and carver, 215 (note)
Clitherow family, 115
Cobham Hall, Kent, account of, 189–90
*Coelum Britannicum,* masque, 35 (note), 54 (and note), 160
Cogan, Henry, squire, 104 (and note)
Coke, Elizabeth Cecil, Lady, 192
Coleshill House, Berkshire, 114, 132, 189, 202, 205, 217, 218; **81, 83, 84**; account of, 211–16
Collinson, John, county historian, 224
Colly Weston slate, 157
Colt, Maximilian, monumental sculptor, 73, 83, 136, 191
Colvin, Mr. Howard, 202 (and note), 206
Compton Chamberlayne, Wiltshire, 164
Compton, Spencer, 2nd Earl of Northampton, 116
Compton, William, 1st Earl of Northampton, 115, 130
Consiglio de' Dieci, 21 (note)
Constantine's Arch, 95 (and note); and Basilica, Rome, 33
Convento della Carità, Venice, 109
Convocation House, Oxford, 148, 152 (note)
Conway, River, 105
Cooper, John (Giovanni Coperario), composer, 29
*Cooper's Hill,* Sir J. Denham's, 162
Cope family, 180 (note)
Cornaro, Villa, 179
Cornbury Park, Oxon, 128, 138; account of, 144–5
Coryat, Thomas, writer and traveller, 31, 79, 109, 226 (note)

Cosimo II, Grand Duke of Tuscany, 29, 40

Cosimo III, Grand Duke of Tuscany, 227

Cosmos Neos, 43

Council and Advice to all Builders, 196

Covent Garden Church (see St. Paul's, Covent Garden)

Covent Garden Piazza, 60, 169, 201; **16, 19**; account of, 83–6

Cranborne Manor, Dorset, 131–2

Crane, Sir Francis, tapestry manufacturer, 121–5

Cranfield, Lionel, 1st Earl of Middlesex, 79, 91

Craven, William, 1st Earl of, 199

Crociferi, Sta. Maria dei, Rome, 109

Cromwell House, Highgate, 126 (note), 201; **74, 75**; account of, 199–200

Cromwell, Oliver, Protector, 44, 51, 94, 96, 132, 154, 175, 224

Croome Court, Worcestershire, 101

Crudities, Coryat's, 31, 226 (note)

Cuer, Cornelius, monumental sculptor, 136

Cuer, William, King's master mason, 76 (note)

Cumberland, Clifford, 5th Earl of, 36

Cunningham, Allan—Life of Inigo Jones, 31 (note), 223, 224

Cupola with clock, Whitehall, 84

Customs House, King's Lynn, 131

Dacre, 13th Baron, 119, 177 (note)

Damporte (or Davenport), John, master carpenter, 104 (and note)

Daniel, Samuel, dramatist, 29

Danvers, Henry, 1st Earl of Danby, 143–5 (and note 144)

Danvers, Sir John, regicide, 141

Davenant, Sir William, dramatist, 40, 43, 184; **4, 5**

Davies, Hugh, mason, 151

de Beer, Professor E. S., 130, 169 (note)

de Caux, Isaac, engineer and architect, 99 (and note), 100 (and note), 101

de Caux, Solomon, drawing master, 30, 99

de Clein, Francis, painter, 127 (and note)

de Clermont, Andien, painter of arabesques, 103

de Critz, Emanuel, painter, 102 (and note)

de Critz, John, serjeant-painter, 72 (and note), 79, 81, 82, 86, 102 (note)

de Critz, Thomas, painter, 103 (and note)

de Keyser, Hendrik, sculptor and architect, 112, 136

de Keyser, Maria (Mrs. Nicholas Stone), 137

de l'Orme, Philibert, architect, 29, 59, 170

de Whitt, Giles, surveyor, 191

Delos, Apollo's Temple at, 232

Denham, Sir John, poet and architect, 162–3 (and note), 180, 183, 185, 190

Deptford–Woolwich highroad, 66

Descritione de le Chiese, Le, 33 (note)

Designs of Inigo Jones, 89, 94 (note), 168 (note) 177

Devereux, Robert, 3rd Earl of Essex, 27, 30, 192

Devonshire, 4th Duke of, 50

Devonshire, 6th Duke of, 33 (note)

Devonshire, library of Dukes of (see also Chatsworth), 26, 164

D'Ewes, Sir Symonds, antiquary, 75

Dietterlin, Wendel—De Quinque Columnarum, 200

Digby, Sir Kenelm, author and traveller, 232

Dixwell, Sir Basil, 193

Dobson, William, painter, 31 (note), 50, 232, 233

Doges' Place, Venice, 54, 79, 102

Donatello, sculptor, 61

Donne, John, poet, 20, 110, 137–8; **45**

Dowland, John, lutanist, 22, 232

Drayton House, Northamptonshire, account of, 176–7

Drummond, William, of Hawthornden, 46

du Cerceau, J. A., architect and author, 106, 210

Dugdale, Sir William, historian, 164

Dunster Castle, Somerset, 225

Duppa, Brian, Bishop, 61

Durham House, Strand, 184

Durkin, Richard, carver, 61, 70 (and note)

Dusart, François, sculptor, 233 (note)

Dutch style of house, 192–4

Dutton, John, M.P., 224

Ebberston Hall, Yorkshire, 105

Edge, William, mason, 111–14

Edinburgh, 22, 71–2, 84, 137, 228

Elements of Architecture, The, 59 (note)

Elgin, Thomas, 3rd Earl of, 157 (note)

Elizabeth, Princess and Queen of Bohemia, 32

Elizabeth I, Queen, 21, 90

Embree, John, serjeant-plumber, 91 (note), 136

Emden, 141

Emmet, William, of Bromley, 164 (and note), 168 (note)

Emmett, Maurice, bricklayer to the King, 164 (note)

Erastianism, 52, 147, 153, 154

Essex House, Strand, 64

Euston, Suffolk, 101

Evelyn, John, diarist, 75, 84, 92, 103, 145, 151 (note), 158, 159, 180, 183, 202, 209, 217–18

Exton, Rutland, 21

Fairfax, Thomas, 3rd Baron, General, 193

Faithorne, William, the elder, engraver, 51

Fakenham Market, 111

Falstaff, Sir John, 25

Fanelli, Francesco, sculptor in bronze, 151 (note), 233

Faringdon, 211

Farnese Palace, Rome, 211

Farnham Castle, Surrey, account of, 190

Felbrigg Hall, Norfolk, 138 (note)

Fellows Building, Christ's College, Cambridge, 158, 173

Fergusson, James, architectural historian, 76, 180

Festival of Light, Luminalia or, 41

Fetter Lane, City of London, 104, 141

Fiennes, Celia, diarist, 99, 216

Filarete, Antonio, architect, 151

Fire of London, 92, 94, 110 (note), 141, 146, 217, 218

Fitzalan library, 30

Flitcroft, Henry, draughtsman and architect, 168 (note), 170

Floors Castle, Roxburgh, 105

Florence, 29, 40, 41 (note), 43, 61, 70, 100, 138, 141, 151 (note), 227

Florimene, masque, 40, 43

Fontainebleau, Palace of, 170

Fontana, Domenico, architect, 54, 83, 93 (note)

Forde Abbey, Dorset, 116; **41, 42**; account of, 132

Foro Romano, Rome, 35 (and note), 53, 54

Fort, Thomas, builder, 131

Forty Hall, Enfield, 119

Foster Lane, City of London, 145–6

Fountain of "Giovanni Maggi", Rome, 73

Fréart, Roland—Parallèle de L'Architecture, 210

Frederick V, Count and Elector Palatine, 32

Frederiksborg Castle, 22 (and note)

French Ambassador, the, 29, 41

Furnival's Inn, Holborn, 202

Galilei, Alessandro, architect, 93 (note)

Gamon, Richard, clerk of works, 104

Gandon, James (and Woolfe)—Vitruvius Britannicus, 132

Gellius, Aulus, Roman judge, 231

Genoa, 34, 199, 202 (note), 208, 210

Gentileschi, Artemisia, painter, 70

Gentileschi, Orazio, painter, 70, 71

Gerbier, Sir Balthazar, architect, 36, 71, 76, 80, 141, 142 (and note), 143, 205, 206, 208, 209, 211, 226; account of, 196 (and note)–201

Gheeraerts, Marc, painter, 30

Gibbons, Grinling, wood carver, 215

Gibbs, James, architect, 72

Gildon, John, monumental sculptor, 136

Giudizio di Paridi, Il, opera, 29, 40

Gloucester, 201

237

Glover, Moses, painter and builder, 125
Goldsmiths' Hall, the 145-6
Goldwell grotto, Oxfordshire, 100
Gonerson, Arnold, mason, 65 (and note)
GooDericke, Matthew, painter, 82, 83, 86, 126
Goor, Anthony, stone carver, 151
Gotch, J. Alfred, 32, 109, 121; *Inigo Jones*, 27 (and note)
Gough MSS., Bodleian Library, 199 (note)
Grange, The, Alresford, Hampshire, 130
Gravesend, 22
Great Brington Church, 206
Great Park House, Ampthill, 157 (note)
Great Queen Street houses, Lincoln's Inn, 201-2, 206
Greenwich, Charlton House, 120
Greenwich, house for Lord Arundel at, 64
Greenwich (*see* Queen's House at)
Greenwich Palace, 66 (note), 69, 79, 162, 163, 164 (note), 167, 169, 170, 177, 178, 216; **68**; account of, 180-5
Greenwich Park, 66
Grimaldo, Don Carlo, 195
Grimaldo, Palazzo Genoa, 200
Grimthorpe, Edmund Beckett, Lord, architect, 110
Grove, John, master plasterer, 71, 184 (note)
Grove, John, plumber, 146
Grumball, Arthur, mason, 157 (note)
Grumball, John, mason, 157 (note)
Grumbold, Robert, architect, 157 (and note), 158
Grumbold (or Grumball) Thomas, mason, 157-8
Guercino, painter, 39, 60
Gunnersbury House, Middlesex, 142, 180; **65**; account of, 179

Haddington, Viscount (*see* Ramsay, John)
Hagley Hall, Worcestershire, 101
Hague, The, 66, 69
Hakewill, Henry, architect, 174, 175
Ham House, Surrey, 129, 146, 148, 200; account of, 125-7
Hampden, John, statesman, 202
Hampstead Marshall, Berkshire, 196-9; **71**
Hampton Court Palace, 30, 125, 169, 176, 178
Hangings for walls, 226
Hardwick, Thomas, architect, 85
Harefield, 136
Harington family, 21
Harrington, Sir, J., parliamentarian, 192
Harringworth, Northamptonshire, 208 (note)

Harrison, Sir John, farmer of customs, 200
Harrison, Peter, American architect, 89 (note)
Harrison, Stephen, joiner, 43
Harvey, Dr. William, eminent physician, 161
Harwood, Doctor, 19
Hasted, Edward, Kent historian, 119, 186
Hatfield House, Hertfordshire, 60, 99, 106, 116, 228
Hatton, Sir Christopher, antiquary, 127
Hatton, Sir Christopher, Lord Chancellor, 127
Hatton of Kirby, 1st Baron, 138
Hawksmoor, Nicholas, architect, 66 (note) 183, 184
Haynes Grange Room, 120 (and note)
Hayward, Sir John, historian, 231
Hearne, Henry, clerk of works, 65 (and note)
Heddington quarry, 151
Henrietta Maria, Queen, 51, 66, 71, 75, 82, 86, 95, 231
Henry VIII, King, 25
Henry, Prince of Wales, 29-30, 31, 32, 35, 52, 56, 99
Herbert of Cherbury, Edward, 1st Lord, 52
Herbert, Mary, Countess of Pembroke, 20, 106, 109
Herbert, Philip, 4th Earl of Pembroke and 1st Earl of Montgomery, 21, 28, 73, 96-7, 100-3, 131, 132, 168, 186
Herbert, Philip, 5th Earl of Pembroke, 227
Herbert, William, 3rd Earl of Pembroke, 20-1, 28, 52, 64, 73, 75, 90, 96, 130
Heriot's Hospital, Edinburgh, 22, 25; **2**
Herrick, Robert, poet, 233
Hicks, Sir Baptist, Baronet, mercer, 90
Highgate, 199
Highnam Court, Gloucestershire, 201
"Hill Difficulty", 106
Hill, William, mason, 151, 152
Hinton St. George, Somerset, 223-4
*History of Architecture*, Fergusson's, 180
*History of Kent*, 119
*History of Life and Reign of King Charles*, 169
*History of Northamptonshire*, 125
Hobart, Sir Henry, 1st Baronet, 111
Hodgkin, MSS., 29 (note)
Holbein, Hans, painter, 36, 103 (note), 194, 233
Holdenby House, Northamptonshire, 127, 157 (note)
Holkham, Norfolk, 101
Holland, Henry, 1st Earl of, 176, 180 (note)
Holland House, Kensington, 127 (note) 180
Hollar, Wenceslaus, engraver, 51, 92; **22**

Holles, Hon. Francis, 137; **44**
Holy Trinity Church, Berwick-on-Tweed, **55**; account of, 154
Holyroodhouse, Edinburgh, 71-2, 137
Honey family of paviers, 138 (note)
Honington Hall, Warwickshire, 141
Honthorst, Gerard, painter, 75
Hook, Mr., assistant mason, 146 (and note)
Hooke, Robert, architect and scientist, 146 (note)
Hooker, Richard, theologian, 231
Hopetoun House, Scotland, 122
Hopper, Thomas, architect, 180
Hopton Heath, Battle of, 116
Horne, Herbert, 62
Horse Guards, Whitehall, 101
Horseheath, Cambridgeshire, 212; account of, 217
Houghton Conquest House, Bedfordshire, 105-6, 109; **28, 29**
Houghton Hall, Norfolk, 232
"House Beautiful", 105
House of Delight (*or* Queen's House), 69
House of Fame, the, 40, 43, 56
House of Lords, 51, 96
Howard, Alathea, Countess of Arundel and Surrey, 32, 34, 35, 64, 96, 145 (note), 226, 227
Howard, Thomas, 2nd Earl of Arundel and Surrey, 28, 32, 33 (and note), 34, 35 (and note), 36, 40, 52, 59, 60, 64, 72, 73, 75, 84, 90, 96, 120, 130, 141, 145-6, 232, 233 (note)
Howard, Lord William ("Belted Will"), 226
Howell, James, diplomat, 46 (note), 59
*Hue and Cry after Cupid*, masque, 28, 43
Hulsbergh, H., architectural engraver, 168 (note)
Huntingdon, Ferdinando Hastings, 6th Earl of, 103
Hyde, Edward, 1st Earl of Clarendon, 96, 145, 206, 217, 222
Hyde, Henry, 2nd Earl of Clarendon, 218
Hyde Park, New Lodge in, 121 (note)
*Hymenaei*, masque, 27-8, 43

*Iconologia*, or *Descrittione di Diverse Imagini*, 26
Ilchester, 163
Ilminster, 224
Ingram, Sir Arthur, 141
*Inigo Jones*, by J. A. Gotch, 27 (note)
Inner Temple, 209
Inns of Court, 32, 109
Intermezzo (*or* intermedium), 40 (note)
Invalides, Paris, church dome, 167
Iseppo de' Porti, Palazzo, Vicenza, 74
Isham, Sir Justinian, 2nd Baronet, 61, 119, 141, 142, 170-6, 177 (and note), 178, 222
Isle of Wight, 169
Isleworth Hundred, Middlesex, 125

Jackson, John, master mason, 146, 151, 152, 153, 210
James I, King, 25, 29, 31, 35, 52, 60, 66, 71, 72, 74, 79, 81, 90, 96, 99, 106, 115, 121 (note), 147, 160–1, 228; 11; his hearse, 83
James, John, carver, 86
James, Thomas, carver, 61, 70, 94
Jansen (or Jonson), Gerard and Nicolas, sculptor, 136
Janus Quadrifons, Arch of, Rome, 128, 144
Jarman, Edward, builder, 146
"Johnes, Mrs.", a sister of Inigo Jones, 32
Jones, Anne (Mrs. Webb), 104, 160
Jones, Elizabeth (Mrs. Richard Gamon), 104
Jones, Eneyo (or Inigo), the elder, 19, 20, 21, 160
Jones, Inigo, portraits of, 39 49–50, 189; 7, 12
Jonson, Benjamin, poet, 19, 20, 21, 22, 26, 27, 28, 43, 45–9, 52, 59; 9, 10
Jordaens, Jakob, painter, 60, 71, 79 (and note)
Jupiter, Temple of, Rome, 56
Juxon, William, Archbishop, 85, 151, 152, 153

Kearne, Andreas, sculptor, 138–41, 143
Kedleston Park, Derbyshire, 70 (note), 122, 185
Keith, W. Grant, 33 (note), 69 (note), 228 (note)
Kent, William, architect and painter, 71 (note), 79 (note), 89 (note), 113, 129, 168 (and note), 170, 177, 179 (note)
Ketton stone, 157
Ketton-Cremer, Mr. R. W., 138 (note), 232 (note)
Kew Palace, 113, 179, 194; 80; account of, 193
Killegrew, Sir Peter, house for, 168
Kineton, 125
King James I's hearse, 83
King's Lynn, 65 (note), 131
King's Messenger, Inigo Jones as, 29
Kingston Lacy, Dorset, 212, 218; 86; account of, 216–17
Kinsman, Joseph, plasterer, 126–7, 146
Kip, Johannes, draftsman, 80
Kirby Hall, Northamptonshire, 138; 38–40; account of, 127–8
Knebworth House, Hertfordshire, 105
Kneller, Sir Godfrey, portrait painter, 79 (note)
Knole Park, Kent, 60, 227
Kynnesman (or Kinsman), Edmond (or Edward), stone mason, 65

Lacrymae, John Dowlan's, 232
Lambeth Palace, chapel, 110, 151, 210; account of, 152

Lamport Hall, Northamptonshire, 141, 142, 157, 177 (note), 185; 62, 67; account of, 170–6
Langley, Batty, architectural writer, 128
Lanscroon, Marcellus, ceiling painter, 79 (note)
Lansdowne MSS., 44 (note)
Lateran basilica, Rome, 54, 93
Lateran Palace, Rome, 54
Laud, William, Archbishop of Canterbury, 52, 91, 93, 110, 147, 151 (and note), 152, 153
Laud's Tower, Lambeth Palace, 152
Lawes, William, composer, 28
Leadenhall St., City of London, 147–8
Ledston Hall, Yorkshire, 194
Lees Court, Kent, 70; 61, 69; account of, 186–9
Leghorn, 34, 184; piazza at, 84; church at, 84
Leicester, Robert Dudley, Earl of, 145
Lely, Sir Peter, portrait painter, 221
Le Muet, Pierre, architect and scholar, 210, 212, 221
Lennox and Richmond, Dukes of (see Stuart)
Lenôtre, André, garden designer, 184 (note)
Lenthall, William, Speaker, 153
Leonardo da Vinci, artist, 36
Leoni, Giacomo, architect, 71 (note), 170
Le Pautre, Jean, decorative designer, 215
Lescot, Pierre, architect, 170
Le Sueur, Hubert, sculptor, 21, 83, 90, 94, 142, 151 (note), 233; 46; account of, 141
Les Plus Excellents Bastiments de France, 106
Lieven, —, Flemish architect, 112
Life of Inigo Jones, Cunningham's, 31 (note), 223
Lincoln's Inn Chapel, 105 (note), 148, 152 (note); account of, 109–11
Lincoln's Inn Fields, 60, 89, 130–1, 201
Lindsey House, Lincoln's Inn Fields, 89, 186; 37; account of, 130–1
Llanrwst, Caernarvon, bridge at, 105
Lloyd, David, Bishop of St. Asaph, 20
Lodge Park, Sherborne, Gloucestershire, 224; 87
Loncellino, Palazzo, Genoa, 200
Londonderry, 169
Lord's Masque, The, 3
Lorenzo (Medici) il Magnifico, 70
Lothsbury (or "Loatsbury"), City of London, 120
Louvre, the, Paris, 167, 210
Love's Triumph through Callipolis, masque, 40, 46
Lovin, John, mason contractor, 207 (and note), 210
Lubenham, 173
Lucy, Sir Thomas, III, 141
Luminalia, or Festival of Light, masque, 41, 43; 4, 5

Luttrell, George, of Dunster, 225
Luxembourg Palace, Paris, 210
Lyminge, Robert, surveyor, 106, 116
Lyndon Hall, Rutland, account of, 207-8
Lynton, Robert, joiner, 109

Machina versatilis, 43
Macrobius, A. T., African writer, 231
Maderna, Carlo, architect, 53, 164
Madrid, 79, 233
Magalotti, Count, traveller, 76 (note), 79, 82, 93, 100, 217
Magdalen College, Oxford, 144, 209; bridge, 144
Maison Carrée, Nîmes, 34
Maltravers, H. F., Lord, 36, 120, 212
Manière de bien bastir, Le Muet's, 212
Mansard, J. H., architect, 167
Maria, Infanta of Spain, 81, 86
Market Harborough, 170
Marlborough House, London, 70; chapel, 1–3, 215 (note)
Marlborough, Sarah, Duchess of, 70
Marôt, Daniel, furniture designer, 228
Marshall, Edward, sculptor, 104, 174, 178–9; account of, 141 (and note), 142
Marshall, Joshua, sculptor, 142, 183 (note)
Mary II, Queen, 66 (note), 183
Mason, William, mason, 95 (and note)
Masque of Queens, the, 29, 39, 40, 41 (note), 43, 56; 10
Maude, Richard, mason, 151
May, Hugh, architect, 145, 163 (and note), 218
Maynard, Sir John, serjeant-at-law, 179
Mayo, Thomas, carpenter, 152 (note)
Meale, George, clerk of works, 74 (and note)
Medici, Lorenzo (il Magnifico), 70, 137
Medici, villa, Poggio a Caiano, 70
Medlay, 20
Memoirs of lives . . . of Excellent Personages, 20 (note)
Memorable Masque, the, 109
Merchant Taylors' School, 160
Merton College, Oxford, 151
Michelangelo Buonarroti, painter and architect, 53, 137
Milan, 32, 151
Mills, Peter, 202, 205–6, 207, 208, 209, 211, 212
Mills, William, mason, 146
Milton, John, poet, 62, 216
Module, rule of, 55 (and note), 86, 93
Molini, Villa, near Padua, 34, 69, 70
Montacute House, Somerset, 226 (note)
Moor Park, Hertfordshire, 71 (note), 185
Moore, Robert, mason, 94
Moore, Thomas, mason, 112, 114
Moorfields, 41
More, St. Thomas, 79, 231

Moretus, Balthazar, house of, 200
Mortlake tapestry factory, 79, 121, 127
*Most Notable Antiquity . . . Stoneheng, The,* 20 (note), 160
Moulton Hall, Yorkshire, 194 (and note)
Moyles Court, Hampshire, 201
Murray, William, 1st Earl of Dysart, 125, 126
Mytens, Daniel, painter, 21

National Gallery, 36 (note), 195
Naworth Castle, Cumberland, 226
Nerva Traiano, Temple of, Rome, 33 (note)
Newdigate, Sir John, 136
Newgate, 84
New Hall, Essex, 80–1, 142 (note), 196, 226
Newmarket, royal manor house, 64–5
Newport, Rhode Island, Market Hall, 89 (note)
Newton, Sir Adam, 1st Baronet, royal tutor, 120
Nichols, J., historian of Leicestershire, 173 (note)
Nicholson, Otto, builder, 110
Nonesuch Palace, 30
Norgate, Edward, picture agent, 35 (and note)
Northampton, 170
Northumberland, Algernon Percy, 10th Earl of, 142, 178–9
Northumberland House, Strand, account of, 178–9
*Note-book and Account-book of Nicholas Stone,* 135 (note)
*Nouvelle Invention de lever l'eau. . . ,* 99
Nys, Daniel, agent, 232

Oatlands Palace, Surrey, 65, 69; **59**
*Oberon, the Faery Prince,* masque, 56; **9**
Oberon's Palace, 56, 59
Odcombe, Somerset, 31, 226 (note)
"Oldborough, Mr.", 35
Oliver, John, surveyor, 164
Orford, Admiral Lord, 85
Osterley Park, Middlesex, 70 (note)
Overbury, Sir Thomas, 27
Oxford (University), 27, 43, 111, 128, 143, 145, 148, 151, 152, 153, 157, 161, 164, 193, 199 (note), 209, 224, 225
Oxinden, Henry, poet, 193
Oxnead, Norfolk, 232 (and note)

Padua, 69, 70
*Palazzi di Genova* (of Rubens), 120, 180, 195, 199, 200, 210
Pall Mall, London, 162
Palladio, Andrea, architect, 21, 32, 33, 34, 42, 54–6, 70, 74, 80, 82 (and note), 83, 89, 93, 102, 105, 109, 137 (note), 144, 159, 164, 167, 170 (note), 180, 184, 186, 208, 210
Palmer, John, monument to, 142
Pantheon, Rome, 33, 93
Panzini, Gregorio, Papal Agent, 36, 52

Papa Guilio, Villa di, Rome, 69
Papillon, David, architect, 173
Papillon Hall, Leicestershire, 173 (and note)
*Parentalia,* the, 184
Parigi, Alfonso, scene designer, 40, 41, 43
Parigi, Giulio, scene designer, 29, 40, 41
Paris, 29, 84, 218
Parker, John, overseer, 146
Parliament, I. Jones a Member of, 52
Parnassus Stanza, Vatican, 39
Paston, Sir William, virtuoso, 138 (note), 232 (and note)
Paul V, Pope, his coronation, 27, 53
Pazzi, Capella, Florence, 61, 62
Peacham, Henry, author, 64, 79, 141, 210, 231, 232
Pembroke, Anne, Countess of, 101, 103
Pembroke, Earls of (*see* Herbert)
Penruddock family, 164
Pepys Samuel, diarist, 75, 82, 128, 152, 183, 192–3, 196 (note), 208 (note)
Pepysian Library, Cambridge, 196 (note)
Periaktoi, 43, 44
Peruzzi, Baldassare, architect, 43
Peterborough, 176, 202, 207, 208, 210; town hall, 207 (note)
Peterborough, Henry, 2nd Earl of, 176, 177 (note)
Peterhouse chapel, Cambridge, 153, 157
Petit Trianon, Versailles, 69
Pett, Peter, shipwright, 70
Petty, William, picture agent, 35, 36
Petworth House, Sussex, 125
Peyto family, 125
Phelips, Sir Edward, Speaker, 226 (note)
Philips, Peter (Pietro Philippi), organist, 232
Physic Garden gateways, Oxford, 128, 209; **47**; account of, 143–4
Pierce, Edward, jun., wood and stone carver, 199, 205
Pierce, Edward, sen., painter-stainer, 89, 102, 103
Pieroni, Alessandro, architect, 84 (and note)
Pindar, Sir Paul, diplomatist and merchant, 91
Pisa, 54 (note), 70
Pisani family of sculptors, 61
*Pleasure Reconciled to Virtue,* masque, 73
Pleydell, Sir Mark, Baronet, 211, 215
Pocoke, Dr. Richard, traveller, 120
Pontefract, 194
Portington, William, King's master carpenter, 74 (and note)
Portland, Isle of, 75, 91
Portraits of Inigo Jones, 39, 49–50, 189; **7, 12**
Pory, John, traveller, 28
Pratt, Sir George, 2nd Baronet, 211, 215

Pratt, Sir Roger, architect, 83, 85, 92, 113, 114, 179, 189, 205, 206, 222, 225; account of, 209–21
*Premier tome de l'architecture, Le,* de l'Orme's, 29
Public Record Office, 63 (note), 82 (note)
Pym, John, statesman, 202

*Quattro Libri Dell'Architettura,* Jones's copy of, 21, 32, 42, 54, 64, 69, 103, 179, 186
Queen Anne's hearse, 73, 83
Queen's Chapel, St. James's (*see* Marlborough House chapel)
Queen's House, Greenwich, 61, 74, 101, 102 (note), 106, 109, 112, 113, 132, 135, 136, 138, 152, 164, 170, 180, 183, 184 (and note), 185, 189, 215; **13–15**; account of, 66–71
*Queen's Masque of Blackness, The,* masque, 25–7, 42, 45

Radcliffe Camera, Oxford, 101 (note), 228 (note)
Ramsay, John, Viscount Haddington, 28, 43
Ramsbury Manor, Wiltshire, 186
Raphael, artist, 39, 70 (note), 79, 82 (note), 232, 233
Raundes, Northamptonshire, 157
Raynham Hall, Norfolk, 65 (note), 128 (note), 192; **31**; account of, 111–15
Raynton, Sir Nicholas, 119
Richardson, Professor A. E., 109, 200
Richmond Palace, 30, 69, 99
Richmond, Yorkshire, 194
Ringwood, 201
Ripley, Thomas, architect, 170, 184
Robinson, Sir Thomas, 1st Baronet, architectural scholar, 115 (note)
Roman Catholicism, Inigo Jones and, 51–2
Romano, Giulio, painter, 70 (note), 71
Rome, 26, 27, 28, 33, 53, 55 (note), 56, 69, 73, 83, 86, 95 (note), 104 (note), 109, 112, 128 (note), 136 (note), 138, 147, 164, 210, 218
Rose and Crown Inn, Wisbech, 206
Rosenborg Castle, Denmark, 22 (and note), 25
Rossi's *Nuova Racolta di Fontane di Roma,* 167 (and note)
Rothamsted Park, Hertfordshire, 194
Rotonda, Villa, Vicenza, 33, 178 (note)
Rowe, Isaac, draftsman, 177 (note)
Royal Commission for Buildings, 51, 59–60, 84, 130
Royal Commission for repair of St. Paul's, 90
Royal Institute of British Architects, library, 39, 64 (note), 101 (note), 177, 196 (note), 211
*Royal Slave,* The, masque, 43

Rubens's House, Antwerp, 195, 199; **73**
Rubens style house, 194–209
Rubens, Sir Peter Paul, 21, 34, 39, 60, 71, 79 (and note), 80, 120, 147, 169, 180, 194–6, 200, 205, 208, 211, 231, 233
Ryder (or Rider), Richard, carpenter and builder, 131
Rye, Old Grammar School, 194; **76**
Ryston Hall, Norfolk, 210; account of, 218–19

Sadleir family, 226
St. Albans, 1st Viscount (see Bacon, Francis)
S. Andrea della Valle, Rome, 218
St. Angelo, Castle of, Rome, 27
St. Bartholomew-the-Great, 74
St. Bartholomew-the-Less, Smithfield, 19
St. Benet, Paul's Wharf, 19, 104
St. Bride's, Fleet Street, 167
St. Catherine Cree, 154; **51**; account of, 147–8
St. Catherine's College, Cambridge, 157
Sta. Francesca Roman, Rome, 53
St. Giles-in-the-Fields, 89
St. Gregory by St. Paul's, 51, 91, 96
St. Helen's, Bishopsgate, door, **52**; account of, 148
St. James's Palace, 30, 175 (note); chapel at, 81–3, 192
St. John's College, Oxford, **56**; account of, 148–52
St. John, Oliver, Lord Chief Justice, 176, 202–5, 206, 207
S. Lorenzo in Miranda, Rome, 54
St. Margaret's, Westminster, 142
Sta. Maria Maggiore, Rome, 33
Sta. Maria dei Miracoli, Venice, 54
Sta. Maria della Vittoria, Rome, 53
St. Martin-in-the-Fields, 104
St. Mary's, Oxford, portico, 151, 154, 209; **49**; account of, 146–7
St. Michael-le-Querne, Cheapside, 51
St. Olave's, Jewry, 215
St. Paul's Cathedral, London, 50, 51, 104, 109, 110 (note), 135, 145, 154, 164, 185, 210, 218, 223, 225; **22**; account of, 90–4
St. Paul's, Covent Garden, 3–6, 91 (note), 132, 154, 186; **20**
St. Peter's, Rome, 93, 167, 218
S. Pietro in Montorio, Rome, 33
Sta. Susanna, Rome, 53, 164; **8**
St. Vedast Foster, City of London, 167
Salmacida Spolia, masque, 43–4
Samwell, William, architect, 130
Sanderson, Sir William, historian, 169
Sandys family, 177
San Gallo, Giuliano da, architect, 70
Sansovino, Jacopo, architect, 54
Sargenson, T., contractor, 174, 176
Saye and Sele, William Fiennes, 1st Viscount, 202

Scamozzi, Vincenzio, architect, 33, 34, 42, 60, 69–70, 82, 102, 106, 164, 210
Schoermann, John, sculptor, 136, 141
Scotland Yard, 96 (and note), 104, 161, 173, 176
Scott, Samuel, painter, 85, 89; **19, 21**
Serlio, Sebastiano, architect, 42, 65, 85, 90, 106, 144, 145, 167, 178, 210, 222
Seymour, William, 2nd Duke of Somerset, 179
Shakespeare, William, poet, 19, 21, 25, 62, 106
Sherborne Park, Gloucestershire, 224
Sheriff Hutton hunting lodge, Yorkshire, 141
Shuckburgh Church, Warwickshire, 175 (note)
Sidney, Sir Philip, 20, 103, 106, 143, 231
Siege of Rhodes, opera, 44
Signet Office, Whitehall, 73
Silver plate, 228–9
Simpson, Percy and C. F. Bell, Designs by Inigo Jones for Masques, 26 (note), 39
Sitwell, Mr. Sacheverell, 40, 41
Sketch book, Inigo Jones's, 33, 39, 211
Slingsby, Sir Henry, Baronet, royalist, 141, 226
Sloane, Sir Hans, Baronet, physician, 80
Slyfield Manor, Surrey, 194
Smith, Francis, architect, 174, 176
Smith, Miss Joan Sumner, 39 (note)
Smith, Robert, mason, 151
Smith, William, painter, 33
Smithson, John, master builder, 59, 74, 75, 81, 125, 192
Smyth, Thomas, M.P., 223, 224
Snowshill Manor, Gloucestershire, 228
Soane, Sir John, architect, 76, 89
Some Designs of Inigo Jones, Vardy's, 178
Somerset House, Strand (or Denmark House), 51, 64, 82, 104, 127, 130, 131, 135, 138, 164, 169, 175 (note); **21**; description of house and chapel, 86–9
Somerset Visitation, 160 (and note)
Sorbonne, Church of, 218
Soria, G. B., architect, 53
South Luffenham Hall, Rutland, 208; account of, 207
Sovereign of the Seas, The, 61, 70, 71, 94
Spencer, Sir Edward, 206
Spencer House, St. James's, 185
Stacey, William, mason, 152
Stacy, Gabriel, pavier, 71, 86, 138, 145, 152
Staines, Church of St. Mary, Middlesex, 105
Stamford, 126, 148, 206, 208, 215; St. George's Square and St. Mary's St. houses, 208–9
Standon Lordship, Hertfordshire, inventory, 226, 227, 231
Stanton, William, sculptor and builder, 212

Stanway House, Gloucestershire, 225; **92**
Star Chamber, designs for, 72
Staunton Harold chapel, Leicestershire, 154
Stickles, Robert, 65
Stiles, Thomas, master mason, 65
Stoakes, Charles, builder, 71, 100, 137, 138, 142, 143, 144, 146
Stoke Bruerne Park, Northamptonshire, 121–5; **35, 36**
Stone, Henry (Old Stone), painter, 138 (and note)
Stone, John, sculptor, 138, 141, 206
Stone, Nicholas, sculptor, 71, 72, 76, 86, 89, 94, 95, 96, 100, 112, 125, 127, 128, 180, 194, 205, 209, 232 (and note); chapter on, 135–58
Stone, Nicholas, jun., sculptor, 95 (note), 100, 128 (note), 136 (note), 138
Stoneheng restored to the Danes, 61, 101
Stonehenge, ruins of, 96, 160–1
Stourhead House, Wiltshire, 141
Stow Wood, 151
Strafford, Thomas, 1st Earl of, 99, 194
Stratfield Saye, Hampshire, 193
Strawberry Hill, Middlesex, 56
Streater, Robert, serjeant-painter, 79, 185 (note)
Strong, Simeon, mason, 151
Strong, Thomas, master mason, 145
Strong, Timothy, contractor, 145
Strong, Valentine, mason, 151
Stuart, James (Athenian), architect, 184
Sturges, John, builder, 208
Surveyor to Prince Henry, Inigo Jones as, 30–1, 32
Surveyor-General of the King's Works, Inigo Jones as, 62
Sutton, John, rough mason, 208
Swakeleys House, Middlesex, 79; **70, 72**; account of, 192–3
Sydenham, Sir John, 224
Syon House, Middlesex, 125

Tables, 227–8
Tailer, Zachary, carver, 70 (and note), 76 (note), 86
Tale of a Tub, the, 20, 46
Tart Hall, St. James's, 145 (note), 228; inventory, 226, 227
Taylor, John, mason, 94, 146
Teatro Olimpico, Vicenza, 33, 42
Tempe Restored, masque, 40
Tempietto, Bramante's, in Rome, 33, 83
Temple Bar, 95, 142
Temple of Love, The, masque, 184
Tethys Festival, masque, 29
Thanet House, Aldersgate, 202
"Theater", the, 41
Theobalds Palace, Hertfordshire, 66, 81, 83, 95, 121 (note)
Thomson, George, mason, 157
Thorney Abbey House, Cambridgeshire, 186, 208; **79**; account of, 206–7

Thornhill, Sir James, ceiling painter, 71, 79

Thorpe Hall, Northamptonshire, 126, 148, 176, 186, 207, 208, 211, 212; **78**; account of, 202–6

Thorpe, Thomas, jun., surveyor, 106

Thorpe, Thomas, sen., mason, 127

Thurloe, John, Secretary of Estate, 206, 212

*Time Vindicated to Himself . . . ,* Masque, 41 (note)

Titian, painter, 35, 103 (note), 175, 233

Top Hall, Lyndon, Rutland, 208

Tower of London, 21 (note), 95 (and note), 104, 146

Townshend, Horatio, 1st Lord, 113, 114

Townshend, Sir Roger, 1st Baronet, 65 (note), 111–14

Trinity College, Cambridge, 31, 131, 157

Tuileries Palace, Paris, 170

Tyttenhanger Park, Hertfordshire, 200–1

Valmarana, Palazzo, Vicenza, 184

Vanbrugh, Sir John, architect, 184

Vandyke, Sir Anthony, painter, 39, 49, 50, 60, 76, 83, 99, 102, 138, 175, 231, 233 (and note)

van Somer, Paul, painter, 22, 64, 65

Vardy, John, architect, 178, 184

Vasari, Giorgio, artist and author, 41 (note)

Veneto, 21, 54

Venice, 21, 22, 31, 32, 33, 35, 54, 79, 80, 102, 109, 127 (note)

Venti Settembre, Via, Rome, 53

Verney, Sir Ralph, cavalier, 173

Verona, triumphal arch at, 90, 167

Veronese, Paolo, painter, 79 (and note)

Versailles, Château de, 42

Vertue, George, antiquary, 19, 20, 51, 79 (note), 96, 100, 111, 119, 121, 130, 135 (note), 179, 180, 189, 202, 233 (note)

Via Aurea, Genoa, 199–200

Vicenza, 33, 34, 42, 54, 72, 178 (note), 184

Victoria and Albert Museum, 120 (note), 141

Vignola, J. Barozzi, architect, 55, 69, 170

Villiers, George, 1st Duke of Buckingham, 35, 36, 52, 72–3, 80, 81, 142, 143, 196, 226, 232

*Vindication of Stone Heng restored, A,* 20 (note), 84, 161, 173

Viner, Sir Robert, Baronet, goldsmith, 192

Vitruvian system, 43

Vitruvius, architectural scholar, 42, 54–6, 85, 93, 105, 144, 160, 210

*Vitruvius Britannicus,* 85, 100 (note), 115, 130, 132 (note), 168 (note), 179, 217

Vitruvius's *I Doeci Libri Dell'Architectura,* Jones's copy, 54 (and note), 144

Vyne, the, Hampshire, 142, 184; **63, 64**; account of, 177–8

Wadham, Mrs., 224–5

Wadham College, Oxford, 151, 224

Wakefield Lodge, Northamptonshire, 71 (note)

Walcot Hall, Northamptonshire, account of, 208–9

Wallace, William, master mason, 25

Walpole, Horace, letter writer and antiquary, 56, 59, 85, 86, 94, 106, 135 (note), 161, 177, 179, 180 (note), 189

Walpole, Sir Robert, 49

Walpole Society, 135 (note), 168 (note)

Ware, Isaac, architect, 89 (and note), 94, 128 (and note)

Ware Park, Hertfordshire, 73

Wase, Christopher, poet, 162

Wase, Maurice, dealer, 175

Webb, Professor Geoffrey, 148

Webb, James (father of John), 160 (note)

Webb, John, architect, 20, 21, 22, 32, 41, 44, 49, 50, 59, 60, 64, 69, 71, 84, 85, 89, 92, 94, 95, 128, 131, 142, 143; 146, 157, 191, 200, 201, 205, 209, 211, 212, 217, 222; **27, 57, 58, 60, 62, 64**; at Chevening, 119–20; at Wilton, 96, 101, 102, 103, 104, 114, 115, 116; **27**; chapter on, 159–90

Webb, John, servant in royal household, 170 (note)

Webb, William (son of John), 164

Weldon stone, 157, 174, 175

West Horsley Place, Surrey, 193

West Woodhay Manor, Berkshire, 223; **90**

Westley, John, builder, 158

Westminster Abbey, 51, 128, 137, 152 (note)

Weston, Richard, Lord, later 1st Earl of Portland, 141

Whinney, Miss Margaret, 164 (and note), 168 (note)

White, Samuel, mason, 153

White, William, monumental sculptor, 136

White House, the (*or* Queen's House), 70

Whitehall Palace, 28, 30, 32, 40, 41, 42, 49, 75–6, 84, 95 (note), 109, 116, 127, 131, 168–70, 184, 227

Whitehall Palace, Lord Buckingham's lodgings at, 72–3

Whitehall Palace, Lord Pembroke's lodgings at, 131

Whitehall Palace Scheme, 60, 164; account of, 168–70, 180, 185; **60**

Whittelsey, Cambridgeshire, gatepiers and market place, 207

Wickes, Henry, Paymaster, 104, 136

Wilson, Henry, mason, 95 (and note)

Wilson, Richard, artist, 99

Wilson, Sir William, mason architect, 205

Wilton House, Wiltshire, 64, 85, 129, 131, 132, 160, 168, 169, 170, 177, 180, 184 (note) 189, 227; **25, 27**; account of, 96–103; grotto, 99–100; **23**; stables, 101; **26**

Wimbledon, royal manor at, 95

Winchester Cathedral, screen in, 90; **24**

Winde, William, architect, 199, 205

Windebank, Sir Francis, Secretary of State, 91

Windsor Castle, 74, 137

Wisbech Castle, Cambridgeshire, 212; **85**; account of, 206

Wittkower, Dr. R., 36 (note), 52 (and note), 55 (note), 70 (note)

Woburn Abbey, Bedfordshire, the grotto, 100 (note)

Wood, Anthony à, antiquary, 43 (note), 148 (note), 190

Woodfeild, David, joiner, 152

Woodstock Palace, 30, 151

Woolwich fortifications, 163

Worcester College, Oxford, 29, 72, 94, 101 (note), 164

Wormius, Olius, antiquary, 161

Wotton, Sir Henry, diplomat and man of letters, 59 (and note), 104 (note), 127 (note)

Wren, Sir Christopher, architect, 19, 51, 60, 62, 71, 89, 92, 94, 95, 102, 105, 110, 129, 130, 142, 145, 157, 158, 163, 167, 169, 178, 183–4, 185, 201, 202, 205, 208, 215, 218

Wren, Christopher, biographer, 184

Wren, Bishop Matthew, 153, 157

Wrest Park, Bedfordshire, 157 (note)

Wyatt, James, architect, 101, 110

Yenn, John, architect, 184

York House, Strand, 81, 90, 142 (and note), 143; watergate, 138; **48**; account of, 142–3

Young, John, stonemason, 183 (note)

Zuider Kerk, gateway, Amsterdam, 137, 146